PARCEL ARRIVED SAFELY: TIED WITH STRING

My Autobiography

Crawford began his professional career as a boy soprano in Benjamin Britten's *Let's Make An Opera*. He became the popular star of *Not So Much a Programme, More a Way of Life* and starred in *The Knack*. He juggled film and stage careers, appearances including *Hello Dolly!* (1969), the long-running comedy *No Sex Please – We're British* and the 70s TV comedy *Some Mothers Do 'Ave 'Em* – which is still running around the world. He starred in, among many other things, the John Barry hit musical *Billy*, the 1981 hit Broadway musical *Barnum* and the widely acclaimed *Phantom*. His solo recording career began in '92 and his three albums have all been huge runaway successes earning him gold and platinum discs. He has been awarded many honours including the OBE.

*To Emma and Lucy, to their mother, Gabrielle,
to my friends and family now gone, to my
loved ones still here.*

What special times we had.

PARCEL ARRIVED SAFELY: TIED WITH STRING

My Autobiography

Michael Crawford

ARROW

Published by Arrow Books in 2000

1 3 5 7 9 10 8 6 4 2

First published in the United Kingdom in 1999 by Century

Arrow Books Limited
The Random House Group Limited
20 Vauxhall Bridge Road, London SW1V 2SA

Random House Australia (Pty) Limited
20 Alfred Street, Milsons Point, Sydney,
New South Wales 2061, Australia

Random House New Zealand Limited
18 Poland Road, Glenfield
Auckland 10, New Zealand

Random House South Africa (Pty) Limited
Endulini, 5A Jubilee Road, Parktown 2193, South Africa

Random House UK Limited Reg. No. 954009

www.randomhouse.co.uk

A CIP catalogue record for this book
is available from the British Library

Papers used by Random House UK are natural, recyclable
products made from wood grown in sustainable forests.
The manufacturing processes conform to the environmental
regulations of the country of origin.

ISBN 0 09 9406411

Typeset in Garamond by MATS, Southend-on-Sea, Essex
Printed and bound in Australia by
Griffin Press Pty Limited, Netley, South Australia

My everlasting thanks and gratitude to Diane Wren, who encouraged me to write, who researched tirelessly and who laughed and cried with me along the path. Then to my editor, Mark Booth, who taught me so much (including patience, well sort of . . .) and saved you all from at least another 112 pages.

CHAPTER 1

FROM THE VERY beginning there didn't seem to be a time when I wasn't completely surrounded by women. I was chin-chucked and kissed, petted and squeezed, hugged and held by my mother and grandmother and an assortment of cousins and aunts. Even in a time of war, it was still the best and most secure of worlds for me, filled with love and laughter, the soft touch of angora wool, the smell of buttered toast and the warmth of an apron-covered bosom.

Then in 1945 the men came home, rationing started, and it was to be many years before this head came into contact with another bosom.

My mother was Doris Agnes Mary Pike, a lively slip of a girl. Happily sheltered within her close-knit Catholic family, she'd grown up on the tiny Isle of Sheppey off the Kentish east coast. She was innately elegant, yet a little madcap, full of life and, as the family says, 'just naturally funny'. I can still picture her coming through the kitchen door and for no reason suddenly putting on a Norman Wisdom walk, still hear the ridiculous impersonations she did. She'd pull a voice out of the air, off the radio, or from something she overheard in the greengrocer's or the chemist's that morning. She loved to make us laugh. The humour was sometimes unexpected from someone so pretty. At eighteen she'd been crowned 'Miss Sheerness' in the local beauty pageant, and with her cloud of blonde hair and wide, blue eyes like Bette Davis, she was something of a minor celebrity on the Island.

When she was twenty Doris had met the love of her life – young Arthur Dumbell-Smith, a tall, good-looking Spitfire pilot from 66 RAF Squadron who had been briefly stationed nearby. Arthur was always called Smudge, although no one seems to remember why.

My cousins and aunts tell me it was love at first sight. Doris and Smudge were married just months after their first meeting, and my grandmother Edith Pike, forever to be known as Nan, held their wedding reception under the morello cherry trees in her little Sheppey garden. I still have faded photographs of the proudly posed couple: a young man in his RAF uniform; just a boy really, barely twenty-one – one of those gutsy, scrubbed-faced young men who go to war armed only with a heartbreaking, thumbs-up air of bravado – eyes squinting hard against the sunlight, dashing moustache decorating an amiable smile. My mother stands close beside him, holding fast to his arm.

Smudge and Doris went to live on the Broads near his base at Duxford, not too far from Cambridge; I can picture them buzzing round the narrow country lanes in their little red MG. But their idyll lasted only a year and ended in one of Britain's 'finest hours', late one summer's day. Smudge's plane was shot down. He had narrowly survived a similar incident a few months earlier when his plane was hit and he was picked up out of the North Sea by a passing destroyer. But his luck didn't hold; he was shot down again over Ashford in Kent and died a few days later of multiple burns.

Years later my mother gave me some of his books, a prized set of classics he won when he passed his exams at Drapers' school before the War; I still have them at home now, kept well-dusted and as good as new. Those few photos, books, his service record and the 'wings' from his uniform are all the souvenirs I'll ever have of their brief life together. And along with the stories my mother told me of their blissful relationship, I kept the image of Smudge as heroic father figure in my mind. I've clung to that image ever since.

The truth is that Smudge wasn't my father, and it's only now in the writing of this book that I've managed to piece together some of the details of what happened. Friends were concerned for Doris after Smudge's death in the summer of 1940; she was only twenty-two and sick with loneliness and grief. They told her all the usual things, of course, about life going on and how Smudge wouldn't want her to be so unhappy, but she seemed entirely lost to the world – until someone at the base arranged a party for her to meet a young pilot-officer. I'm told he was very charming, and from a very good family. Doris saw him a few times and they spent one brief night together. She never met him again after that, although when she found she was pregnant a short time later, she tried to make contact and even travelled to Cambridge to find him, with Nan's sister, Auntie Ann Cleary, along for support. They saw him, just for a moment, walking through the lobby of their Cambridge hotel on the arm of another woman. 'Doris never said a word to him,' Auntie Ann said later. 'We just got on the next train and came home . . .'

My grandfather, Monty, and my grandmother, Nan, sent her off the Island, away from the reach of scandal, to

3

stay with Auntie Ann and her husband Jim Cleary in Wiltshire. And when her time came it was their daughters, Eileen and Peggy, who kissed and waved her off to the hospital in a taxi, anxiously watching the car's slippery progress as it crept away through a heavy snowfall. Several hours later a friendly hospital orderly rode his motor bike up the Bulford hill to bring the news to the Clearys.

'It's a boy,' he shouted. 'Born at four am.'

It was the morning of January 19, 1942. I was to be christened Michael Patrick Dumbell-Smith.

Getting the news from Bulford back to the family on Sheppey was a fairly tricky business: a standard telegram sent to the little Sheerness post office was bound to start loose tongues clacking. So with her usual foresight, Nan had composed a coded message to be sent when the baby arrived, so the family would know if the 'parcel' was a boy or a girl. A girl would simply have 'arrived safely'. But if it was a boy, the telegram would read: 'Parcel Arrived Safely – Tied With String.'

While the heavy bombing continued along the coastline of Kent, Doris was persuaded to stay on in Wiltshire for safety's sake, with only the occasional weekend foray to Sheerness to see her parents. It helped that her Cleary cousins were also her best friends. We were all housed together in the civilian quarters in one of the Army camps, my mother caring for me at home with Auntie Ann, while Uncle Jim, Eileen and Peggy worked in the Ordnance Depot on the assembly of camouflage nets.

During those war years, there was an air of adventure and camaraderie never equalled since. Women were suddenly working in positions for which they had been considered totally unsuitable before the War, and while it may have been a time of danger, it was also an exciting and happy time. There were dances held in Bulford almost every night to boost morale, and my mother and the Cleary women went along, leaving poor old Uncle Jim baby-sitting. 'I'm sure he knows when you walk out that door,' he said to my mother. 'He's up the minute you leave! The little bugger does nothin' but cry all night!'

A lot of the young men stationed there knew my mother and the Clearys. After taking me to Mass on Sunday, it wasn't uncommon for the family to find a group of young officers waiting for them when they walked up the hill from church. Straightway I'd be taken from my mother's arms: 'C'mon, my lad!' -- the cheery red-faced Mess Sergeant would bounce me about -- 'We'll take you into the mess. Let's give the lad a drop o' stout!' (That Sergeant may well have been the source of my lifelong passion for Guinness.) The piano lid would be lifted and, like a newborn giraffe taking its first shaky steps, I'd be danced on skinny little legs up and down the keyboard.

So the family escaped the worst of the War, except for the occasion when a German plane dropped a bomb on Beacon Hill near their house, creating an enormous crater. For reasons never made clear to me (it makes for a good war story, I suppose), people there were still convinced the Luftwaffe pilot dropped the bomb on unpopulated countryside, not wanting to hurt innocent civilians. Those were less cynical times, and the general feeling of trust in man's goodness still prevailed. My mother and Eileen shared the same bed in one tiny room, with my cot beside them. In the instant the bomb dropped, and with the sound of hell breaking loose around them, they grabbed me and scrambled frantically under their bed.

To this day I have incredibly tactile memories of the Bulford house, especially of my bare feet hitting the icy floor on a frosty morning. (Central heating was, of course, an unheard-of luxury in those days.) Somehow I'd find a way to wriggle through the sides of my cot to get to the warmth of the kitchen stove and my family of women sorting out my clean, freshly pressed little outfits, still warm from the iron. Uncle Jim would be hunched over the fire, browning thick slices of bread speared on a long brass toasting fork, while my mother cooked porridge for breakfast, and then she would see me and hand me a mug of milk. In those days fresh milk was delivered in great galvanised metal jugs. I can still feel the smooth, wet chill of those heavy cans on my fingers, kept cold just sitting on the porch. Milk has never tasted as sweet to me since.

Bulford winters, as I recall, could also be a time of great humiliation; I lost my mittens so often that I was made to suffer the indignity of wearing them attached to a strip of elastic sewn into my jacket and running down both sleeves. I even had to wear one of those muff things that girls wore to keep their hands warm when everyone dressed up to go to church. It was like a big fluffy white rabbit with no legs. God, how I dreaded that muff coming out of the drawer!

By 1945 the bombing had stopped, so Mum and I left Bulford to return home to Nan and Monty on the Island – and to a new courtship and another marriage for my mother.

There was never a question in anyone's mind that Nan was the Pike family's strong, tough centre. Born Edith Emaline Kathleen O'Keefe in Londonderry in 1885, she died in Bedfordshire almost a hundred years later, holding my hand. I thought she was absolutely marvellous, and I am shameless in the way I love her still.

After her death I discovered a 'diary' of sorts left in her room among her treasured possessions. Written on a child's lined school notebook, she described a Nan I'd never known, her long-ago self 'tall for the times, with large hazel eyes, raven black hair and milk and roses complexion'. The daughter of an amiable Army man from Wales and his fierce-tempered, hard-working Irish wife, Nan was one of eleven children. Before the turn of the century her father's Army company was posted out of Sheppey to the Mediterranean, so Nan lived most of her early years in the warmth and sun of Gibraltar and Malta.

But it was a hard life, with long hours, little money and few frills. Nan and her mother and sister took in washing for the regiment's officers. 'We did the [household] scrubbing and the laundry as well,' she wrote. 'There was never any recreation for me, like dancing. All that came after I was married.' She didn't speak of it often, but she wrote vividly about the beatings she endured from her unstable mother. Even her father feared the outbursts. 'He'd be for it too,' Nan wrote. 'We all protected him ... he had such an even temper and was of a quiet disposition.'

The last hiding came when she was seventeen: 'In her temper she hit my head with a lump of wood until a gash opened and then she chased me until I ran and hid in the lavatory. She yelled at me that I was the most idle creature under the sun, and banged on the door until it split ...' Afterwards, determined to find a 'situation' away from home, Nan became nursery governess to the children of a wealthy Maltese family.

In 1904 she married a soldier posted to her father's camp in Malta. Charlie Murphy was a plain-spoken Irish soldier who loved his drink. Nan never pretended it was a great love match, but it gave her a permanent escape from her mother. She bore Charlie eight children but lived to see most of them die before her. Toosie, the eldest, her greatly loved daughter, died just a few months past her fifth birthday as the result of peritonitis after an accidental fall, and was buried the next day in the Addolerata Cemetery on Malta. 'She was gone from me in a day,' Nan wrote, 'the light seemed to go out of my life and I was never the same.' She was pregnant with her third child at the time and, when the baby was born, Nan wrote that 'he had eyes like a Japanese . . . all the crying I had done made his eyes look like that.' She carried the pain of that first loss all through her life, and even in her eighties her eyes would fill whenever she spoke of her dear, long-dead golden child.

Nan was less than enthusiastic about her 'marriage duties'. 'I was very ignorant of sex,' she wrote. 'I told my husband that if I had known what married life was, I would have gone into a convent . . .'

When I read that, I was reminded of being a guest on the *Pete Murray Radio Show* in London, along with a handwriting expert. He pored over a sample of my handwriting, closely examining every dotted I and crossed T. 'Ahhhh,' he finally announced, 'this is interesting. You've got very cheeky bulbous, lower loops! That means,' he said, 'that you're coyly virile!'

'Coyly virile?' I said. 'Does that mean I like to turn the lights out, or what!'

I laughed loudly at my own joke, but Pete Murray just cleared his throat and swiftly brought the interview to a close.

Nan was waiting for me when I got home, and fixed me with a meaningful look. 'What does that mean, when he said you've got those loops!'

'No,' I said. 'Cheeky, bulbous lower loops. You know

. . . when I write a "*y*" or something, it looks . . .'

'No, I heard that. What was the next bit?'

'Well . . . He said I was coyly virile . . .'

'Yes, I know!' she said impatiently, her distant Irish accent coming more to the fore, as it always did when she was excited. 'But what after that?'

'Well, I was asking did it mean that I like to turn the lights out . . .'

'Yes, that's it!' she said. 'I was like that! I could never bear to look at it!'

And to think she had all those children.

When war was declared in 1914, Charlie, Nan and the young Murphys were posted home again to England and stationed at Dover Castle. Charlie's drinking ate up whatever extra money there was, so life was hand-to-mouth. Later on, when he was posted to Bermuda and then to the Continent, Nan and the children were left behind and from then on, judging from the notations in the little diary, her life was taken up with making ends meet.

Charlie Murphy was killed in France at the beginning of 1917, and before the year had ended Nan was married again, to an old friend of her husband who had promised to look after the family in case anything happened to Charlie. He was a Lance Corporal in the Military Foot Police, my grandfather, Montagu Pike.

I grew up hearing Nan's hints about the circumstances of Charlie's death. She told us the Brigadier General in charge of his unit had a terrific crush on her and used any pretext to flirt with her whenever she was out walking with her children. She said the Brigadier had asked her to marry him, and I think she was convinced that Charlie had been sent off to serve in the front line because the Brigadier wanted to get rid of him. He lost no time, she said, in proposing again after Charlie was killed. I don't know why she married Monty instead of the Brigadier, but I think part of her always regretted it.

The family often laughed about it, but Nan never did.

When Monty Pike left the Army at the war's end, he took Nan to stay with his family in Southampton where my mother, the only child of that marriage, was born in 1918. A short time later the Pikes moved to the Isle of Sheppey.

I knew little or nothing of this family history as a boy. Nan was simply Nan to me, white-haired now, with the warmest dark Irish eyes. She had beautiful, healthy skin, having grown up washing with soap and cold water, and I can still feel the heat of her flesh between shoulder and chin where she held me scrunched against her to whisper a good-night. When I was tiny she sometimes let me share her bed. A child always has an eager eye for the grotesque; and I can well remember the fascinating sight of Nan's false teeth in a glass on the bedside table, and also craning my head underneath the bed to inspect the rusty patch on the springs that had been caused by the steam rising from the chamber pot placed below it.

Made for a child to snuggle against, Nan was my personal hot water bottle and back-tickling machine. She exuded a comfortable air of protection. She did her best to spoil me – and she succeeded overwhelmingly. Despite all the abuse she'd suffered at her mother's hands, I never saw her do anything that wasn't motivated by love.

There was an old lady, a Miss White, who lived around the corner from Nan in Sheppey. Nan used to go and visit her three times a day, just to make sure she was eating enough and had someone to talk to, and she did this until the day Miss White died. So you see why I loved her so much.

*

Even though my grandfather Monty died when I was a child, I remember him very vividly.

Montagu Pike. I love that name. Rather grand, don't you think? But in fact, Monty worked as a porter for a fish shop in Sheerness. Physically, at least, he was a little man (Nan was five-foot-eight and she towered over him). Trim and dapper in his Sunday best, his normal expression could make him look severe – until he smiled, that is, and then he had the warmest face imaginable. He'd sit in his chair in the parlour, first polishing his brogue shoes to a mirror-finish, then trying desperately to find the basis of a shine on his old lace-up work-boots. I've always remembered those particular boots; they had a living sadness about them, and I used that image many years later to create my boots in *Phantom of the Opera*.

Mont was the son and grandson of Dorset coachmen; he had worked around horses himself before the war, as a stable boy and sometime jockey. Now he carried fish, picking it up from the station and bringing it to Cassell's fish shop in the Sheerness high street. It was hard, heavy and often dirty work, which must have been an irritant to someone so fastidious.

I loved combing his silvery hair, endlessly parting and re-parting it, pretending to be his barber while he sat by the window trying to read the paper. The moment of warning would arrive. 'Come on now,' he'd say, 'I've had enough of this!'

'I'm sorry sir,' I'd tell my customer, 'but I haven't quite finished yet' – I can never leave well enough alone – 'You really need a little more off the top sir!'

'I'll give you more off the top, my boy!'

And still I'd keep on, teasing him relentlessly, until he suddenly rose from his chair with a dangerous gleam in his eye – my cue to run like bejeezus. With Mont at my heels I quickly learned to become a good runner, and also developed the knack of diving through the ground-floor parlour window. My very first stunt work was motivated solely by the wish to avoid a thrashing!

A new face began to appear with great regularity in my grandparents' home in 1945. I used to sit in the window seat of their front parlour to watch and wait for him. His name was Lionel Dennis Ingram, but everyone called him 'Den'. A rather handsome, dark-eyed man, he was already quite bald at twenty-eight, which contributed to his air of early middle age. Den's family lived further up the hill from my grandparents' home on Southdown Road. (As far as Den's mother was concerned, they lived 'up the hill' from us in every sense of the word.) Den had never married – twenty-eight was very late to be unmarried in those days – and his mother, a very determined woman, acted as a sort of matchmaker between her son and my mother.

Den was a Sergeant in the Army's Buffs Regiment stationed at Canterbury, where his job was drilling new recruits. In retrospect, it seems as if he trained half the troops in Kent. For years after the war, whenever we walked together down the Sheerness High Street on our way to the beach or wherever, it was perfectly normal for Den to stop and call out to somebody on the other side of the road. Invariably it was someone from his Army days, who he'd trained years before.

On Den's early courtship visits, he always brought along a gift of a toy for me – airplanes mostly. Once he brought a plane that I could actually sit on, carved for me by someone in his regiment. It was of solid wood with a wingspan of over three feet and I've never forgotten it. I, of course, reasoned that I loved planes because I was Smudge's son. Planes provided a kind of mystical bond between Smudge and me, a kinship with the young romantic hero of all my mother's stories. For years I clung to the dream that some day I would follow in his footsteps by joining the Air Force as a pilot.

So I never missed having a living biological father, nor was I ever lonely because of it. In those days there seemed to be a purity and a completeness in this secret relationship with Smudge that nothing would ever be able to touch. Like all children, I suppose, I lived in my imagination, and there he was my constant companion. We'd fly imaginary sorties together over the coast of Essex towards Holland and onward to Germany. Arms outstretched and running as fast as my legs would carry me, I'd scream down the Halfway Road, with Smudge right alongside me, vocally machine-gunning the Co-op and the paper shop – both munition factories just outside Berlin – then, mission accomplished, we would lean to the right and start flying home.

Mike Sierra (Michael Smith), Good job.

Alpha Sierra (Arthur Smith), You too! Roger & Out.

As for Den, I suppose, looking back on it, that there is a sense in which he bought my love with his gifts. Still, even as a three-year-old, I would have preferred him to be in the Air Force rather than the Army: the blue uniforms were far better looking than the khaki.

Thus, with the end of the war, my comfortable world of women began to change as the men returned. There was enormous excitement when my cousin Eileen's fiancé, Tony Weir, came home from a Japanese prisoner-of-war camp and their long-delayed marriage was set for July 1945. For me, dressed in a pageboy's suit of cream satin, it was a day of total humiliation!

Six weeks after Eileen and Tony were married, my mother and Den were married too, with Eileen as the matron of honour. No one believed it was ever the great love match Mum had had with Smudge and, by family accounts, she had her doubts about it right up to the first moments of the ceremony, but I think that more than anything else she wanted me to have a father and a proper family life.

So at age three I was given a new name, Michael Ingram. And my one overriding memory of that time is of sitting on Nan's carefully polished stair waiting for my mother and stepfather to return home from London on the last day of their wedding trip. I was intrigued that my mother had given up taking sugar in her tea while she was away, a piece of news that raised all sorts of dire suspicions about honeymoons in my child's mind.

Looking back now, I'm not sure I wasn't also feeling jealous of Den, worrying that from then on I'd have to share my mother's love. Or could it be that, at the end of the happiest and most carefree days of my life, I had some premonition of darker days to come?

CHAPTER 2

SOON AFTER THE marriage Den left the Army to go into
the grocery business in the small town of Bexleyheath, in
Kent. He was to manage the Bexleyheath branch of
David Grieg's, a large Scottish-based chain of grocery
stores – the thistle was its logo – with branches all over
Britain. Den's new job meant moving away from Nan
and Mont, but there was rarely a weekend or holiday that
we didn't return to the Isle of Sheppey for a visit.

Thus it was that Friday evenings marked the beginning of what became a permanent family ritual – the
journey from Bexleyheath down to the Island to see Nan.
We didn't own a car, so we took the Maidstone and
District Coaches, great green and cream buses, real old
bone-shakers, that picked us up from the grass verge at
the side of the A2. It was opposite the Black Prince,
Bexley's large and elegant public house built in the style
of a great Edwardian manor house.

I'd jump on the bus, hoping the seat behind the driver
was empty. It never was; the coach had come all the way
from Victoria Station and by the time it got to the Black
Prince, there were only a few mid-section seats left. As we

rolled and bounced our way through the dark night, I'd pretend to be the driver on the long journey. I don't know why, but even on the rainiest nights there seemed to be more moisture inside the coach than outside. Neither was the heating adequate, and for each mile down the A2 you had to wrap up that much warmer.

From the Black Prince onward there was rarely a sign of light until we reached Rochester. Then we'd drive through Chatham, then Gillingham and Sittingbourne, until, finally, the Kings Ferry Bridge led us onto the Isle of Sheppey and Sheerness. The bridge I knew then was a massive wooden structure that would part in the middle for ships to pass through on their way to the Bowaters Paper Mill. It was always an event driving on and off the Island, if only to find out whether yet another passing ship had rammed into the bridge, which was always being battered and broken down.

I was off the bus the second we arrived, but still had to wait a minute or two while the driver retrieved our luggage; I followed fast on his heels when he went round to unlock the two great doors on the back. Handed my suitcase, I'd be off, flying from the bus stop way ahead of Mum and Den, up the Halfway Road – so called because it's halfway to everything on this Island – across the Queenborough Road and up the Crescent to Sydney House – painted a beautiful pale seaside green and cream – to bang on her window and hide when she parted the curtains.

As soon as she opened the door, I'd jump around like a crazed Irish Setter, wanting only to run around the house, to sniff it, explore it, and rediscover the place all over again.

The excitement of those Friday night homecomings never dimmed, and just the mention of them still makes me smile; I'm grinning to myself as I write this.

'I'll get the fish 'n' chips,' I'd tell Nan. Then I'd rush off into the night to the little shop around the corner to pick up our rock salmon and chips, liberally sprinkled with vinegar. There was no light in the Crescent at that hour so I ran like hell for fear the bogie man might be following behind . . .

Saturday morning, I'd be up at dawn and out the house. The Island was my paradise, my own personal kingdom. At the top of Southdown Road, where the concrete disappeared abruptly into grassland, the hill rose another sixty or seventy feet above the street, coming eventually to an isolated place where the donkeys grazed and only the gypsies ever seemed to venture; for as long as memory served, there had always been a band of Romanies on the Island, eking out a living by giving donkey rides on the beach to tourists.

After breakfast, I would scramble up this hill – my hill – climbing hand-over-hand until I reached the top. I'd sit awhile, chewing on a blade of grass – it had a wonderful taste to it, a bitter taste, a country taste – and look out over the estuary to the docks and the boats beyond.

I can see it now. To the left, there's the River Swale coursing around the Island and flowing out into the English Channel. Straight ahead is the entrance to the Thames Estuary, and Southend with its mile-long pier. I can see the ships coming in from all over the world, going up to Tilbury and the London Docks, up to Tower Bridge, in fact. To the right there are fortresses, protecting the entrance of the Estuary. They were built on top of what look like giant's stilts with vast underwater nets stretched in between to block any incoming enemy ships bound for London. They're all gone now, but when I was a child those fortresses still stood balanced all in a row.

Far out in the middle of the Estuary, you can still see

the wreck of an ammunition ship that went down during the war, its masts reaching upwards through the water. When the tide is down you can actually see the ship's bridge. My Uncle Fred was once part of a group organised to board the wreck and try to defuse the ammunition, and as a boy I would have given anything to have been a part of the boarding party.

That lonely hulk served as a summer attraction on the tour-boat rides from the beach. We always opted for the small white motor launch, *The Rosemarie*, for our adventure trips. It carried about thirty-five passengers and had mahogany-like slatted benches. We used to lean over the edge, arms outstretched to catch the wake. From the boat you could see Sheerness Dockyard, which used to employ thousands. It was the lifeblood of the Island.

Inland from the fortresses, wedged in the middle of the Island's slowly receding shoreline, is Minster, with its ancient history and medieval abbey. I remember as a child hearing an old Island story about an evil, rich nobleman who rode along its beaches. One day, it was said, he stole a horse from a gypsy who cursed him and warned that because he had stolen it, the horse would be the death of him. The nobleman scoffed, but soon had nightmares, so he took the horse to the beach and shot it dead, believing he had broken the power of the gypsy's curse. Five years later, as he walked the Minster beach, he tripped suddenly and fell onto a bone from the skeleton of that very same horse. It plunged into his chest, killing him instantly. So I never, ever again walked along the Minster beach by myself; instead I always took the long way round, up and over the cliffs – just in case I happened to be a distant relation of that long-ago gentleman.

*

I remember the two cherry trees in Nan's garden. One was filled with wild cherries, the other with morellos, the cooking kind, but both were so sour that just a taste threatened to pucker my lips. Taste buds still tingle and sharpen at the memory of apples eaten not-quite-ripe from the big bowl on Nan's oil-cloth-covered kitchen table, or 'scrumped' from a nearby orchard with my best boyhood friend, Tony Clayton. Tony, like me, had a lot of Irish in him. We got on like a house on fire. He was slightly taller than me and a bit more beefy. But then, who wasn't? Two-fields-and-a-wood beyond the orchard was a field with a giant haystack built by the farm workers at harvest time. Tony and I, and sometimes John Wood, another friend, would hide in the hedgerows, waiting and watching until the haystack was finally high enough to suit us. Then, in the evening when all the labourers had disappeared, we rushed from our hiding place to climb our straw mountain. The journey home would be down Southdown Road, racing along on an orange box with two small pushchair wheels at the front and two large pram wheels at the back, speeding up to twenty miles per hour with our backsides two inches off the ground. As the road curved into the Crescent, we'd often run out of control and find ourselves embedded three feet into the privet hedge belonging to Mrs Yardley, the ironmonger's wife.

At lunch-times there was the smell of Nan's sausage-meat pies made for the family's beach picnics with the lightest, most beautiful pastry in Kent, and a bottle of Lea & Perrins sauce kept near at hand – Nan called it 'Woosesser sauce'. She never could say it properly. We had great flasks of tea, filled to the brim to last the whole day, and there were winkles too, hundreds of them, dug from the mud at Scrap's Gate, a little place on the coast near Minster. We'd take them home to boil in a great chipped black enamel saucepan, then use needles to dig out the treasured morsels from inside the tiny shells and quickly gobble them down with a thick slice of bread topped with fresh dripping.

I remember, too, bright-coloured blankets spread wide along the beach to accommodate everyone in the family, and conversations conducted to the rapid click of knitting needles and punctuated by a sudden, worried, 'Where has that boy gone now? Has anyone seen Michael?' Michael was somewhere in the water with his friend Tony. We were as inseparable and as full of the devil as Tom Sawyer and Huckleberry Finn.

In the summer the seashore was always crowded with barefoot holiday-makers from the city, bouncing over the hot, shiny, grey pebbles that covered our beach like so many Indian fakirs running over fiery coals. The end of their tortuous journey was the shoreline and the cool, slimy edge of the Thames Estuary. But you never knew what you might be stepping on as you sloshed your way, calf-deep, out towards a steadier surface. Anyone treading on a broken cockleshell en route would be certain he had stepped on a live, nipping crab and would leap about terrified and splattering mud on his unlucky neighbours.

I well remember those painful journeys down to the water's edge; my eyes forever seeking an oasis of sand, a relief to the aching soles of my not-yet-summer-hardened size fives.

Tony and I wore the old-fashioned swimming trunks, the thick woollen kind which guaranteed that once we went into the water, we wouldn't be dry again for the rest of the day. Sometimes I'd take my trunks off and sit on the beach with a towel wrapped round me, then try to dry my trunks on the hottest stones, moving them around to face the sun, but they stayed obstinately damp no matter what. The real indignity of wearing them was knowing that anybody walking by could see my private parts, which tended to peep straight out of the leg-holes. I tried to walk about the beach with a casual air, sometimes holding a large beach ball to hide behind, but I knew the girls could see *everything*.

Then I'd slide down the sea wall or dive off a ramp and sometimes, in the splash, my trunks and I would part company. My family would laugh at my little white bum as, spluttering and bobbing under the water, I went frantically searching for the wayward trunks. Finding them I'd pull them straight on-and-up, only to discover that both legs were squeezed into the same leg-hole. I'd disappear under the water again, put things right, and eventually re-emerge onto the shore. There my mother would be waiting, to give me a whack with the comb for stretching my bathing suit again.

Let me digress for a moment to touch briefly on my mother's weapon of choice: a brown bakelite-toothed comb! Whenever she combed my hair into a quiff, she would use Lorelox. It came from a wide-necked screwtop bottle big enough to dip the comb in and coat its teeth in the gooey mixture, which then hardened like a lacquer, holding my much-despised quiff in place all day; a hurricane couldn't have ruffled it. I hated the quiff and the combing and the Lorelox. My mother, standing in front of me as she combed, would quickly get fed up. 'That's right, *start*!' she'd say. 'It'll all end in tears!' and to prove her point I'd get a wet sticky slap on my cheek with the comb.

'Aoww!'

'Don't answer back!'

The script might vary – 'You never know when to stop,' or (I loved to cross my eyes as a kid) 'You'll stay like that!' or 'You know where you're going, don't you . . .' (I never actually did, but it's a marvellously threatening thing to say.) The result was always the same; I'd spend hours with my cheeks covered in a residue of Lorelox, and I couldn't answer back then – my face was so stiffly lacquered, I couldn't move my lips at all.

Tony and I did absurd, harebrained things playing our war games, the preferred boys' pastime in those days. Everyone on the Island had been involved in the war in one way or another, and even in those postwar years the Island had the appearance of a military base. There were soldiers everywhere; a large contingent of the Navy was stationed at the shipyard in Sheerness, and the RAF was constantly overhead, flying surveillance up and down the Estuary.

The two of us would climb the cliffs as marine commandos, and slide back down again as ourselves and the idiots we were. More than once, we nearly drowned playing Cockleshell Heroes, using thick planks of wood as our make-believe submarines. They would turn over, of course, and we'd be clunked on the head and almost knocked senseless by the floating driftwood and the waves that pounded relentlessly against the shore.

For years a rubber inner tube was the perfect substitute for the boat I yearned for. Ordinarily a boat would have been entirely out of the question – there was never any extra money to buy such a thing – were it not for my uncles, Fred and Charlie, who worked at the Sheerness Dockyard at the time. They managed to find a war-surplus rubber dinghy for me. It was the ideal vehicle for our great sea adventures and I treasured it. Tony and I used to paddle like fury far out to sea then turn the dinghy over, pretending to have been hit by a submarine. We dropped down underneath, treading water frantically, and lifted the dinghy a fraction from time to time to see what was happening on the beach. I knew it wouldn't be long before Mum began to look for me, walking frantically up and down the beach; then suddenly she'd catch sight of our upturned boat and Den would be pushed into action. Nan would start to say her rosary, while Den hopped about, hastily pulling off his trousers as he splashed his way through the mud along the water's edge to look for me. He'd spy us as soon as we laughingly reappeared. 'Bugger it,' he'd shout. 'Get in here before I kill you both! We'd thought you were drowned!'

'Bugger it' was the favourite expression in our household. When someone burned the toast, or Nan dropped a stitch, or Monty passed wind, it was always 'bugger it'.

I was nine the first time I said those words, delirious with a case of sun stroke, lying on the bed in Nan's room, my head rolling side to side with the fever. Nan and Mum sat on either side of me, pouring out sympathy, until the moment I murmured 'Jeezus . . . Mary . . . and Joseph'. That was a shocker, of course, but when I capped it with 'oh, bugger it', I lost the sympathy vote. Nan waited just long enough for me to regain my wits before fiercely asking, 'Where did you ever learn that word?'

'From you Nan!'

Wallop! She said she rued the day her grandson would ever use such language in her home. Then Mum took over – and out came the comb again.

Sometimes Tony and I walked on the wooden breakwaters that jutted into the sea. They were covered in mossy seaweed, slippery and treacherous. More often than not, I slipped the moment I stepped out and cracked my skull in the fall. I very nearly drowned once in just that way. Worse still for me, after gulping and clawing my way to the surface, was the embarrassing realisation that I had almost drowned while other people were actually watching. As a nine-year-old I lived in a constant state of embarrassment.

One day my big chance to be a hero arrived. A little girl's beach ball had floated out to sea, and I swam like hell to get it, buoyed by the shouts of 'Atta boy!' from the beach. I rescued the ball, but then I suddenly couldn't get back to shore; the tide was on its way out and taking me further and further out to sea. Of course, I was too embarrassed to shout for help; I would rather have drowned than make a fool of myself. At one point I thought about discarding my trunks, which kept pulling me down. Dear God, all I ever prayed for was a proper pair of swimming trunks! Drowning or not, the mind kept racing; if I take off my suit, what will I do when I get back to the beach? How can I hand the ball back to her? I'll be naked! If I do give the ball back, her father will come down and beat the hell out of me for exposing myself! Somehow I made the shore, but the swim had completely exhausted me. I scraped up the strength to say a few words of acknowledgement for all the hurrahs on the beach: 'Oh,' I mumbled, 'it was nothing really.' Then I keeled over on the mud in a dead faint.

Nan's little home in Sheerness was called Sydney House. It was a very simple place, but in my mind's eye the house was filled with so many well-loved colours, shapes and textures that it has taken on a certain permanent grandeur in my memory. I thought it was lovely, and however plainly furnished it may have been, there was a kind of spotless pride about it.

In Nan's time, if you peeked from the street behind the stiff-starched curtains that covered the big left bay window, you would see the front room where we sat in the evening listening to the radio. On Saturday nights we'd sometimes get jugs of Guinness from the 'snug' at the Halfway House pub at the end of the Crescent, then we'd all sit round the table singing Irish songs about angels coming from heaven to take this poor child's mother away, or about a minstrel boy who to war had gone and in the ranks of death you'd find him. If anyone *had* looked in through the curtains they might have been dismayed to see us all sitting there with tears streaming down our cheeks, but the truth was we were having a whale of a time.

There were gas lamps in the room (gas mantles they were called) with beautifully etched glass shades that were one of Nan's joys. She kept that room especially tidy, with the *Sheerness Times*, *Tit-Bits* and *Reveille* stored well out of sight under the furniture cushions. The gloss of brass was everywhere and always kept gleaming, including a magnificent used mortar shell that was employed as a giant door stop. But it was a comfortable room too; I could drop an occasional crumb down the back of an armchair without getting my head knocked off.

This was years before the arrival of modern, designer chairs. They were the grand days, when you could sink deeply into comfortably pillowed chairs and creaking sofas graced with handmade shawls or starched lace antimacassars. (My mind runs away on the exotic sound of that word, 'antimacassars'; as a child I thought those coverlets had been sent by some unknown relation in Malta.) And depending on the amount of reading material kept under the cushion and the age and condition of a chair's protesting springs, people sat at different heights around the room. A lot of character left our homes and lives in the fifties, when all those chairs and shawls and antimacassars were thrown away and replaced by ultra-functional furniture with all its boring uniformity; forever after everyone sat at exactly the same height.

Behind the right bay window curtain was the spare bedroom where Nan used to sell secondhand clothes to the neighbourhood. That room always had its own special character and the musty, comforting smell that belongs to old clothing. Nan kept a lot of secondhand muskrat coats in there, or 'mushquashes' as she called them. God knows where she bought the furs; they were from very old, very tired animals – definitely the non-pedigree variety, and certainly not big game – and they had obviously done more than their share of sitting; there was always a remarkable shine on the rumps, and very little hair.

Tony and I used that room for our 'Mass'. We were both altar boys at St Henry and Elizabeth Catholic Church in Sheerness, and on Sunday mornings after church we'd go home to Nan's and 'do' Mass our way, singing our own hymns.

We took turns at being the priest, of course, but even then I loved top billing, and insisted on playing the priest most of the time. We had some wonderful homemade props at our disposal. Monty's shirts made for perfect vestments and there was a dressing table that served as an altar. Candles were lit in a dark corner of the room and once one of Nan's unfortunate handbags was set aflame as well. It was the perfect size to serve as an 'incense holder'. We set a match to grass cuttings placed in a tin can deep inside the bag. We had to swing it to get a proper amount of 'incense' smoke in the room while we sang our hymns. But the bag itself actually caught fire, and the stink of the smoke was enough to convince the family in the sitting room across the hall that the whole house was in flames.

The door swung open and my mother stormed in, ready for trouble – 'What's going on in here!' – closely followed by the action of that comb being propelled across the room straight at my head. My mother had an unerring eye: Thwack!

'Aaaaoooooowww.'

I read somewhere that for those of us who view the passage of time through 'the astigmatic' lens of memory, yesteryear's England assumes a gentler, softer outline – no matter how contradictory historical facts may be. That might have been written specially for me.

CHAPTER 3

BUT IF I talk about weekends and holidays on the Island as paradise, that's not to say life in Bexleyheath was all bad. Mum and Den settled into flat-life over the David Grieg's shop on the High Street.

The shop and flat were combined in three storeys plus a basement. Now most people, I suspect, think of a grocer's shop as a fairly dull affair, but for a child it can be the most exotic place imaginable. The basement was a subterranean world filled with mysterious creaks and shadows and the occasional scuttling of a rat. Heavy sacks of coffee were stacked in dark corners; there was sugar down there, held in thick blue two-pound bags of a kind you never see anymore. Everything had been packed in England, but shipped originally from ports in Jamaica, Ceylon and Brazil, places that conjured up marvellous palm-tree images. There were great dark chests of tea from places with intriguingly melodic names like Darjeeling, Assam, Yunan and Keenum. And the smell of it all! Years later, while wandering through the street markets in Singapore, all the exotic aromas took me directly back to the delights in David Grieg's cellar.

The store placed great emphasis on what I suppose today is called 'personalised customer service'. It was at street level and had wooden, sawdust-strewn floors and brass fittings. I remember delectable meat pies kept fresh behind a glass case – the best pork pies in the world – and fresh creamy butter, patted from great tubs of the stuff, and later cut up and thwacked yet again into more butter pats to be sold in half-pound blocks. It's only now I realise how lucky we were in that time of postwar food rationing; because Den worked in the trade, we rarely lacked for anything.

An iron staircase twisted its way up from the back of the shop to the flat above. I never went up those stairs other than three-at-a-time, and I fell down them far more often than I walked. Once I missed the steps completely and plummeted straight through the railings, landing on the thirty-foot-long aviary underneath, that Den had lovingly built to house his budgies. After the accident it was difficult to say who was more apoplectic – Den or the hundred and twenty-two budgerigars. We always kept one budgie in a cage in the flat (I don't know why) and it was always called Mickey. When it died and was replaced, the new one was called Mickey too; even the cat was called Mickey.

My great friend in the shop was Sam, the man hired to help around the shop. Not an assistant really, but more of a sweeper, he was a man somewhere in his thirties, but he was like another kid for me to play with. Nowadays I suppose Sam would be adjudged retarded, but he was routinely accepted by everyone in those days, his innocent simplicity protected – at least by most people! I used to play hide-and-seek with him, teasing him mercilessly from some dark cranny in the shop. 'Sam – I'm here, Sam, you'll never find me . . . Ssaaaaamm-mmm!'

'I'll get you, you little rascal,' he'd say. And he'd try to find me, but never could.

'Ohhh, Saaammm, I'm over here now . . . !' Then I'd dash away with Sam fast on my heels chasing me with his broom, but he was never quite quick enough to catch me.

Sam saved my life countless times. Whenever the prisoner-of-war escape tunnels that I'd dug under the aviary collapsed, he'd see a pair of brown Clarks sandals protruding from under a pile of rubble and drag me to safety. Then he'd help me fill in the tunnels and he never, ever told Den. Sam would never split on a friend. I've never forgotten him. Years later I used my memories of his kind, gentle disposition as a framework for the role of Charley, the retarded hero in *Flowers for Algernon*.

Our sitting room, always called the lounge, took up the entire front area over the shop. It was a vast place, which Mum did her ingenious best to 'stretch' our new G-Plan furniture to fill. There was a big bedroom on the floor above, directly overhead. When we first arrived at Bexleyheath, Mum and Den had the use of it, with my small bed placed at the end of theirs, but it wasn't long before they had to shift from there to the smaller bedroom at the back of the flat, adjoining an even smaller one for me, to accommodate the arrival of Den's parents.

Maurice and Ethel Ingram appeared one day, complete with bag-and-baggage, accompanied by their prized upright piano, and stayed on with us for the rest of my mother's married life.

Everyone called Grandpa Maurice Ingram 'Pop'. I liked him. Quiet and unassuming, he was a nice man, a gentle man, never given to scenes and upsets. In the evening the family used to gather in the lounge and listen to radio shows like *In Town Tonight* and *Henry Hall's Guest Night*, a variety show. ('Good evening! This is Henry Hall's Guest Night! and this *is* Henry Hall speaking!') The radio was replaced, years later, by our Logie Baird television set with a heavy bifocal-like lens set in an imitation-mahogany case that weighed a ton. I used to sit, quite mesmerised, at about four in the afternoon, watching a clankety puppet called Muffin the Mule. Pop Ingram was entirely bamboozled by the telly and never quite grasped the concept of the tube; whenever he watched football matches and the ball was kicked off the screen out of the camera's eye, he'd get up to look for it behind the television set.

Pop and Ethel were great movie fans. Early on in their stay, while they still felt active, they went to the pictures every week, like clockwork, and never missed a new film, especially if it starred Victor Mature or Robert Mitchum. Those were the days when even the smallest neighbourhood cinema was designed as a kind of 'Arabian palace', the walls decorated with pillars and elaborate gold-painted scrollwork, the ceilings dotted with dozens of puffed pink-painted clouds and a galaxy of eternally twinkling stars. When the lights went up, I could see that the clouds were peeling, the ceiling needed repair, and the musty-smelling maroon carpet was badly in need of cleaning, but never for a moment did I think the place was anything less than magical.

Saturday was my favourite day of the week; no fear of dreaded school the next day. There was free time to read my new comics, the *Beano* and the *Dandy*, with characters like Abbott and Costello, and Roger the Dodger (my hero, he could get out of anything). Or I'd put on my cowboy costume and join the crowd of Saturday Morning Minors at our local cinema to watch *Batman* and *Tom Mix* and *The Lone Ranger*. All us

Minors were issued our own badges; we even had an anthem to sing. The cinema would darken, a spotlight would suddenly shine on the front of the stage and, from a hole in the ground, there would appear the head of the organist who thumped away on the keys of this great Wurlitzer. The music would swell, filling the theatre, and as he rose into full view there were cheers from every corner of the building and we all began to sing, 'We are the Minors of the Odeon ...' After the Saturday morning matinée, I'd get on my imaginary horse, which I'd left tied up in the car park, and begin to run a crazy zig-zag course down the very crowded High Street, making believe that 'Tonto' was breaking in a very tricky young stallion. Usually he'd have it under control by the time he arrived at Burrow's sweet shop, where his sixpence pocket money would be enough to stuff his pockets with sweets. Then he'd say 'kimo sabbi' to Mrs Burrows and gallop off home.

People would see me coming and step into doorways. 'That poor woman, he must be such a handful!'

The family trusted me with an unusual amount of freedom as a child, and I took that freedom and ran with it, relishing absolutely every moment. I was constantly inventing games of adventure outside. On top of the wall at the back of the shop were bits of broken glass embedded in cement designed to deter burglars – I suppose we were hoping they wouldn't notice the gate. I'd scale the wall and crawl along the top on my belly, invariably ripping my sweater, which I'd then try to hide from my mother. (When she caught me, I'd blame moths.) I also loved to steal the occasional ride on the two-wheel shop bike used to make deliveries – how I longed for one of my own! I'd remove the big basket in front and ride it up the High Street, sitting sideways, one leg straddling underneath the crossbar. Den was always getting telephone calls about me: 'Mr Ingram, do you know your son is riding the shop bike again? He's just gone past our window . . .'

When I was nine, my grandfather, Mont, fell ill and died. The Kings Ferry Bridge wasn't working on the day of Monty's funeral – it had been bashed by a ship again – so the family had to transport his body from the Island to the mainland in a row boat; there was no crematorium on Sheppey at the time and the service had to be held in Charing, Kent. My mother made the sad journey from Bexleyheath by herself. Just the thought of her father being so unceremoniously hustled and jostled about – taken out of a hearse and put on a boat, then rowed across rough waters to the mainland – must have added awful distress to the deep sadness of the occasion. Always so precise and tidy, poor Mont would have hated all that bouncing about inside his casket.

I waited at the gate for hours for the bus to drop my mother off at Bexley after the funeral. She was in tears when I caught my first sight of her as she turned the corner, and I remember being terribly embarrassed because she was crying in the street where everyone could see her.

That same year I almost died from scarlet fever. I was ill in bed for eight weeks, spoiled by all the attention and the feel of new pyjamas, a hot water bottle, and the luxury of clean flannelette sheets changed every morning about eleven o'clock. *Music While You Work* would be playing on the BBC Light Programme, followed by *Workers' Playtime*. The priest used to visit me regularly – as much for a taste of my mother's home cooking, I suspect, as anything else – although I do remember him praying in my room. Little did I know that he was giving me the last rites! After two months I had recovered sufficiently to be allowed to walk about and experience the thrill of reacquainting myself with the flat all over again, but I relapsed after only two days and was sick in bed again for another four weeks.

If everyone liked Pop, he was inevitably completely dominated by his wife, Ethel. My nickname for her was Queen Ethelred. A fussy, prim and brittle sort of woman, querulous and highly strung, she was never anyone's idea of a cuddly Granny. (Nor indeed would I ever be her idea of the ideal grandson!) I remember she used to chain-smoke, and her jerky gestures made it look as if she'd learned the habit while watching old Barbara Stanwyck films. When she was irritated about something – which seemed to be most of the time – she'd take an extra-long drag on her cigarette and quickly, petulantly, huff the smoke into the air. She'd spend the mornings in bed, sitting bolt upright in her grey hairnet, smoking, and smelling of a mixture of tobacco and the lily of the valley scent she always wore. Wearing tinted spectacles that hinted at neurosis, and with the crooked finger on the hand holding her cup of tea indicating false gentility, she'd occasionally look up from her newspaper to call for my mother to bring her another cup of tea or to plump her pillows.

Ethel's early morning routine is one of the things I remember best about her; it never varied during all the years she lived with us, and everything was done on the dot. From my room I could hear her morning cough – her 'calling cough' – like the sound of reveille in our house. It meant Ethel was awake, ready and waiting. I'd hear Pop draw the curtains, then a door would bang and Pop would go to the kitchen to pick up the breakfast that my mother had already cooked. I'd hear his scuffing footsteps as he carried her tray back to their room; another door would slam. A new day had begun.

And God help anybody who hadn't used the

bathroom before 0900 hours; after that it was strictly Ethelred's jealously guarded terrain and everyone else was out of luck. She used to spend at least an hour in the bathroom, and in the same way that, as a child, you have difficulty with the idea of your parents having sex, I just could not imagine what she was doing in there all that time. I used to worry that if I tried to imagine it too hard, I'd go mad.

Ethel had limited tolerance for children and their habits, so we tended to avoid each other in the main. She wore layers and layers of chalky white make-up, but despite its thickness I never saw any of the powder rub off on the pillow or, indeed, on Grandpa Pop. At the end of the day Ethel would offer me her heavily powdered cheek in an absent-minded goodnight gesture; I thought her face had a slightly mummified feel to it, so I never lingered long and our goodnight kisses were apt to be slightly slapdash.

My mother's never-failing sense of the ridiculous helped her cope with the situation, but she felt trapped, held prisoner to Ethel's beck and call, and it rankled. She had to be up and ready to make breakfast for her in-laws; lunch was at noon, and tea on the dot of four. Whenever Mum broke away for an afternoon's shopping or a visit with Cousin Eileen, she was sure to hear Ethel's injured whine: 'Well what'll happen about tea?'

'I'll leave something out in the larder.'

'Oh?' Ethel would respond, taking a long drag on her Kensitas filter tip. 'We're getting *cold* again, are we . . . ?' She'd turn to Pop with a look of enormous dismay and the battle lines were drawn.

I find it amusing now that Ethel was such an avid reader of the *Daily Herald*, the Socialist newspaper of the day. She was always quoting it as though she spoke ex-cathedra. She completely failed to see the paradox of this, as she led the life of a colonial memsahib, waited on hand and foot by her husband and daughter-in-law. When the *Herald* went out of business she took to reading the *Daily Mirror* and her political opinions, at least, became considerably watered down.

Mum's only regular release from Ethel's demands was on the weekend when just the three of us went to Sheerness, and it made that time on the Island all the sweeter for her. Den liked the weekend away as well; he worked a long, hard week at the shop and could relax on the Island. It was at his insistence that for those few days his parents had to fend for themselves. I can't blame Den for continually taking Ethel's part in order to keep the peace; I just hated it always being at my mother's expense.

One day, Den's nephew, Gerald Ingram, a boy some six or seven years older than me, came to stay. In later years, as a scientist, he became the famous Ingram family member, working with William Penney on projects involving the atom. I can scarcely remember Gerald, however, only the results of his visit.

I've already mentioned Pop and Ethel's beloved upright piano; it was their pride and joy and occupied a place of honour by the window in the lounge. After Gerald's departure Ethel discovered that someone had defaced the entire middle octave of the piano by scratching the appropriate letters into the ivory of the corresponding keys. Ethel was out for blood. She convinced herself and everybody else that I was the villain and nothing I could say or do would persuade her otherwise; she was determined to skin me alive. My mother, on the other hand, was equally determined that Ethel was never going to lay a finger on me – so to make everybody happy, in a kind of community thrashing, Mum proceeded to beat the bejeezus out of me while the whole family looked on approvingly. A letter came later (we had no home phone in those days) confirming my dark suspicions about Gerald, but it had arrived too late: I'd already had my beating. I felt like one of the victims in *The Ox-bow Incident*, the old Henry Fonda film where the lynch-mob punish those who they *feel* are guilty, then the posse arrive too late with the *real* villains. I had already been hanged.

Filtering through the walls of my room in a jumble of angry, mostly unintelligible words came the sound of late-night arguments between Mum and Den, whose temper was legendary. When I heard his fist hit the table, I knew it was trouble.

Den was never a bad man, but he was a complicated and volatile one. Life's confusions and inequities seemed to bewilder and frustrate him, but I can only guess at the root cause of his violent eruptions. Perhaps Ethel's influence on his life was not an entirely healthy one? Here was a Drill Sergeant Major, used to commanding hundreds of soldiers, not a big man but stocky and incredibly strong. Yet when Ethel spoke to him he was thoroughly emasculated. Perhaps when my mother complained that Ethel was overbearing, he felt as though she were questioning his very manhood?

I used to sit by my bedroom door in the dark, listening, opening the door a crack, holding my breath in the effort to concentrate and make sense of what was happening. One night I couldn't stand it any longer. I went into the front room where Den was screaming at my Mum. 'If it was your bloody mother it wouldn't be any bloody trouble would it?' Beads of perspiration were breaking out on his reddening forehead. Then he hit her. I ran and stood between him and Mum. 'Don't you hit my Mum!' I screamed, tears running down my face. 'Don't you ever hit my Mum!' With that, he hit me hard around my head, sending me flying across the floor. I'd never been hit as hard as that in my life. His hand felt like a steel bar as it landed. Mum came rushing to my side. My ear was stinging madly and it felt wet. There was blood dripping on the carpet.

Although my childish attempts to stand between them and shield Mum were laughably ineffectual, I just couldn't stand by when Den hit her. The divisions between them grew deeper over the years, their arguments continuing in the same vein and usually centring on the same subject, the in-laws.

CHAPTER 4

MY MOTHER USED to tell me I had St Vitus's dance. The truth is I was hyperactive, always running, always busy, taking things apart, putting them together; always imagining and inventing; endlessly competing, challenging, and questioning. So school was bound to pose some real adjustment problems; for me, all the promise of life lay outside, in the world beyond the classroom. My first experiences of school as a five-year-old, though, were actually quite pleasant. It was a Catholic convent, a large Victorian building called Stoneyhurst in Bexleyheath, a place with vast (to my child's eyes) buttercup-filled fields and loads of conker trees. Sadly, those lovely fields and trees of Stoneyhurst are all gone now, replaced by a dreary housing estate.

Despite having been told it's a medical impossibility at such an age, I swear that it was at this age that I had my first erection. (Perhaps it was one of those miracles the nuns were always talking about.) I distinctly remember being in the boys' toilet, attempting to wee, wondering what was going on with this *thing* that had suddenly taken on a life of its own. It wouldn't point downwards, only up, and I was afraid to come out of the toilets because I didn't know how to hide it. I was wearing short trousers and the damn thing would poke out round the bottom of my pants as though, now that it had come to life, it was absolutely determined to see where it was going. Eventually one of the nuns came to find out why I was taking so long. She saw my dilemma, and her solution was to give the offending member a smack with the back of a wooden spoon.

My real problems began when I was nine and started attending the London Choir School, another institution since replaced by rather uninspired housing, but in this case it is no great loss. I recall the chill of the place. I was often sent outside to freeze for an hour or more as punishment for not doing well enough. It was at the Choir School that I experienced bullying by other children for the first time. The older boys seemed to travel in packs, preying on the very tiny kids. The school head was called Father Ingram – unluckily for me as, of course, my name was Ingram too – and some of the bully-boys, taking me for one of his relations, had another reason, apart from my size and freckles, to use me as a human punch bag.

They were always there, every morning, waiting outside the school gates to steal our pocket money and generally make life a real hell. I so dreaded the trip to school, and fear affected me so deeply that I now refused to sleep without a night light, a chubby little candle like those used under a chafing dish, which Mum put in my room.

The school provided choirs for places like the Savoy Church on the Strand, the Brompton Oratory, and St Paul's Cathedral. I was very slow in learning to read music, so, in the beginning, the choir master thought the best way to make use of my very special 'gifts' was to let me carry the cross. I liked to think of myself, with those aforementioned freckles and fair hair, as every inch an innocent cherub, straight out of central casting. I walked in front of the processional line, loving the limelight – until that horrid day when I lost control of the top-heavy cross, and it crashed onto the Archdeacon's head at St Paul's Cathedral. After that, it was suggested I try harder to speed up my efforts to read music.

I had my first taste of travel in March 1952, when the Choir School went on a week's tour of Europe. I clearly recall falling out of my top bunk (I still have the bump on my head to prove it) on the boat that left England's east coast, travelling across to the Hook of Holland. From there we boarded a train to Germany and moved on to sing in Bremen, Hamburg and Lüneburg. Mum had read that because the Germans were suffering under severe postwar rationing restrictions, coffee was still completely unobtainable there, so in a sort of goodwill gesture she armed me with tins of it to give to the people I was staying with in each city. I'm not sure how much good will it fostered; we used to travel by bus, and more than once some of the other passengers spat on us simply because we were English.

When I was about ten Den was given a new position as manager of another, much larger, David Grieg store in the London suburb of Herne Hill, some distance from Bexleyheath. For the family it meant climbing another rung up the ladder from working class to upper working class. It also meant that if I was to finish the term at the Choir School I'd have to travel two-and-a-half hours each way by bus and train, leaving at six each morning and arriving home at six-thirty in the evening. It made a very long day, but it was a marvellous way to become independent at a very early age.

With my passion for any kind of transport, I quickly

learned to love train travel even though I continued to loathe going to school, and it wasn't long before most of the station masters on the route began to call me by name and watched for all my comings and goings. When I was given a small model train set at Christmas, I started going by myself to London to the British Rail office on Oxford Street to collect as many free railway timetables as I could carry. I used them to help me run my own private railway, the one I kept in my head. I was station master, booking agent and customer, holding intense phone conversations and doing all the voices:

'No, I can't handle it this week . . .'

'What about next week, what have you got . . . ?'

'Well, madam, I can't do a London–Blackpool, direct . . . but there is a London–Crewe–Blackpool . . . or a London–Manchester–Blackpool – but you don't want to change at Crewe, I take it?'

'No, I hate changing at Crewe . . .'

'Quite right, Madam, I can understand that . . . It's the *sandwishes*, isn't it? . . . You're lucky you're not travelling from St Pancras . . .'

My mother later told me she used to stand outside my bedroom door, listening to all of this. How many times must she have wondered, 'Should I call the doctor?'

When my parents found another school for me, closer to our new home at Herne Hill, I was finally able to leave the nightmare of the Choir School behind. Later, there were stories in the press that Father Ingram had engaged in 'improper behaviour' with some pupils, but as I was one of the younger children at the Choir School and a day-boy, I was shielded from most of it. There was one incident, however, that should have given me a clue to what the gossip was all about. After a long day at St Paul's Cathedral singing the *St Matthew Passion*, we were on our way back to Bexley. I couldn't help but notice that a few of the other choristers were kissing each other. My curiosity piqued, I interrupted my neighbour in row 6A, and asked if, when he had a moment, I might try it. He pulled himself away from Tibitz Minor and, without so much as a by-your-leave, sloppily kissed me full on the lips. I promptly threw up over his shoes, which gave me a fairly clear indication that it wasn't something I wanted to try again.

Later on it came out that 'Father Ingram' wasn't a clergyman at all. One of the Sunday tabloids published complaints about some of his alleged 'unsavoury practices' – what other newspapers went on to describe as 'interfering with some of the young pupils'. The case eventually became something of a neighbourhood *cause célèbre*. There were emotional meetings held in the church by various parent groups, with many people swearing to defend and stand by 'Father Ingram' to the end. After his trial, of course, everyone conveniently forgot all about their fervently sworn oaths. I believe he was sentenced to a ten-year term.

I attended the Choir School for only a year, but to a child that's a lifetime.

Our new flat in Herne Hill was again over the local David Grieg shop. It was in Half Moon Lane, right by the main Southern Region railway line that ran from Victoria to Sheerness. The flat was a bit larger now – a nod to Den's new status – although the lounge was not nearly as big as the one we'd left in Bexleyheath, so Mum had far less 'stretching' of the furniture to do. Herne Hill was a noisy area of London, but I found the clanking railroad sounds almost soothing. I could lie in bed at night and watch the lights from passing trains as they flickered across the ceiling of my room. It was never dark; there was always a glow from the yards or the street lamp on the corner. I continued to hate the dark.

I was enrolled in a small preparatory school called Oakfield, in Dulwich, just a short bus ride from our new South London home. Oakfield was a mixed school, which was my dream come true; everywhere I looked I would see girls. Alas, the girls at Oakfield soon made it abundantly clear that I wasn't at all their idea of a 'catch'. Worse still, within a year of my arrival, I was also viewed as a scholastic washout; I was one of the pupils who failed the important eleven-plus exams (partially due to the inadequate Choir School training, I think, which left me wretchedly ill-prepared). Failure meant I couldn't go on to a grammar school but had instead to go either to a technical college to learn a trade, or to a local secondary modern. I'm sure the family despaired of their dreams for my future.

The question of what to do with me was solved when I was allowed to stay on at Oakfield, which was opening its own upper school and needed students to fill it. The family had been paying fees up till now, but the upper school was much more expensive. Nevertheless they felt they had little choice; I'd stand a better chance of survival in a private school than in a state-run institution where the kids were often a lot tougher and there might be as many as fifty in the classroom (as opposed to fifteen or twenty at Oakfield).

Mum and Den scrimped and saved, giving up many small pleasures, like cigarettes. I know Mum gave them up; Den seemed to find it a little more difficult. He always swore he'd stopped smoking, but everyone could plainly see smoke escaping through the bathroom window whenever he was in there. Suspicions were only aroused because he was generally in there twenty times a day.

Despite my family's sacrifices, I wasn't a success at

Oakfield Upper School either. I wanted to learn, but it was more important to me to be noticed – and that I did any way I could. A child easily recognises that clowning, which serves to cover all the thousand real-and-imagined schoolboy humiliations, will guarantee a degree of popularity among his peers, and I willingly became one of the school jesters.

It should be said that, as a result, my actions at school were enough to provoke any teacher to the limit of endurance. I objected to the obvious boredom of some of the staff, and yet, clearly, there were some very dedicated teachers at the school let me speak only of them.

Mr Harold Passey was the best teacher I ever had. A Yorkshireman through and through, his broad accent seemed to burst its way from the back of his nasal passages and travel down the large red nose that dominated his face. He was rarely without a cigarette, outside the classroom, which would hang from the side of his mouth waving wildly up and down dispensing ash onto what appeared to be the only suit he possessed. I had more ruler-wallops on the hands from him than from any of the others, but he broke down my inability to concentrate and even I could see the results.

Then there was Mr Rainer, the English master, who dribbled when he spoke. When he was expounding a particularly passionate point, he'd launch a splattering two-pronged attack from both sides of his mouth. He also had a fascinating yellow smoke stain right under his nose – Mr Passey had it too – from the Craven A cigarette he kept clasped in the side of his mouth.

The geography master, Mr Steele, had a metal arm, rather appropriately, which would find itself pointing in my direction as surely as a compass finds magnetic North; and the history master, Mr Chandler, reminded me of a campaigning Conservative MP. He was every bit as uptight as the rolled umbrella he carried, rain or shine: 'Ingram,' he'd say, 'come here . . . I've heard things about you, Ingram . . . and I do not like what I hear . . .' Well he certainly didn't hear them from me!

And there was Mrs Oram. She always wore a T-shirt and a whistle that dangled between her breasts. Our class used to sit transfixed, bodies slumped forward across our desks, all heads turning left, then right, like watching a tennis match, as we followed with goggle-eyed amazement the mesmerising tick-tock action of Mrs Oram's whistle. It was better than Wimbledon! In the interests of historical accuracy, I wish I could remember what she taught in the classroom but I doubt that anyone can – though, God knows, she always managed to keep our attention.

Mr Briggs was the sports master and sport was a joy for me. There were two houses at Oakfield, Raleigh and Grenville, locked in fierce competition throughout the year. First there was the football season. I was goalkeeper for Raleigh A team and I can honestly say I don't think there was a match that I wasn't ejected from. It's not something I'm proud of, but my passion for every game was second only to Nobby Stiles's commitment to winning the World Cup in 1966. Verbal abuse of the referee (Mr Briggs) was the usual cause of my weekly dismissal. Then there was cricket. I loved getting dressed up, but quickly became rather bored standing around waiting for something to happen. My favourite was athletics. Cross-country runs dominated the cold winter months and I seemed a natural at this. It must have been all the practice I got, avoiding thrashings in my early years.

The highlight of the year was sports day – the day when all the parents were invited, and the chance for everyone to show what they excelled at. I had to make my mark on sports day somehow. I was already entered in the high jump. In the qualifying round I had managed, with the help of Mr Briggs's boot, to clear the unimpressive height of four-foot-six. But what I really needed was to be in a blue riband event. I had an idea. The relay race! The highlight of sports day. After my recent success as a lonely long-distance runner I had been appointed, rather rashly, as Raleigh sports captain and, as such, I knew I had the power to actually put myself in the relay team. I was never much of a sprinter, but I was determined to be part of the team.

I soon discovered that Raleigh A Team was considerably faster than Raleigh B Team. And that both were at least twice as fast as the two Grenville teams. I therefore appointed myself the runner who takes the final acceptance of the baton on the Raleigh A Team, so that I'd be the heroic recipient of all the cheers as I came in the winner. All went well in two practice runs the day before, when we beat the three other teams handily. Then came the day of the race.

The first leg went perfectly; the second leg was fine, but not *great*: the A Team's pace was off. I began to worry. Bugger it, this isn't going to plan at all! On the third leg the Raleigh A Team was slower still and by the time I took over Raleigh B had, unbelievably, overtaken the A Team . . . In best sportsmanlike fashion I hurled abuse at the two runners who had preceded me for letting the whole side (translate that as *me*) down. Then I grabbed the baton and ran like hell, screaming to the Team B runner in front of me, 'Slow down! Slow down! The A Team is coming through!' Much to his credit, he did slow down, but I still couldn't catch him. As I ran the last hundred yards, I seriously contemplated tackling him. But it was the runner from Grenville A Team who indisputably settled matters; he ran through and devastatingly beat us both!

In a last desperate act to milk a little glory from the debacle, I dramatically tripped and fell, pretending to injure myself. I could have saved myself the effort. When I looked behind, I saw that all the other runners had taken their cue from me; everyone was limping and grimacing in pain, rubbing their calves.

Not surprisingly, I was booed and pelted with everything that came to hand from the sidelines; this was the first time our house had lost the relay since the school had opened.

Because I'd had some musical training at the Choir School I was automatically put into the choir at Oakfield Upper School. It was my job every year to sing 'Once In Royal David's City', the opening solo at Christmas in Dulwich College chapel. I was always terribly nervous about doing it and couldn't sleep for days beforehand. I was plagued by the anxiety that my voice wouldn't be there when I had to hit the top note in the last two lines that began, 'Mary was that mother mild . . .' But in the event it always went well, and whenever I sang in the chapel I felt truly special because I knew I was finally doing something well.

It was Mr Passey who saw I could also act. He gave me the chance to prove it in our school production of Benjamin Britten's *Let's Make An Opera*. Mr Passey was the director, but even before we opened he told my parents he was beginning to have last-minute doubts. Lately, he said, the boy hasn't put much effort into his performance, and he went on to complain that I'd only been walking through rehearsals. 'When he tries, he's brilliant, but since he's learned the part, he hasn't tried at all,' he sighed: 'And now I don't know what he's going to be like.' It was only after I stepped on stage that first night that both he and I found out what I was about as an actor. I heard the laughter for the first time; I could see and feel that living organism that is an audience, and my love affair with it began at that instant.

We did a week at school with a cast made up of pupils and teachers. It was such a success that two months later the headmaster agreed that we would do a performance on a proper stage in South London at the Town Hall, Brixton. The public was invited, tickets were sold, and it was a very proud night for the school. The local newspaper sent a reporter who took photos, and there was coverage in the South London press, including a picture of me melodramatically posing with Henry Livingston, the Oakfield headmaster, who postured over me, pretending to beat me with a broom.

The second half of *Let's Make an Opera* is a rather dark and Dickensian tale, telling the story of one of the children who were forced by sweeps in Victorian England to climb up and clean the narrow chimney passages. It was grim work and most of the children died at a tender age, their lungs congested and diseased with soot. I was Sam, the young sweep boy and the opera's hero, who is rescued from his terrible fate, brought into a loving home, and turned into a gentleman.

In the first scene of the opera little Sammy is pushed out on the stage while everyone sings, 'Up the chimney you go . . .' In response Sam pleads, 'Please don't send me up again! Please don't send me up again . . .' and the company keeps singing, pushing their brushes, 'Up the chimney, up you go . . . !' After the first verse the two villainous sweeps (played with relish by Mr Livingston, the headmaster, and Mr Anderson, our French master) come along and rip off poor little Sammy's shirt. At the end of the second verse they rip off his raggedy pants and he is left standing in his tattered shorts, a miserable tyke with soot all over his pathetic frame. Then they push the poor boy up the chimney.

On opening night, the hall was filled to capacity with parents, teachers and pupils; Mum and Den were in the audience, and Nan as well. The night was in aid of the Church of England Children's Society. The audience included representatives of the Church, local dignitaries and, top of the list, the Mayor of Lambeth.

Behind the curtains I was manic with stage fright. (Nothing much has changed on that score.) I can barely recall getting ready for the performance. At last the moment came, the curtains opened and the opera began: 'Up the chimney, up you go!' They ripped my shirt off. 'Up the chimney, up you go!' But this time I grabbed my trousers and absolutely refused to let go. Little Sammy stood firm, grasping his drawers with an iron grip. Mr Livingston was convinced I was overacting, and decided to take matters into his own hands. 'Ah-ha,' he ad-libbed, lunging across the stage at me. 'Little Sam doesn't want to go up the chimney!' Then he cuffed me on the head and pulled off my tattered trousers. There was nothing on underneath, not a stitch. I was so nervous beforehand, I had simply forgotten to put on my shorts.

So I stood there, stark naked, in full view of the audience and the Mayor, completely surrounded by chaos. Apparently my poor mother began chain-smoking again on the spot; there was anarchy in the stalls, as pupils started cheering, the girls whistled and pennies were thrown onto the stage.

Mr Livingston was livid, of course, and using his bare hands he pulled the curtains across on the performance. The noise from the audience died down, and for the next few minutes the only audible sounds in Brixton Town

Hall signified that the mother of all beatings was being administered to my backside.

The curtains parted once more. I stood centre-stage, dressed in the hastily borrowed pair of trousers that covered my bright-red rear end. It felt like heavily peppered steak tartare. I heard my cue: 'Up the chimney, up you go!' They didn't have to sing it twice; I went up the chimney as if I had been shot from a cannon.

For a little while afterwards I was a minor hero at school. But my relationship with our head, never warm, went completely downhill from then on. He never, ever forgave me for that night and refused to believe I hadn't done it on purpose. My record was such, I suppose, that he had every right to think as he did, but I must plead my innocence.

By all that's right my acting career should have ended that evening on that Brixton stage, were it not for the guardian angel who appeared later on in the rather improbable guise of our new next-door neighbour in Herne Hill.

A year or two after we had first moved, Den was promoted again. This time he was made manager of the much larger Brixton branch of David Grieg (there were three shops underneath the railway arches in Atlantic Road, Brixton), and we were able to move to a house of our own, round the corner in Herne Hill at Winterbrook Road. It was a momentous event for the family. That house and its garden became my mother's pride and joy. It was great to have a garden to play in – this opened the door to all sorts of new adventures. It had an apple tree, roses and blackberry bushes; Den could never understand why they never had any fruit on them – it was because I ate them so fast! Neat suburban borders of dwarf marigolds, nasturtiums, petunias and the ever popular alyssum were hoed on a nightly basis. Then there were the prized shrubs, azaleas, lavender, lilies, and Mum's special lilac bush.

Inside the house, everything was given a daily dose of elbow grease. I remember that the sideboards, in particular, even the scratched ones, shone with a mirror-finish. We had our first fridge at Winterbrook Road; they were just beginning to become popular in the fifties, making the larder redundant. A strange, stark white obelisk, far too large to fit in the kitchen, it was kept in the hallway.

Just down the hall from the fridge, off the breakfast room, there was a very large cupboard with deep shelving and a light inside. This became my workroom. I made model airplanes in there, brilliant little Spitfires, from model kits that supplied the wood and special stickers for decoration. I always kept the door shut tight whenever I worked, and with the complete absence of air, I'm sure half the time I was high on fumes from the glue.

I also built a puppet theatre in the cupboard and made glove puppets from the instructions I found in the 'How To Amuse Yourself' section in the *Eagle* comic. I put on intricately staged Sunday afternoon puppet shows for Mum and Den. I wrote the script, painted the scenery, sewed the curtains and supplied the puppets; there were even some battery-driven lights for the stage and an occasional special effect like an explosion. I served tea at the interval, but once tea was over I'd disappear again until the finale. Afterwards, when I poked my head round the curtain to get the audience reaction, it was always the same – I'd find the two of them fast asleep, absolutely dead to the world.

Mrs Gray was our next-door neighbour on Winterbrook

Road, one of those kindly people with an instinct for gaining a child's respect. She never minded when I kicked a ball over to her side of the fence, so I paid her the ultimate boy's courtesy of knocking on her door to ask for it back. With anyone else I'd have just scrambled over the fence, grabbed the ball, and run like hell.

Mrs Gray wore her silvery hair cut in the fashionable pageboy style, and she had to be middle-class because my mother always used her 'telephone voice', winching it a few notches up the social scale whenever Mrs Gray rang. We were two very different neighbouring families; we read the *Daily Sketch*, they took the *Telegraph*, and it was that ridiculously insignificant fact that completely changed the future course of my life. She happened to see the notice in the *Telegraph* that the English Opera Group was looking for boy sopranos to play in a production of Benjamin Britten's *The Turn of the Screw*. She must have heard me practising through the walls, because she urged my mother to let me have a go. So I went along to join the hundreds of other children who auditioned. I sang 'Early One Morning' and recited a poem about a donkey, Walter de la Mare's 'Nicholas Nye', managing quite painlessly to get through that audition, and several more, until it got down to the last four boys.

But the pure terror of stage fright overtook me at that last audition and my voice left me completely. I couldn't sing a note. David Hemmings won the role, which marked his debut as a performer. These days he's most often thought of as a dramatic actor and director, but he had a very fine, very strong voice, much stronger than mine, and he was certainly far more suitable for the role than I would have been. Both he and that production of *Turn of the Screw* enjoyed well-deserved success.

The English Opera Group remembered my audition, and a few months later they contacted my mother about my availability for their production of *Let's Make an Opera* which starred Trevor Anthony. This time I managed to get through the last big audition at Benjamin Britten's home in Regent's Park; Malcolm Arnold played the piano and Normal Delmar stood by, murmuring, 'Ah, yes, yes, very good' while he conducted. (It's heady stuff to realise that I worked with that calibre of musician at such an early age. Of course I didn't appreciate any of it at the time.) I got the part. I still have the letter that says they've chosen me as 'Sammy 2' in *The Little Sweep*. (David Hemmings was 'Sammy 1'; he played the role on opening night, and then we alternated every other performance.) I was to be paid eight pounds per week. Fantastic!

I must say something here about Benjamin Britten – indeed, I cannot say enough about the kindness of that great man. I was twelve when I met him, and he was at the time by far the poshest person I'd ever seen – the poshest before that was the chairman of the local Bexleyheath Labour Party, when he'd called to say my stepfather's application to join had been turned down. Benjamin Britten was the pre-eminent British composer of his time and he had a wonderful patience and affinity with young people. He loved music, and loved youngsters caring about music. I remember being mesmerised by his mouth – it hardly moved at all when he spoke, so that making himself heard and understood seemed a tremendous exertion for him. When he began a sentence, his words at first came carefully, and very, very slowly, then he'd build up steam, getting faster and faster as he became more enthusiastic, and at the end, his sentences often seemed to fade away, in a kind of dying fall.

From the very start he showed me enormous consideration and tolerance. I remember an incident when, in the midst of the studio recording of *Let's Make an*

Opera, the engineers began to pick up a crunching sound on one of the mikes. Everything stopped until the technicians could figure out what it was or where it was coming from. An engineer finally discovered the source of the problem off in a corner – me cracking chestnuts. As I wasn't singing I thought it was perfectly alright to eat, never realising it was all being picked up on the studio microphones. Mr Britten never scolded – the humiliation alone was enough to make me never do it again – but only gave a kindly word of advice about appropriate studio behaviour, which in its way was far more effective. We began our tour in September 1955 at London's lovely old Scala Theatre in Charlotte Street off Tottenham Court Road. It was torn down in 1969, but still revered by generations who, as children, went to the Scala production of *Peter Pan*, traditionally presented as a special Christmas treat. From there, the company moved on through Oxford, Cambridge, Birmingham, Wolverhampton, Norwich and Blackpool, and ended the run at the Royal Court Theatre in Sloane Square. That tour was the beginning of a previously unimaginable life for me. For one thing, to my utter jubilation I was taken out of Oakfield to tour with the production.

The icing on this very rich cake was a girl in the show named June, for whom I developed a passionate case of puppy love. The extent of our physical relationship was in seeing exactly how long we could kiss. We were sometimes stuck together, like guppies, for twenty minutes at a stretch. I was almost inconceivably innocent in those days.

David Hemmings, on the other hand, was more precocious, and far more adventurous than I would have ever dreamt of being. When I was fourteen, David was fourteen going on thirty! He was always disappearing into the bathroom with his girlfriend: I imagined that they were 'doing it', but I didn't have the faintest idea what 'doing it' entailed. David was a gentleman, never indulging in locker-room confidences. Still, we all knew that whatever it was he and his girl were doing behind the bathroom door, you could bet your life that she'd emerge with a smile on her face.

In fact David would arrive anywhere as if he had just come from 'doing it'. He had a rolling gait like Robert Mitchum's in *Build My Gallows High*, and had the upturned collar too. His voice was always a little deeper than mine; he sounded as though he'd been smoking from birth. 'I think it's *bloody*,' he'd say. It was his favourite phrase – he said it about everything. It's difficult to appreciate just how cool that phrase sounded. He was everything I wanted to be. Whenever there was a woman around, he was there first. And what a dancer! I remember he moved his hips a lot inside his very sharp trousers. David was doing the Lambada before anyone ever thought of it. I admired him enormously. Looking back now, I think David was in the process of re-inventing himself – he was standing outside himself, trying on new personalities for size, tongue in cheek all the while.

At the end of the tour I was sent back to Oakfield kicking and screaming all the way. Predictably, I returned to the classroom as David Hemmings, swaggering in, collar turned up. First period of the day: geography. Mr Steele addresses the class. 'The Suez crisis – what are we to make of it?'

From the back of the class I offer, 'I just think it's *bloody*.' My classmates turn away, sniggering loudly.

'It's "bloody" alright,' Mr Steele agrees: 'Get out!'

Having had a taste of life on the stage, I was absolutely miserable about returning to my former life. I started to press Mum and Den to let me leave school.

I had never dreamed of becoming an actor (I was mentally gearing myself to take on the role of Herne Hill's first test-pilot hero) – it was almost as if the profession had chosen me; one job always seemed to lead to another, and by the time I was fourteen I was working steadily.

I even found an agent during the *Opera* tour, an odd and confusing man in a long beat-up raincoat. He seemed to use a coffee bar for his paperwork, on Shaftesbury Avenue next door to a secondhand saxophone shop, whilst most of his negotiations were conducted via a public telephone on Charing Cross Station. I don't remember much else about him, although we did the rounds together, visiting casting directors, and he actually managed to get me quite a considerable amount of work. It was he who decided that I needed to change my name (to avoid confusion with a television newsman called Michael Ingram who was registered with British Equity). One afternoon while walking down Sheerness High Street I saw a large biscuit lorry with an enormous sign along the side, reading 'CRAWFORD'S Biscuits are Best.' I don't know why, but the name jumped out at me. 'Michael Crawford.' I liked the sound of it.

It was Mr Rainer, the smoke-stained English master at Oakfield, who may have provided the key to my release from school. He convinced the director of a radio play he'd written to give me a part in it. (I sang 'Ramona' as I recall.) The show's producer, David H. Godfrey, had been rather amused watching me mess about during the breaks and cast me in another radio play he was doing, *The Same Sky* by Yvonne Mitchell, with Thora Hird playing my mother. Other radio shows quickly followed: the part of Greenwood in the radio series *The Barlowes of Beddington*, which starred Patrick Barr; *Children of the Archbishop* with Gladys Young and Hugh Manning, and

Invitation to Murder with Joan Sanderson. They were all marvellous learning experiences; I played absolutely everything and I was even cast as Henry VIII and two of his wives in the same programme.

Mum and Den finally gave in to all my arguments. I know they were disappointed, but they must have realised it was senseless to throw their money away on schooling I hated. Besides, with all the work I was getting, it was obvious I was learning more doing broadcasts than I was in the classroom. So I was allowed to leave school at fifteen, when I was legally able to do so.

Shortly thereafter, when I was still fifteen (looking all of twelve), I did two films for the Children's Film Foundation, an organisation which unfortunately no longer exists. One was *Blow Your Own Trumpet*, in which I got my first screen kiss (from a dog); in the other, *Soap Box Derby*, I experienced the thrill of performing my first stunt work. The Foundation budgets were far too small to allow for a stunt man, so when the script called for me to dive into the Thames to save another boy from drowning, I was the one to do the diving. We did it by the old Nine Elms Railway Yard, where the water was absolutely filthy; the director made sure we had our stomachs pumped as soon as we were brought out. I loved it. It's every boy's dream to dive straight off a crane wall into the river to save someone from drowning. The whole crew made me a hero: 'Well done boy, you were great . . . really brave . . .' I'd have done it a hundred times even if it meant facing the stomach pump each time. The thrill of it, the love of it, made it easy to bring a real drive and intensity to everything I did. The work has never been a hardship – it's doing what I love to do.

The film had its world premiere at the Savoy Cinema, York Road, Wandsworth on Saturday January 4, 1958 at 10:45 am – by invitation only. I was in the big time.

Mum and me.

Me at 18 months in home knitted sweater and Adolf Hitler haircut.

Nan and husband number one Charlie Murphy.

Above: Monty, Nan and Mum.

Left: The Right Hon Montagu Pike – fish porter.

My mum – Miss
Sheerness.

Below: Mum and Arthur
('Smudge') on the Broads.

Mum and Arthur
on their wedding
day.

(*left to right*) Uncle Jim Cleary, Peggy Cleary, Uncle Tony Weir, Eileen Cleary, the best man, Auntie Anne Cleary. *Front row*: totally humiliated white satin – me.

Left: Mum and me.

Below: Look at those trunks! Look at those legs!

Above left: Candyfloss kids – Tony Clayton and me
Above right: Another day in paradise.

Below: Note the cool cycling shoes.

Quiff without Lorelox, aged 9.

Quiff with Lorelox, three years later.

Daytrip to Eastbourne.

Nan, Mrs Pollard, Mum, MC Den, Pop, Ethelred – Christmas at Bexleyheath.

(*Left to right*): Mr Anderson bending down, in middle Mr Passey refereeing, on the right Mr Chandler – MC left hand team second from front.

Gladys Parr, Owen Brannigan and MC in *Noyes Fludde*, Aldeburgh.

Peter Butterworth and MC in *Blow Your Own Trumpet*, 1957.

CHAPTER 5

ODD THOUGH IT may seem, it was my bike that got me my first job in rep.

I had been eleven when I finally got my longed-for, prayed-for, pleaded-for bicycle – a shiny, red Raleigh two-wheeler – and from the moment it was mine, I spent almost every waking hour riding it. That was my joy, to ride out every night and perfect my skills, navigating between the cracks in the road, practising my 'figure 8s' as a skater does. Pitting myself against myself, I was relentlessly my own competition; every night another challenge, tomorrow night I'll be back for more.

Over the next couple of years, and at an age when most parents would think twice about letting a child out of sight on a bicycle, I had already started doing long one-day trips on my red Raleigh Junior down to Kent and points beyond. I'd simply disappear for a Sunday, with only a brief 'I'm going cycling for the day, don't worry about me.' I'd be up at six, pack some sandwiches and water bottles, and then off to bike the fifty-five miles from London to Sheerness, spending two or three hours at the seaside before pedalling home again. Or sometimes

I'd take off with school chums on a marathon cycle, doing the fifty-odd miles from London to Brighton or to Southend. The London-to-Brighton route was always the worst. It took about four-and-a-half hours each way, and there are more hills on that run than in all of San Francisco. When I was tired, I'd hang on the back of a lorry and let it pull me for a bit – a stupid and dangerous thing to do, but I was thirteen, you see, and therefore immortal.

I was so chafed the first time I did that trip, it took me fifteen minutes to get off the bike saddle when I got home. I crawled to the bathroom and climbed on top of the sink to have a look at the damage in the only mirror available. I stood on the edge, trousers around my ankles, with my head hanging, bat-like, upside down between my legs – not an attractive position – but it seemed to me the only way to assess the situation. I spread some Savlon antiseptic cream between my legs to ease the agony. The skin was just at the point of breaking and it stung as much as if I'd sat on a beehive. I spent the next few hours half-crippled and totally bowlegged – there was enough room between my legs to accommodate my mother's weekend shopping – but the pain eased, and, miraculously, there was scarcely a trace by the time I set off for school the next morning. I can give Savlon no higher endorsement.

When I returned home in the evenings and told my mother and Den where I'd been, the response was usually a very casual, oh good, and you had a nice time? I was perplexed and, I suppose, a little hurt.

When I was thirteen Den bought our first car. Driving, incidentally did nothing to help Den's temper. When he drove, he swore at absolutely everyone on the road – quite an education for a young man. It was a very secondhand Humber Hawk, pale green, and filled with the mixed aromas of leather and wood and pile carpet, the sort of smell one pays a fortune for today. It was only then, when I was able to give them detailed directions to Sheerness without a map, along with the shortcut hints that cycling teaches you, that they finally accepted I had often been cycling up to a hundred miles on those day trips. It turned out that they'd simply assumed that my tales were products of my wild imagination.

It was to be expected, I suppose, that I would splurge on a new bike with the very first money I earned from the radio broadcasts. It was a twenty-six-inch-wheel Armstrong, with drop handle bars, quick-release wing nuts, a twelve-speed Campagnola gear system, and it cost thirty-five pounds. As I was earning only a little more than two pounds per broadcast, this was a fairly sizeable splurge, but it turned out to be one of the single best investments I ever made; that bike and I travelled a long way together over the next few years, rolling from audition to audition, and it was partly responsible for my first success in repertory theatre. And therein hangs my tale.

There was very little extra money to be had for transport in those days, which is why I cycled to auditions. It was certainly cheaper, and besides, when the traffic was bad, it was usually faster than the bus. I'd speed away from Winterbrook Road, wearing long white socks that covered madly pedalling spindly legs in short trousers, and a yellow oilskin cape billowing high behind me in the gusting wind. I was half man, half lamp shade. As soon as I reached the hall I'd unwind the long, wrinkled trousers I kept rolled underneath the bike saddle and go in to do the audition. I must have looked as if I'd slept in my clothes. It was even worse when it was raining; I used the cape to prevent the back wheel from splattering mud on me, but invariably I'd arrive with a mud streak up the back of my head, as if I wore a damp Mohican long before that haircut became the rage. Yet my scruffy appearance rarely seemed to hinder me professionally. (It was quite another story with the opposite sex, but I'll get to that later.)

That bike travelled a few thousand miles. One of the hardest trips as I remember was up to Suffolk. The English Opera Group called again, this time with an offer to appear with Owen Brannigan and Gladys Parr in the premiere of Benjamin Britten's *Noyes Fludde* as part of the Aldeburgh Festival and, later, in Southwark Cathedral. My voice had already started to change after the tour of *Let's Make an Opera*, not cracking exactly, but rather sliding slowly from soprano to tenor, which should have effectively ended my chances of performing in this new production. Rather than have me left out, Mr Britten – in a typically generous gesture – spent an entire weekend transposing and reworking my role to accommodate all the changes. Looking back, I'm still amazed he took the time for such a thing, but he thought I had pluck and determination and he encouraged that spirit.

Then, one morning, the call came to Herne Hill with an audition for the Belgrade Theatre, Coventry: Would Michael Crawford be available to see Belgrade director, Bryan Bailey, before the close of auditions today at one o'clock in London? By the time I got the message I had less than twenty minutes to make the audition. By bus, it would have easily taken forty-five minutes to reach the venue. Instead, I hopped on my splendid maroon-coloured Armstrong and sped through the pouring rain, plastic cape flying, and arrived with five minutes to spare. And that, to cut a long story short, was the day my bike repaid my investment a hundred times over. I got the part – my first 'grown-up' role – and graduated into repertory theatre.

For the theatre actor in England, the experience of performing in rep is not unlike doing your National Service: you acquire a basic theatrical training, some versatility, a little professional polish and a lot of discipline. The Belgrade Theatre in Coventry, the site of my first, limited experience of rep, was the first civic theatre to be built (in 1958) in England since the war. A lot of the more seasoned actors there tried to instil in me the basics of the craft. Actually, some of them couldn't have been blamed if they had been tempted to *beat* the craft into me; indeed on one occasion I remember my head being soundly cuffed by Richard Briers. I can't remember why, but I was a smart-aleck kid, always teasing my elders and betters.

I'd been given a wonderful lead role in *Head of the Family* by the French playwright André Birabeau. The play was about a schoolboy who gets his fourteen-year-old girlfriend pregnant; most of the play follows the boy's efforts to provide for the birth while trying to keep it secret from his parents. It was a strong, serious drama with some occasional comedic bits, and gave me the opportunity to work with such eminent actors as Frank Finlay, who played my father, and Richard Briers as the family doctor.

Our producer was the scholarly, much esteemed author/director James Roose-Evans. Jimmy was a well-known believer in using acting exercise classes to develop improvisational technique and to stretch the actor's imagination and vision. I'd never had an acting lesson in my life.

When the company gathered for class one day in the rehearsal hall, Jimmy suggested we all pretend to be trees. I remember thinking Frank Finlay looked particularly uncomfortable: with his arms outstretched like an ungainly ballerina, he swayed ever so slightly. I sidled through the room at snail's pace, placed myself next to Frank, and slowly lifted my leg. After a few seconds one of the other actors noticed me and began to snigger. James Roose-Evans, who took such exercises very seriously, said, 'Michael, may I ask what it is you're doing?'

'I'm a dog, Jimmy,' I said. 'Out for a walk in the park, and I've just seen this very nice tree . . . !' He suggested I went and had a coffee in the canteen. But he was a dear man with a wonderful sense of humour, and I'm certain I heard him laugh just as I closed the door.

Jimmy always had a compassionate eye for the sensitive kid hiding beneath the air of bravado. He reminded me not so long ago of a day in his office when he and Frank Finlay gave me a little pep talk to give me confidence after a bad review; they tried to persuade me to look on the criticism in a constructive manner. 'Just keep saying to yourself,' they said, 'I am resilient, I am resilient.' And they had me chant it to myself, mantra-like, for days on end.

Displaying much forbearance, the Coventry manage-ment invited me to stay on for their production of *Julius Caesar* (which featured a very young Alan Howard). I would serve, they said, to plump-up the crowd scenes and play the small role of the young musician, Lucius, servant to Brutus.

Those Shakespearean matinées were always an adventure; the seats were either filled with groups of senior citizens or, more likely, with youngsters on a school outing, a popular excursion except when it came to Shakespeare. Anything remotely fey on stage was met with wild shouts of derision, and as you may imagine, I was asking for it when I stepped on stage as the young musician, dressed in a short-skirted toga and carrying a lute.

The role called for me to 'play' the lute in one scene (while a musician hidden in the wings did the actual strumming). My cue was '. . . And touch thy instrument a strain or two . . .' I recall one particularly uncomfortable performance when I ran my fingers over the strings, and nothing happened. There was dead silence, the lute was mute. Richard Martin, the actor doing double-duty playing the guitar, was obviously late turning up. I whispered to the wings, hissing in heated embarrassment, 'Dick . . . Play! DICK! DICK! DICK!' 'YEAH, WE CAN SEE IT FROM HERE, LUCIUS!' some kid shouted from the balcony. I hurriedly crossed my legs. When a harassed Dick Martin finally arrived, I tentatively plucked again, and this time there was life in the old lute. We somehow got through the scene with a minimum of further comment from the audience.

I was also designated as one of the pallbearers at Caesar's funeral, supposed to help lift and remove the somewhat well-upholstered carcass of our star from the stage after his big death scene. In order to create the maximum effect of an enormous pageant for our audiences, we pallbearers were required to carry Caesar's body, slowly, slooowwwly, circling the stage, once, twice, and then off. The solemn procession moved with great stateliness, with only the occasional groan from us hard-pressed pallbearers, until that fateful performance when our 'corpse' lost his battle with his digestive system and farted rather explosively.

Discipline went to hell as the audience was treated to the astonishing sight of a bouncing Caesar resting on what appeared to be an undulating waterbed. The pallbearers' laughter got so out of hand that a kind of demented hysteria prevailed until finally, on our knees, we had to give up, lower our cadaverous burden to the ground and crawl off into the wings, leaving the 'corpse' alone on stage. I then reached from behind the curtain, took hold of Caesar's ankles and pulled him, inch by inch, across the boards. His toga went along for the ride – it was up around his neck by the time he reached the wings – and our gleeful audience of OAPs and schoolchildren enjoyed a long, steady close-up of his dazzlingly multi-coloured Y-fronts.

I felt my acting days at Coventry were about to be terminated, but for some reason I got away with only a mild reprimand, perhaps because it was obvious the audience had had a ball. Our Caesar eventually left the company, and though I can't absolutely swear to it, I heard he was doing Alka Seltzer adverts in Southern California.

Some marvellous things came from those days at Coventry Rep; the experience of playing with a first-rate company, some exciting reviews for *Head of the Family*, and the appearance in my life of a lady named Adza Vincent, a London theatrical agent who had come up from town to see her client, Sarah Long, the lovely, caring actress who had played my teenage girlfriend in *Head of the Family*. Adza's first glimpse of me was as the musician in *Julius Caesar*. I can't imagine what she saw in me in that tiny role – it may have been my legs that did it – but it was enough for her to take me on as a client. She became my agent as well as my great friend and protector.

There was always something wonderfully large and theatrical about Adza, so very Margaret Rutherford. She was given to great gesturing and wild swooping of hands and arms, and she didn't so much enter a room as whoosh into it like a mini-cyclone. Smartly dressed in a chic tailored suit and with a cigarette, sans cigarette-holder, delicately poised between her fingers, Adza looked the picture of a sophisticated older woman. (I say older, although she could have only been in her early forties, but anyone over the age of twenty-one seemed positively ancient to me.) 'Michael, daahhling,' she'd say, and she referred to me as her 'Daahhling boy'. Adza would barrel around London in her Riley Elf, with her whippet, Alexander, by her side. With only one hand on the wheel (the other waving about as she made a point), she'd drive me to some audition or other.

Adza toiled twenty-four hours a day for her client. I doubt she ever slept, and I know that's just the sort of agent I've expected to have ever since, God help them. (Over the years I freely admit to having driven all my agents absolutely crazy, suddenly having an idea and calling them at all hours of the day and night.) Adza cared for me like a doting parent. Her kindness was indefatigable. She never married, and her life was devoted to helping others; especially her mother, Katherine Vincent, once a well-known opera singer. She lived with Adza, who looked after her until the day she died. Adza had already had a varied career before she decided to become an agent (she'd been private secretary to the playwright Christopher Fry for over twenty years), and she cultivated and used her many lifelong friendships with various celebrities to help her clients. Her friends were always more than happy to oblige.

The British film director Anthony Asquith was a particular friend of Adza's, and it was through him she got me a small part in one of his films, to be shot on location in Sweden. This was my first experience of flying, and you can perhaps imagine the stir it caused in Herne Hill and Sheerness. Not only was it a plane, it was a jet – the Comet, no less. Mum and Nan had Masses and Rosaries said for me in churches all over Kent. The idea of a jet flight seemed especially traumatic for my mother who, in all her life, had never once travelled beyond that little area of England in which she had grown up and lived out her married life.

I kissed the family goodbye at Heathrow airport, fully expecting, in a dramatic scene of farewell, to be able to turn and wave to them again as I boarded the plane. But I couldn't see them at all. And since non-passengers were restricted to an observation roof, they couldn't tell which plane was mine. So for an hour they waved and wept at each departing flight until someone wisely decided it was time to go home.

I know I wrote home every day; I was miserably homesick. Yet all the company's well-known actors were very protective in the way they looked after the young people, the newcomers, making certain we were included in museum excursions or in any evening get-together. They couldn't, however, protect me from some of Scandinavia's more surreal sights. There was a group of Eskimos staying at our hotel, and on more than one occasion I walked into the loos in the lobby to find two Eskimos, their trousers rolled down to their ankles, sitting facing me on the urinals, into which they were emptying their bowels. Isn't it amazing the bizarre images that stay in our memories?

The film I had gone to Sweden for was called *Two Living, One Dead* and starred Bill Travers, Virginia McKenna and Patrick McGoohan. God bless Patrick, I used to drive him crazy. I love to mimic people, and in Patrick McGoohan I found mimicking heaven. He speaks almost in a monotone; very quickly, very precisely, in an elegantly deep voice, clipping his words distinctly, almost abruptly ('Ek-scus-me-pleez'). I followed him everywhere, imitating him behind his back. I flatter myself now to think I got quite good at it, and later used this impersonating device to great effect when trying to make my way through Saturday morning shoppers on a crowded Clapham High Street. 'Ek-scus-me-pleez. Ek-scus-me-pleez.' People would start and stand aside. Was that *Danger Man* they'd heard? Had *The Prisoner* escaped? They'd turn and see not the suave Patrick McGoohan, but a skinny, freckle-faced fool.

Peter Vaughan, that great character actor, famous for his air of menace, was part of our movie company and another of my targets. We all used to gather in the hotel bar at the end of our shooting day. One of the company mentioned to me that Peter had been seen talking to the same attractive Scandinavian lady over the past few evenings. We knew it was perfectly innocent, but I seem to be unable to leave well enough alone, and so one night I made it my business to discover the mysterious lady's name and then went to one of the phones in the lobby to have Peter paged to take a call. Using my best Swedish accent, I barked into the phone, 'Eye understahnd you're zeeing Greta, my wife!' At the other end I heard Peter Vaughan's voice, and from the sound of his gasps I knew I'd really gone too far.

'Uhhh! . . . Huuhhh . . . Aargh . . . !'

Dear God, I thought, he's having a heart attack! I decided to put a quick end to the conversation, now clearly out of hand, and hung up. When I got back to the bar, I saw an ashen-faced Peter hurriedly saying a final goodnight to Greta. I felt a bit guilty and thought, how can I tell him, how can I walk up to the man and say, 'Hey, Peter, you remember that phone call you had just now . . . well, that was me!' It took me a day to pluck up the nerve to speak to him, indeed, to find him; he was obviously avoiding the hotel lobby. When I finally spoke to him, confessing all, he emitted a series of gulping sounds in a massive release of tension. 'You (gasp) little (gulp, gasp) bastard!' was all he said. I got off lightly that day.

Recently turned sixteen, I was everyone's first choice for the role of juvenile pain in the ass.

CHAPTER 6

HERNE HILL WAS a working-class life with limited experience of places or people beyond the family and the immediate neighbourhood, and light years away from the world of grease paint and film studios and West End auditions.

I know my mother began to entertain some dire suspicions about actors in general, especially after her first encounter with the fourteen-year-old David Hemmings. I had brought him home to meet the family one day during a rehearsal period for *Let's Make an Opera*. He stood on tiptoe to reach her, gave her a kiss full on the lips, and told her he thought she was 'very tasty'. She gasped. I gasped. My mother! Very tasty! Good grief!

As far as my sexuality was concerned. Mum may have wondered what I was up to, but, if so, it wasn't something she'd dream of discussing with me. Emotions and experiences were not analysed then as is so fashionable now. In a way the fifties were a totally innocent time 'when people guarded their emotions more closely, spoke of them less openly, but felt them no less deeply', and the plain fact was you didn't talk about your own sexuality, let alone anyone else's. Mum and Adza tried to protect me from anything other than 'normal' life – and I could never find a way to tell them I didn't want to be protected!

Of course, there were a few things they didn't know about, like those summer afternoons in Sheerness when a group of seven or eight of us, including Tony Clayton and John Wood and his girlfriend, Betty, sat in a field after scrumping for apples. John and Betty would kiss, and the rest of us, in between bites of a Golden Delicious, were sometimes allowed to touch the breast of a particularly friendly redhead called Hazel, blessed with the firmest, most sumptuous bosoms on the Island. Just touch, mind you, that's all you're allowed! We never even kissed her.

And there was that red-letter day when I was fifteen. I had a fight with, God forgive me, the pigtailed Girl Guide who lived down the road. It wouldn't be exaggerating to say she was a robust girl, about five inches taller than me and with a weight advantage of about thirty-five pounds. We'd been playing explorers at the end of our garden, building a shelter in the 'jungle'. I can't remember what was said, but suddenly words turned into a wrestling match, and when she obviously saw no other chance of victory, she suddenly grabbed my parts through my shorts and gave them a violent squeeze. To my astonishment I became immediately erect and experienced an incredible craving for this enormous girl who seemed intent on annihilating me. I felt a sudden burning sensation that rapidly spread from my head to my toes and all points in between, and I kissed her so hard, I must have almost eaten her alive. Then as we thrashed around in the bushes, my whole being went into spasm and the centrifugal force of my universe seemed to whirlpool down into my groin. As the feeling went from absolute ecstasy to unbelievable shame I tore myself away from this delectable Girl Guide. I'd had my first orgasm and, in the process, had completely devastated my mother's prized lilac bush.

All the same, I remained pretty innocent about life and women and, as heavily 'mothered' as I was, opportunities to explore further never seemed to arise. Even if they had, I would have been too shy. At that time, I couldn't even make the first move on a Monopoly board.

In between auditions I made myself useful at home. I used to plan great 'Do It Yourself' projects for the house; I built the garden shed, put in a new sink and built-in cabinets in the kitchen, and one weekend, while the family was away at Sheerness, I redecorated the entire kitchen, painting and wallpapering, staying up the entire forty-eight hours so that when they walked in, Sunday evening, it would all be finished. Naturally the family became quite cautious about leaving me at home after that; they never knew what they might find when they walked through the front door.

I was able to earn a little money on the side packing Horizon Holidays brochures for shipment to travel companies around the country, or helping Den at the Brixton store on Saturday mornings, selling eggs to the old ladies; they were always fond of the brown eggs, I've no idea why. I sold woven baskets that I made at home, and I also made inexpensive marcasite and rhinestone jewellery for a small London arts-and-crafts shop, inserting stones into the designed pattern. Mine tended to come out a bit askew. When I was carpeted, I defended myself with Well, if the stone's a bit crooked, it picks the light up that much more. Of course I'll keep the stones straight if you *want*,' I added, 'but most people like it a little crooked to catch the light!' The manager saw things differently and suggested I find another line of work where my creative theories might be better appreciated.

The first year out of school was a fairly depressing time of sporadic work, and more than once I thought of cycling out to the local RAF recruiting station. But a breakthrough of sorts came with a job I landed as a waiter in London at the Westminster branch of Lyon's Corner House, opposite the Houses of Parliament.

Because the boss was pleased with my work, I was determined to become the world's best waiter, and redoubled my efforts by trying to prove I could clear five times as many tables as anyone else. The rest of the staff didn't bother to hide their contempt, but even there I eventually managed to ingratiate myself; with me around to pick up the slack they could always count on the occasional extra cigarette-break. ('Don't worry about the tables, "Crackers" is doing 'em.')

Then my role as world's speediest waiter brought me to the attention of a television director who stopped at Lyon's, for breakfast every morning. When I told him I was an actor, he offered to give me a bit-part in the live television show *Emergency – Ward 10*. I was cast as 'Eddie', a motorbike accident victim. He was seriously injured but according to the script had every chance of recovery. All I had to do was point to a gift box that someone was supposed to have brought me in hospital and say, 'Have you seen this, nurse?' Mum was thrilled at this chance to see me on the tube, but I had to warn her I might be totally unrecognisable. 'I'm bandaged from head to foot,' I told her. 'There's just enough space to show my mouth and my eyes. But you'll know my eyes, won't you Mum!'

On the day of my television debut, I – well, Eddie – lay in a 'hospital' bed, swathed in bandages, baking under the hot studio lights, sweat pouring. I tried to quash thoughts about it being a live performance and the size of the live viewing audience. Eight million people. I'd taken precautions against nerves by writing down my only line of dialogue, and hiding it under the sheets.

The moment arrived when the 'nurse' came to my bedside. 'And how are you feeling today, Eddie?' It was my cue; I froze. I couldn't think. 'Uhhhh . . .' I said, then I suddenly remembered I'd written the line down. I whipped up the sheets, looked down, and said, 'Have you seen this, nurse?' The television camera started to shake while the whole crew howled. Off in a studio corner I could hear the producer scream, 'That little bastard!'

Eddie died later that night.

Luckily another casting director gave me a job in a television series called *Probation Officer*. For the next few years I went on to enjoy a life of crime, playing every conceivable kind of juvenile delinquent. And as name and face became better known in the casting offices, my career began to pick up. I'd already done some small parts in the occasional, forgettable low-budget films like *Two Living, One Dead* in 1960 (it was never released) and something called *The French Mistress* later the same year. It was filmed down at Shepperton Studios where Bob Hope and Bing Crosby were also working in *Road to Hong Kong*. The two of them practised driving golf shots on the back lot and, whenever possible, I'd go out there and hide behind the bushes to watch. Sometimes they'd hit long balls far out to that remote area where I was crouching, back of the rhododendrons. If the coast was clear, I'd nip out and pocket the balls, keeping them as souvenirs. (It was quite a thrill to work with Bob Hope later on; the most peculiar look came over his face when I told him I'd run off with his balls thirty years earlier.)

It was on the basis of some positive reviews for *The French Mistress* that I was booked in for a film called *The Villa*, produced for the series *The World Beyond* (a kind of early British 'Twilight Zone'). But the real breakthrough happened in March of 1961 when, thanks to the generosity of Patrick McGoohan, I was approached to appear in a television series called *Sir Francis Drake*, starring Terence Morgan. Patrick knew the producer and put in a good word for me and an audition was set up. Ultimately I was cast in the ongoing role of the cabin boy, John Drake, and paid the fantastic sum of forty-five pounds a week. ('John Drake' was the name of Patrick's character in his own enormously popular television series *Danger Man*, or *Secret Agent* as it was later called in America; the name brought luck to both of us.)

On the strength of that television role, I was called in to audition for an American film, *The War Lover*, which was being shot at London's Elstree Studios. When the producer, Arthur Hornblow Jr, asked me if I'd ever done an American accent before, I had to admit I'd never even tried it. 'Well, do you think you can try one now?' he asked. 'Let me come back tomorrow and do it then,' I said, and he agreed to hear me the next day. I rushed home and spent the next twenty-four hours listening to a Woody Woodbury comedy album and then, armed with a string of American-drunk stories, I auditioned again for Mr Hornblow. He didn't laugh too much, but evidently savoured my accent. He said it sounded like a cross between Wapping High Street and Brooklyn. I was very proud when he cast me.

The War Lover was based on a story by the American novelist John Hersey, and starred Steve McQueen and Robert Wagner. The story revolved around Steve playing an emotionally mixed-up pilot who tries to steal his co-pilot Wagner's girlfriend. It was still early days in the careers of both actors and I doubt the film did much to speed their way to the top. The film's female love interest was supplied by the English actress Shirley Ann Field, who had a difficult time, as scathingly commented on by McQueen:

'You'd have made a great man!' he told her.

She looked at him. 'What are you talking about?'

'I mean,' he deadpanned, 'the way you screwed that last scene.'

I had only a small role in the film, but it was my dream come true; I was in the Air Force at last – albeit in the American Air Force. The production also provided my first real insight into the very serious business of creating Hollywood fantasy. Steve McQueen wasn't as tall as he appeared on the screen and Hollywood fantasy dictated that the star must always be taller than everyone around him. I dreaded shooting the scenes on the old windswept airfield which had been transformed to resemble an American air base; I thought my feet would drop off with the cold when I stood alongside him, dressed only in flying suit and socks.

I would hardly call myself a friend of Steve McQueen's, but he was agreeable and professional, and I liked him. Like all of us he had a thornier side, though, and it was sometimes difficult to judge his motives. I continued my pursuit of the 'perfect' American accent by always using it around the set, never letting on I was English. But someone told Steve, and from that time on he always seemed to find me just before it was time to go on for a shot. 'Watch the Limey accent, kid,' he'd remind me. I don't know whether he did it to intimidate me, but if that was his intent, he nearly always succeeded. Still, he had a certain street-smart charm.

The most alarming thing about Steve was the way he drove. I think he drove at high speeds because driving race cars was what he really wanted to do in life, and indeed did in between filming. I was very flattered when he asked me if he could give me a ride back to London. 'You sure you fellas don't want to go . . . ?' I asked the crew. 'No, no, go ahead,' was the reply. 'You enjoy yourself, Mike.' After about a mile and a half I realised why they had taken the bus. 'How're ya doing, kid?' Steve asked. My knuckles were white as I gripped the dashboard. I think I learned my nervous machine-gun laugh during that jeep ride.

By the time we wrapped production on *The War Lover*, our director Philip Leacock thought my American accent was good enough to recommend me to Cy Endfield, who was about to direct Neil Simon's comedy, *Come Blow Your Horn*, for the West End.

I was asked to audition for the London theatrical impresario Bernard Delfont, who was producing the play. Midway through the audition Mr Delfont asked me to drop my trousers. Oh my God, I thought, Mum's told me about things like this. But as he was sitting some distance from where I was standing, I felt reasonably secure, so I complied.

Mr Delfont looked at my legs, then, puffing his cigar, he looked me in the face. He took another giant puff on his cigar and looked down at my legs again. I looked down at my stilt-like pipe stems, and stammered – 'Well, comedically,' I said, 'they could be, well, you know, uh, sort of, good!' 'Comedically,' he exulted, 'they're bloody marvellous!' And he walked out of the room and down the corridor, mumbling all the while, '. . . comedically . . . ha . . . bloody marvellous . . .' I got the part.

The play starred Bob Monkhouse, with Nyree Dawn Porter, David Kossoff and Libby Morris, and revolved around the relationship between two brothers, Alan, the elder (Bob was superb in the role), living a carefree bachelor life happily surrounded by women, and his younger brother, who leaves home to move in with him. I of course played Buddy, this twenty-one-year-old virgin.

I make my entrance, suitcase in hand, telling Alan I've left home.

'Permanently?' he asks.

'I took eight pairs of socks,' I reply. 'For me, that's permanent.'

That was my first laugh on a West End stage. From that moment I knew it was comedy for me. Nothing on earth can duplicate the sound of laughter. Mum and Den and Nan were all there for the opening night, the audience loved the play, and the critical response was equally joyous.

Come Blow Your Horn represented more than a few 'firsts' for me; it marked the first time I met Noël Coward, a very kind, always encouraging man. He had come backstage to visit Bob Monkhouse and stopped by my dressing room to introduce himself. I was in absolute awe of him, and hung on his every word. 'Dear boy,' he said to me, 'you have a presence and an economy, and I like it.' I'm afraid that for a brief, embarrassed moment, I thought he was telling me I'd been tightfisted – what could I possibly have done to him to make him believe that? I was only just then meeting him! Perhaps he saw my confusion, because he explained that he felt I had an ability to convey a multitude of comic meanings with a minimal of display and pauses. It was a very big deal for a newcomer like myself to get a plaudit like that from the Master, and I remain inordinately proud of it to this day.

Our opening-night cast celebration lasted well into the wee hours, and Bob Monkhouse and his wife put me up for the night. I remember leaving their flat in the light of early dawn the next morning, riding the bus through the silent London streets, home to Herne Hill, then tiptoeing through the dark house because everyone was still asleep. In my room I found a long brown envelope my mother had left for me, sitting on my pillow. She had written a few words in pencil on it: 'My wonderful, wonderful son.' That's all it said, but it was like an award for me; something I still treasure. I have it wrapped in tissue, kept in a dark place so the writing doesn't fade.

I celebrated my twenty-first birthday during the run of *Come Blow Your Horn*. The family gave me a party to mark the occasion and as a treat Adza took me to Paris a few weeks later. I remember having a few misgivings at the time; I was nervous about the sleeping arrangements which Adza hadn't discussed with me, and I had a mental picture of two beds in one room, and Adza leaping out of hers and into mine!

I'm sure this anxiety was the result of conditioning by my mother, who continued to warn me about 'those theatrical people. Never turn your back on anyone!' (I was forever spinning round on people like a manic whirling dervish.) 'You never know what she (or he) might do,' she'd say. 'She (or he) may run off with you! You know what they're like.' I did, but I wondered how she knew. Obviously there was more in *Tit-Bits* than I thought.

I need not have worried. Adza had obviously made the rooming arrangements to save money. She had flown me to France entirely at her own expense; if we used her percentage of the money I was earning, we wouldn't have made it as far as Dover.

As the *pièce de résistance* of our trip, Adza arranged for

us to have supper at the Paris flat of Philippe de Rothschild. This amazing woman had apparently been an intimate friend of the Rothschilds for years. We were ushered into a small, highly decorated baroque private dining room, complete with chandeliers. The master of the house had business elsewhere, so Adza and I sat in solitary splendour, waited on by a butler, enjoying the most beautifully prepared five-course meal imaginable. It was all so incredibly extravagant. (God, if only Sheppey could see me now!)

The butler didn't speak a word of English, so Adza acted as a kind of semi-interpreter. 'Por favor, oh, beg pardon, s'il vous plaît!' was all she had to murmur and, as if by magic, yet another course would appear. And the wine! A Rothschild '45 Bordeaux. It was unbelievable.

'Do you think he'd let me have the label off the bottle for my scrapbook?' I asked Adza.

'Of course he would, darling,' she answered in her most magisterial tone. 'It's no problem,' she said. 'Garçon! S'il vous plaît!' She pointed at the bottle. 'Le, uh, label, pour M'sieur!'

'Oui, oui, Rothschild,' he answered, looking blank.

'Pour, M'sieur,' she said, gesturing at the bottle. 'He would like . . .' (enunciating very slowly now, and loudly, as if the man had gone suddenly deaf).

'Non, non, non, c'est impossible . . .' he gasped, horrified that we might be ordering another bottle of his '45 Bordeaux.

'Well, I'll take the bottle . . .' I said, and I reached out to pick it up. But the butler grabbed my hand before I could touch it. After much picture-drawing – I had the gall to soak the bottle in the finger bowl to show him what we were after – he was finally convinced to give me the label, but I don't think Adza and I did much to improve Anglo-French relations that evening.

My mother always kept a cheerful silence about her relationship with Den, mostly for my benefit I think, to keep up appearances while I still lived at home. And on the surface their marriage was never anything less than successful. How many times have I heard someone say about a couple, 'We would never have guessed . . . they always appeared to be so happy . . .' Then the doors close, the smiles fade, and the couple retires into their own silent world where nothing is shared. I was always aware that Mum was never fully happy with Den, and just as aware that divorce was never a consideration. In those days, for better or for worse meant just exactly that; people stuck it out. That was the way life was; it was what we were brought up to do. There are many who'd say that sticking it out does no one any harm. Perhaps, but I know there were those who suffered for it all their lives.

I'm glad she had that opening night, that she was there with me to share in the success. It was the last thing I was able to give her; she died within a year.

CHAPTER 7

I'VE OFTEN BEEN accused of being somewhat susceptible to superstition. Perhaps I am, but I still believe everyone has experienced a sixth sense – feelings, presentiments, whatever you want to call them – that simply can't be explained away in the normal course of events; these things do occur, and I accord them a certain belief and healthy respect.

One night, during the run of *Come Blow Your Horn*, I'd been out with some friends at the Earls Court flat of an old friend of mine, another of Adza's clients. She was a county girl, from a very good family. I'd known her for a couple of years and she knew my family. This particular evening had been all quite pleasant and we'd entertained ourselves by messing about with a ouija board, trying to get a lead on the name of the next Derby winner. Late in the evening, for absolutely no reason, the 'ouija pointer' went completely out of control and my friend became hysterical, crying uncontrollably, shrieking and thrashing about; at one point she started to smash up things in her kitchen. It took forever, but in the end I managed to quieten her down, though she still refused to say what was the matter. I eventually left and drove home. She had really frightened me.

Months later, she revealed that she had suddenly 'seen' my mother ill and dying.

But that same evening, as my car turned into the end of our road I saw another car parked outside our house, unusual for the area because in those days there weren't that many cars to be found in our neighbourhood. Inside the house everything was in a terrible state of upset; my mother was upstairs in her room with our family doctor, and I could hear her crying in pain. Den and I sat downstairs, feeling helpless, and waited for the doctor. He came down at last and told us my mother had to go to hospital immediately. The ambulance came and took her off to Dulwich Hospital where she was diagnosed as having had a gall stone attack.

It was a terrible shock for Den and me to visit her over the next few days. She was pinioned to the bed by a frightening array of intravenous tubes and drips. I had never thought of Mum as being vulnerable before, and she had never had a day of illness that I could recall. But now she was helpless and an agony to watch. After several days it was obvious to all of us she wasn't responding to treatment.

One night at the theatre, I sought out Bob Monkhouse for counsel. He'd become a great friend and was far more worldly-wise than I. He unhesitatingly recommended we get a second opinion. Like so many ordinary people we were intimidated by the medical profession, too timid to ask too many questions.

When I arrived at the hospital the next morning, I tried to convince Mum that we'd got to get someone else to come and see her. She refused, as I knew she would – no matter what her condition, she simply couldn't conceive of offending our family doctor by questioning his judgment. But for the first time in my life, I ignored her wishes: Bob's advice had seemed so eminently sensible. I suppose I acquired my first bit of worldly wisdom at that moment, but it came a week too late.

With the help of Libby Morris, another caring friend in the show, I was able to find a specialist who came to see my mother and advised that she be transferred immediately to another hospital to undergo emergency surgery. Without waiting another hour I had her removed, quite literally from under the disapproving nose of our family doctor, and taken by ambulance to St George's Hospital near Hyde Park Corner. I remember holding her hand during the ride on a beautiful March morning. When we passed Buckingham Palace she glimpsed the surrounding treetops through the ambulance window and she commented on the new green leaves and that spring would soon be coming.

The doctor told us she had acute pancreatitis which should have been operated on days before. Afterwards I wept outside the ward. For the first time I felt something dangerous was happening – what had always been the most important thing in my life was suddenly at terrible risk.

It was a long, hard operation; when we saw her again she was heavily sedated, in and out of consciousness, although she knew Den and me when we sat with her and when I held her hand. But she didn't improve over the next several hours and a decision was made to operate again, this time to close an opening in the pancreas through which poisons were leaking into her body. That night, when I left her to do my show, I couldn't touch her because she was housed in an oxygen lung tent, and I could only kiss her goodbye on the chilly plastic that separated us.

The next morning, at some black hour before dawn,

the sudden ringing of the phone ripped through the silence of our house and sleep. Then it stopped. I heard Den answer, and the continuing murmur of his voice in muffled conversation. Then I heard him hang up, and his footsteps scuffed up the stairs; the sound stopped at my door. When he came into my room I knew what he had to tell me before he said a word; his tear-marked face said it all. Then he closed the door and left me.

She had just turned forty-four.

At that moment grief, that most selfish of emotions, took me over. I couldn't think of Den or anyone else, only my own hurt. I've never felt such overwhelming loneliness before or since, like a black cold pain in the middle of my gut. I wept until my face throbbed with it and then I was suddenly engulfed in the most soul-destroying rage. I beat and beat and beat my fists against the wardrobe door, wanting to smash it apart. I couldn't bear the injustice of my mother's death or conceive that a good God would let such a thing happen. And I could weep at this moment for all the things I never knew – and will never know – about her, and for the thousand-and-one questions I want to ask her now that I am grown older than she was when I last saw her.

Den and I went to see her in death that morning. I was afraid of what we might find, yet when I saw her body I almost believed she would begin to breathe again. She was absolutely beautiful, with a look of serenity on her face I could never recall having seen during her life. I kissed her, but all the warmth I had known was gone. There was such a terrible finality to the touch of her that it compounded the agony of loss.

When we left the hospital, Den and I drove my car to Victoria to register her death. I remember we couldn't find a parking space, so I sat outside and waited in the car while Den did what had to be done. I heard a voice: 'You can't park here . . .' A policeman poked his head inside the window to order me off. 'Piss off', I told him. 'What d'you say?' he barked. 'I said, piss off.' 'Just what's your problem, boy?' he said to me. 'My problem,' I answered, 'my problem is my mother has just died and my father is inside registering her death. That's my problem!' I didn't care if he arrested me on the spot. He said nothing, but put a hand out and I could feel a pressure where he squeezed my arm before he walked away. Even now, I thank him for that small gesture of understanding.

Then Den and I drove to Sheerness to see Nan, who was, for the first time in anyone's memory, completely distraught; she couldn't be comforted. My Uncle Fred – now her only surviving child – was with her, along with Auntie Ann Cleary and the rest of the family. No one could help her. Nan had endured the death of so many children, eight in all, but my mother was her youngest, her baby girl. Nan and I clung together like babes in the wood.

Later that day Den and I drove back to London. The company and management at the theatre were wonderful and encouraged me to take time off, but I felt I had to work that evening. It was possibly the hardest show I've ever done, particularly at that point in the play when I said goodbye to Libby who played my mother.

Mother:	Buddy, darling, you do whatever you want sweetheart. You're not a baby any more.
Buddy:	Thanks, Mom. (He kisses her.)
Mother:	But be up for dinner Friday night.
Buddy:	I will.
Mother:	And bring your laundry.

The company was incredibly supportive and understanding that night and helped me to hold back the tears
until after the curtain fell.

The house was silent for days after my mother died.
Occasionally, I wondered if Pop or Ethel missed her. Did
they realise now how much she'd done for them? I never
asked. Later, as we drove to the cemetery I watched
people go about their daily business seemingly
unconcerned. I wanted to shout, 'Don't you know what
a special person my mother was? Don't you know?' I
wished people still doffed their caps as we passed, as they
used to do when I was a child.

We're not trained for mourning. It seems we are only
taught the trivial things – like geography, or how to ride
a bike. We're left to work out the great events of life and
death for ourselves. Those not affected by a death
murmur conventional words of sympathy, but there is
often an air of pretence about it, as if they don't really
understand the pain of bereavement – which they may
well not if they haven't experienced the loss of a loved
one themselves. Often they encourage you to 'move on'
and forget about everything as quickly as possible.

Personally, I don't believe that's the way to handle it.
My son-in-law lost his mother recently. I said to him –
and I hope not too clumsily – every day it will get a little
easier to deal with her not being here physically. But
don't ever get over it. Don't let her ever leave your
thoughts, and that way you'll always have your mother's
love inside you and alongside you. The love that a
mother gives to a child *never* stops.

Shock and intermittent numbness soon wore off, to be
replaced by a clear knowledge of what had happened: the
suddenness of my mother's passing had overwhelmed the

whole family. The death of someone so young and alive, with such humour and vitality, had a lasting effect on all of us. It's still a kind of watershed in our lives. Until her death, I hadn't realised how much of an emotional anchor my mother had been in our household. She was the light of our family life, and although it may sound melodramatic to say it, at the time I couldn't conceive of living without her.

I recall a particular day when the pain of grief was so acute that I became frantic for help. As a child I had been brought up as a Catholic, which taught me all the basic rights and wrongs of life, but now, in my misery, I wasn't sure what I believed anymore. This was the first time in my life that my belief in God's goodness was put into doubt. In desperation I went into Westminster Cathedral and asked to speak to a priest. My mother must have been looking after me because the priest, Monsignor Murphy, a really kind man, came to talk. He suggested that if I came home again to the Church, perhaps I would then be able to find the solace I needed. I went to confession then and embraced the Church again – and with a vengeance – desperately holding onto it for comfort. I went to Mass every day and found consolation in the sad painted faces of the saints, the Stations of the Cross, and the marble walls and columns of the building itself. I used to stare at the walls hoping, believing, that if I prayed hard and long enough, my mother's face would one day appear to me in the marble. I still look for her face sometimes, but now I don't have to look very far; it's there on my daughter, Emma.

Den and I began a new life together, along with the in-laws. In a way, Den had always done his best for me and I owe him a debt for all the years of sacrifice he made for a boy who wasn't his son. He was the only father I'd ever known, but I was my mother's son, and I was always very conscious that he was my stepfather. Our relationship was further complicated by a certain lack of chemistry between us and the image I clung to of my dead hero father. Ultimately, my mother's death, and my own intuition about their increasingly strained marriage in the last years of her life, resulted in an angry estrangement between Den and me.

I was fortunate that I was able to do a television programme for CBC in Toronto, which took me away from Herne Hill for some weeks. I returned afterwards, but with my mother gone there seemed to be nothing, not even grief, to hold the family together. Den and I were like two strangers living in the same house, going about our lives in close proximity but rarely connecting. He was working nights, by this time as a manager at the David Grieg factory, and we only ran into each other for a brief time each day around lunch time.

The strain of life under the same roof pushed us to the limit until, one day, it exploded and we fought, dredging up old hurts, both real and imagined, along with my bitter accusations about Den's harsh words to my mother. Ever since I was a small child Den had known only one way to answer me, to settle anything – with the back of his hand. Again, it was as strong as a piece of iron when he swung his arm through the air and knocked me to the floor. From that moment, the last threads of family that bound us were broken.

I waited until Den left the house for work that night to pack up what I owned. Ethel watched me as I stuffed some clothes into an old suitcase, and offered me her cheek for one last goodbye. So, at age twenty-one, I left Herne Hill for good, with no clear plan except to start a whole new life. I went back to Sheerness for a while, just as Mum and I used to do, back home to Nan. And in those few summer months I stayed with her, I started to grow up a little, and all the love I had for my mother, I now gave to my grandmother.

I realised that during her long life Nan had never had another person to really hold her, to be there for her. She had always been the one who had to be strong, holding up her family through troubled times. There had always been such a feeling of comfort and healing when Nan had her arms around me. Now she needed hugging as tightly as I did.

I knew I would have to leave soon to find my own life, but even then we never entirely left each other again until the day she died.

CHAPTER 8

I HAD BEEN seventeen when I first met Cavan Kendall, a young actor well known on children's television programming (and one of the original Railway Children). We were both cast in the *Billy Bunter* series starring Gerald Campion. Cavan was from an old theatrical family. His grandmother was Marie Kendall, one of the great Edwardian music hall stars who continued to make nostalgic appearances until her death at the ripe old age of ninety-one. His father, Terry Kendall, was a popular song-and-dance man in the twenties, and the beautiful film star, Kay Kendall, was Cavan's half-sister. We quickly became friends but, at the time, I would never have predicted that the Kendalls would become like a second family to me.

The thing was that we both suddenly found ourselves all at sea when Cavan's mother died in 1963, shortly after mine, and we both moved into his father's tiny one-bedroom flat in Clapham. It was a horrible time for Terry as well. So all our lives were completely torn apart and we were depressed as hell but, in spite of that, life among the Kendall men turned out to be pure comedy.

I was lucky to arrive in London when I did. It was the era of the Beatles and Carnaby Street, the so-called Swinging Sixties and an amazing time that brought a whole new sense of freedom. America might have been the birthplace of Rock and Roll, but Britain was the land of the Beatles and their wildly irreverent way of looking at life. What a fabulous time to be young, and in London, the centre of all the excitement.

In physique at least Cavan and I were poles apart. He was terribly proper-looking, tall and very handsome, with the long-legged stride of a greyhound. I used to have to trot alongside him just to keep up, but we were both the sort who dressed in cavalry twills and a sports jacket while everyone else was fitted out like members of the Mod-Squad. When we went to concerts we'd dance and shout like everyone else, but we stood out like two candles in a black-out. We just didn't belong with the in-crowd. And we both suffered the same agonies and frustrations about women.

Bugger this, I thought one day, it's time to step out. This is the Sixties! I want to be Mod, I want to be cool, I want to be now!

So while Cavan still refused to dress in anything but his Prince of Wales checked suit, I bought a tailored black leather jacket and pointed leather shoes and a snappy Lambretta 150 scooter. I used to sit on it at the proper Mod angle, keeping my feet turned in fifth position, jutting my needle-sharp toes round the sides of the mudguards in front. I even took to sleeping on the scooter in the garden, my feet resting on the handlebars and my head cushioned on the luggage rack. This was considered a very cool practice at the time, though there were a couple of drawbacks if you were accustomed to rolling over in your sleep. The three-foot fall to the ground was the first and the eight-hundred-pound machine coming over on top of you the second.

I still went to Mass every day and was in and out of the confessional with all the regularity of a cuckoo clock. Sometimes I'd use a different accent, hoping the priest wouldn't recognise me. 'Bless me, Father . . .' I'd whisper. 'Haven't you just been in here, my son?' was the soft response from behind the dark screen. 'Yes, Father,' I'd answer, 'but I had another impure thought as I left the church . . .' It was spring, you see, and all the girls wore soft loose dresses.

Eventually I was relieved of my virginity through the noble ministrations of an attractive actress – an 'older' woman of about twenty-eight, who I met while doing a show in Bristol. After our last night the company gathered in one of the actors' hotel rooms for a few beers and the post-mortem that usually follows the recording of a big TV production. You all work together for some weeks and you get to know each other rather well. So we're saying our goodbyes when this woman asks if I'd like one more drink. She accompanied me down the corridor and simply said, 'Would you like me to come in for a little while?' This innocent-sounding enquiry made my brain start to pound; and then the stuttering started: 'Uh, yes, I mean, umm, yes, I've uhh, got an early start tomorrow . . .' (IDIOT!!!!) Luckily she came in anyway. We sat down by the fire awhile, and she started to take my clothes off and all I could think was *IT* is going to happen, *IT* is actually going to *Happen*. Frankly I was so overwhelmed, I was absolutely no help to her; I didn't know whether I should try to remove her clothes or not. In fact I thought she might hit me if I touched her. Instead, very kindly, she told me what to do, whispering in my ear, and I'd never felt anything so wonderful before as this woman's legs so close around me. I was so pathetic I think she felt in the mood to do a good turn for the day.

Afterwards, she asked my age, but I couldn't, wouldn't tell her; I didn't want her to know I was twenty-one and terribly inexperienced, something I'm sure she'd figured out for herself.

I waited around for her the next morning, having developed an insatiable yen for a complete re-enactment of the night before, but she'd have nothing to do with me. I stayed madly in love with her for the duration of the train journey back to London and thought about her for months afterwards, trying to recapture her touch, her smell. Let me hasten to add that the episode made absolutely no difference in my continuing non-success with women. As for the lady in Bristol, alas, I never saw her again.

Cavan and I used to try our luck with girls at the Streatham Locarno ballroom in South London. Standing on the edge of the dance floor, 'The Unlikely Lads', we'd examine the local talent with the cool detached Mod air we'd developed. 'Right,' I'd say, 'those two in the middle! They look great!' 'I want the short one, Crawford,' Cavan would argue. 'No,' I said, 'let me take the vertically impaired one. You take the other one, with the legs like oil drums.' Then we'd saunter out to the centre of the dance floor in super-cool pursuit of our quarry. 'Excuse me ladies,' Cavan would say, sounding for all the world like Professor Higgins ordering a taxi. 'Are you free?'

'No, get lost!'

'Oh . . . uh, fair enough,' was our pathetic response. Crushed, we made a humbling retreat backwards off the dance floor. The humiliation of being rejected at a

'Mantovani favourites' evening was mortifying. Our pace quickened until we caught sight of the exit, then made a mad dash for the safety of the night air, away from all those scary women. Cavan then strode off at double his usual pace, shouting all the way up Streatham High Road. 'Bugger, bugger, bugger, bugger and bugger.' I threw in a 'sod it' just for support.

Of course, in all the days and months that went by, I don't suppose either Cavan or I ever once gave a thought to Terry Kendall, who was every bit as much on his own as we were. Creeping home late one night, the two of us went through the front door to the sitting room. We found the door bolted and from behind it we heard the muffled moans of someone in an agony of pain. 'OOOoooh – Aaaagh . . . Ohhhh . . .' There was no sign of Terry. Frantically we pushed at the locked sitting room door.

'Pa!' we called. 'Are you okay?' There was no answer.

'Pa! Pa! Is there anything wrong?!' No sound. Nothing. Then, 'Ahhhh . . . Ooooh . . .'

'Pa! Are you in there?!!' We were suddenly fearful and started to hammer on the door.

Terry's roar burst from behind the door.

'SOD OFF!'

'Pa, are you in there?'

'OF COURSE, I'M IN HERE! SOD OFF!'

We finally got the message and, doubled over in laughter, we staggered into our room. Suddenly Terry stood in our doorway, dressed in Y-fronts and black socks.

'You pair of bastards!' he howled. 'That's the first woman I've been with in eighteen months, and you two bastards come in the middle, just as I was about to . . .'

He never finished his sentence because, just then, the sitting room door opened and out walked this gorgeous-looking woman who could have been Anna Magnani's slightly older sister.

'Stone the crows!' we gawped.

'I'll stone your bloody crows!' Terry bellowed. 'You're like two big . . . bloody schoolgirls! Why don't you bloody well stay out like other men and find yourselves a bloody girlfriend . . . !'

God knows I was never anyone's idea of a Romeo. Since Bristol only the occasional opportunity had arisen and the experience was rarely as romantic as I hoped it might be. I remember one girl, a school teacher who appeared backstage with her girlfriend one night after a performance of *Come Blow Your Horn*. We started going out together accompanied by a friend of mine who was an usher at the theatre. The four of us would go off to Ronnie Scott's on an occasional Saturday night to listen to jazz till three in the morning. I had a car, and we'd drive the girls home, dropping them at their front door with just a friendly goodnight kiss. And that was it.

One night my usher friend, who'd had a lot of practice in the art of frontal attack, cheerfully told me his plans for our double-date that night. 'Leave us alone in the car,' he instructed. 'You go off somewhere with your school teacher because I'm onto a real certainty.'

'Well, what the hell am I gonna do? I complained; it was my car he was using.

'Oh, c'mon,' he said. 'You're not on a real dead cert, are you? I am.'

'Alright,' I said. 'But if it's raining, forget it! I'm not gonna be walking down the bloody towpath while it's pouring with rain!'

That night, the four of us drove to the river side and in a lame attempt to carry out the plan, I asked my date if she'd like to go for a walk. We walked down to the towpath, and sat down on the ground along the embankment of the river. We talked and talked and hugged and then we kissed and before I knew it, my trousers were unexpectedly around my ankles – and what had seemed very uncertain had turned out to be very certain indeed.

When we finally returned to the car we found my friend and his date sitting together in stony silence. 'Uh, hullo,' he said. It was obvious his dead cert hadn't come through after all.

On the short drive home after dropping off our dates, I began to experience the most extraordinary discomfort. Within minutes the itching around my privates was almost unbearable, and I was really shaken. 'You know, if you catch something,' I asked my friend, 'what does it, uh, I mean, what does it feel like?'

'Well, you get itching . . .' he replied.

'Itching?' I yelped. 'I'm itching like crazy!'

'Well,' he said, 'I think it takes a few days.'

'Oh, my God, I've got it bad – it's itching right now!'

Within minutes the fiery sensation in my crotch forced us to pull the car into a lay-by and, by car light and the aid of a torch, we inspected the damage of my offending parts. 'It's all around here,' I cried. 'Look at the spots!' A hurried trip to a doctor eased my mind; my manhood would remain operative and intact. But, he cautioned me, young man, when you make love, try not to do it while lying in a bed of stinging nettles.

This was my second grown-up sexual experience and it was as fraught with anxiety and guilt as the first. In fact, my youthful zealot's brand of Catholicism was beginning to test everyone's patience. Many friends grew fed up with me, and I think I frightened a lot of girls off because of my intensity. The problem seemed to be this awful tug of war between my two awakenings, the spiritual and the sexual. I was obviously far too wide awake in both areas. It was though I had been born again again. Instead of just again.

And then I met a beautiful girl, a model named Virginia who sometimes wore woolly black stockings. Not the sexiest of garments, I grant you, but they were dazzling on her because she had the most beautiful body. Virginia was fast losing patience. You see the thing was, that on the Saturday evenings I went out with her, I'd always been to confession earlier in preparation for Mass on the following morning. So whenever I contemplated launching myself on top of that beautiful body, in my mind I couldn't help seeing my evangelical mentor, my priest wagging a finger of disapproval at my none too divine intentions, and, unfortunately, Virginia's Jewish faith didn't give her much insight into my predicament. Well, in the end I decided that God would be forgiving enough to take into account all my struggles with my conscience, and wouldn't judge me too harshly if I just slipped every now and then. I slipped alright, but I'm not complaining in the least. And there's no doubt in my mind that Virginia in her sexy tights was my sexual Waterloo.

CHAPTER 9

Adza had a call from Frank Dunlop, who was directing *The Importance of Being Earnest*. The production was scheduled to open the brand-new Nottingham Playhouse, home to the rep company whose artistic director, John Neville, would star in Wilde's famous comedy. Dunlop wanted me to take over the part of Algernon from another actor. Almost as an afterthought, I was also assigned a minor role in the production of Shakespeare's *Coriolanus*.

That year the Nottingham company was an impressive group. Ian McKellen was its newest rising star and cast to play Tullus Aufidius, which was to prove his great breakthrough performance; Helen Ryan and June Ritchie were also part of the company. So was Leo McKern, whose party piece at the local Chinese restaurant was to remove his glass eye and place it in one of the freshly served dishes. The waiter was called back to the table, then we all turned and watched his horrified expression as he saw an eye staring at him from among Leo's prawn balls.

We began rehearsals for *Coriolanus* in late November

with the already legendary Tyrone Guthrie as guest director. He was an astonishingly theatrical figure to me; a towering six-foot-four-or-more inches with a handsome face distinguished by a jutting beak of a nose, a promontory so large it would have done honour to a curlew. His military brush-cut and ramrod bearing only served to exaggerate his dramatic 'Your Country Needs You' persona – he was all resonant, booming voice and arm-waving enthusiasm. It was easy to see why he was said to be the only person apart from Elizabeth Taylor who could control Richard Burton. He provided some of the most exciting and testing rehearsal-time I've ever experienced.

I arrived at the London rehearsal room for the read-through totally ignorant of the role I was to play, and was only then handed the script of 'Cor-RYE-u-lanus' (as Guthrie pronounced it). It was decided that I would play Second Citizen and Second Serving Man.

I didn't know a thing about the play or my parts in it, so I decided to run the gamut of my limited accent reper-toire in order to make one character so entirely different from the other that the unsuspecting audience would never imagine that both were being played by one-and-the-same actor (and with such amazing dexterity!).

I never thought to ask, but I'm sure if I had, I would have discovered that everyone perceived the Second Serving Man as a fairly uncouth type, more at home in the local alehouse than in the drawing room. I decided to make him the ultimate Jeeves.

I heard my first cue from my counterpart – a rough-and-ready First Serving Man with an accent to match – to whom I proudly gave my response. It must have sounded as if my character had mistakenly wandered into the wrong theatre: we sounded like a production called 'The Admirable Crichton Meets the Artful Dodger'.

I was a boy among men. This was my great opportunity to prove myself, and I was trying to grab it by the horns. I began to hear some stifled chuckles and coughing around the rehearsal room but still I droned on, mentally flailing about for a way to extricate myself from this preposterous accent. But I was so far gone, I couldn't stop. Having left the jetty, no way would I miss the water now.

Youthful humiliation is a particularly messy sight. I felt like such a fool – and in front of the Great Guthrie! My head sank lower and lower into the book; my ears turned scarlet and glowed like Vesuvius the night before it erupted over Pompeii.

Without even bothering to pick up my coat, and rigid with embarrassment – I couldn't look to left or right in case I caught someone's eye – I left the rehearsal room at the end of the read-through, and headed straight for the tube station. I got on the Circle Line and stayed there the rest of the day riding round and round London, miserably hunched in the corner of the car, a dismal figure of dejection. It was the only place I felt safe, where no one could get to me, where there would be no more humiliation.

When I emerged from my hideaway hours later, I wandered about to find a telephone booth to call Adza. 'Adza,' I quavered into the phone, 'the most terrible thing has happened . . .'

'Michael? Where are you, daaahhling?' she asked.

'I've been on the Circle Line all day,' I said.

There was a long pause at the other end. You could almost hear the cogs turning: What's he doing on the Circle Line? Didn't he start a new job today?

'This is all your fault,' I wailed to her. 'You should've told me what I was going to play!' I told her what I'd done and she laughed. 'Look,' I said, 'it's not funny

Adza. This is it, my career is at an end. I've made a total fool of myself.'

'Dahhlling boy,' she said, 'you know you've got to go back, you're under contract.'

'I'm never going back. I'm not. They were laughing at me. I'm just no good. Adza, I'm giving up acting. I'm joining the Air Force.' (Mum used to keep plenty of applications on hand for just such occasions. It never occurred to me, of course, that one had to pass all sorts of exams to be accepted. I suppose I expected to just take off like Peter Pan.)

With her usual graceful blend of good humour and tact, Adza persuaded me to return to the company a few days later. I walked in, pretending nothing had happened, and mumbled my hellos, and was amazed to discover that everyone knew my name no company had ever learned a minor supporting player's identity as quickly as that company had learned mine.

It was at that next rehearsal that I got to know my counterpart, the 'First Serving Man', John D. Collins. He was another young, struggling actor who became a good friend and, eventually, my long-suffering roommate. He was as impoverished as I was. Out of his slightly undernourished frame came an unexpectedly deep voice, well-suited to expounding the rich music of Shakespeare's language. Tall, with a receding hairline and dark eyes set back in his head, my favourite memory of him is his rocking with laughter, backwards and forwards from the hips, like one of those laughing-sailor figures at the seaside.

Nineteen sixty-three marked an exceptionally cold winter in England. The icy air felt like a glacier and both John and I suffered from chilblains as well as terminal poverty; consequently we seemed made for each other. We were paid the handsome sum of eight pounds a week, but with rent to pay and the expenses that keep body and soul together, we were usually broke by midweek. The occasional cigarette was a luxury. Domino's was our brand, because at the time you could buy a packet of just two. When I was terribly broke, I'd apply as much negotiating skill as I could muster for the purchase of a single cigarette, or else I was reduced to picking stray butt-ends from strangers' ashtrays.

Our first flat was in what had formerly been a none-too-successful brothel. Our landlady was almost always on her own now, and both she and the establishment had seen much better days. Just to keep her hand in, she'd make some enthusiastic grabs at either John or me – depending upon who was in the door first when we came home at night – offering the 'free sample', so to speak. Climbing the stairs at night was like running the gauntlet.

I had a higher priority – food – so I tried to make sure John went through the door first. 'Allo, boys!' came that cheery voice from the front room. With a shove I'd propel him inside and into our landlady's motherly clutches, which left me free to take first-grabs at leftovers in the fridge. Every now and then I would call out from the kitchen, 'He loves you, Missus! He really loves you,' just to egg things on a bit. John, ever the gent, always visited her for a few minutes. I think it was partly that he was terrified she might raise our rent, but he always swore to me that nothing ever happened.

Many a night we were forced to sleep in the same bed, wrapped in our coats to keep warm. The place was freezing. (I think the first time I truly believed that I had achieved some professional success was when I was finally able to afford a centrally-heated flat.) Conditions were so bad that even when we actually found girls willing to come back to the flat with us, we often had to borrow a shilling from them for the meter, to keep us warm. This didn't exactly enhance our image, and the girls would routinely take off halfway into the evening when they realised they could do much better with the local boys.

Eventually John and I decided that desperate measures were called for; we had to find new digs. I don't know who had the idea first but it suddenly seemed so obvious: we would sleep in the theatre. It was newly built, clean and modern and, besides, there was all that central heating going to waste.

It would be so easy. Just hang around at night until everyone leaves, then dive into the top of the hanging space in the dressing room and pull the curtains across. (There were great open coat-hanger areas for the costumes, with wide racks above where hats and suitcases were stored, and while breathing conditions weren't exactly optimum, they seemed preferable to freezing to death.) John and I did just that.

There was no night watchman. Someone would simply lock up and turn the lights out, except for the work lights downstairs. John and I brought in flashlights, and a cache of food during the day, and a little radio for entertainment.

After a few days of timid exploring we found new kitchens in the building, not yet in operation, and this glad discovery allowed us to pull off the occasional hot meal. It was practically paradise; we might be living there still had it not been for an unfortunate accident with one of the new stoves. After the firemen left, the police arrived and patiently explained the paramount importance of our finding new accommodation.

Tactfully, no one in the company mentioned anything the next day. But that night on the notice board the

Artistic Director posted a rather cryptic message: 'May I point out it is forbidden for any member of the company to sleep in the theatre.'

Rehearsals with Guthrie began in earnest. He knew how to get the very best from the company, giving us all continuous encouragement.

One look at me in tights and anyone could see why Guthrie envisioned my minor role in *Coriolanus* as a running gag. (I looked like a stick-legged Lowry figure come to life.) Guthrie positioned John and me at either end of a long ladder which we carried back and forth, trotting across the apron of the stage, making dry little comments about life.

A rectangular hole had been cut into the covered stage apron, with steep steps placed inside descending down into the orchestra pit. John held the ladder in such a way that it was fully balanced on his shoulders, although to the audience it appeared as if I was supporting the back half. John walked in front of me and blithely passed over the open hole as if it didn't exist. I followed behind and fell straight into the hole and down the steep stairway. John carried on walking with five feet of ladder behind him and no one supporting it. It looked both ridiculous and impossible, and the audience would gasp, and stand up to see where I'd disappeared to.

John and I worked on that routine for hours at a time. We were always trying to invent some new bit of business to offer the always receptive Guthrie. For my part, I was trying to make up for the debacle that had been my 'Jeeves' read-through.

Our small stunts were a minor sensation with the audience. I relished hearing their gasps and the relieved, delighted laughter that followed my reappearance. My ambition to do more – much more – was firmly planted at those moments. Happily, our 'Serving Men' were favourably mentioned in *The Times*, and I still think of that small role in 'Cor-RYE-u-lanus' as one of the happiest and best things I've ever done.

When I left Nottingham I joined the cast of *March Hares*, a new comedy by Ronald Harwood that starred Ian Carmichael, and toured England for four weeks. The production was summed up by the critic in the Manchester *Daily Express* who began his brief essay with the sentence, 'How I lost 120 minutes of my life . . .' (It's a favourite of mine, among my bad reviews. I keep those notices; they are entertaining to read, given a few years vantage.)

Then Colin Graham called me. He had known me since I was fourteen, when he was stage manager for the *Let's Make an Opera* tour (he is now the renowned director of the St Louis Opera Company in America). He offered me an opportunity to join the New Shakespeare Company for a tour that included Michael Blakemore, Stephen Moore, Jane Ryan and Annette Crosbie in the company. Colin wanted me for the role of Feste in Shakespeare's *Twelfth Night*, which he was directing.

Frankly, I've always found the classics a little daunting and I recall racing out to buy a Lamb's *Tales From Shakespeare* – a re-telling of the stories in simple prose for children – to read up on the play. I'm glad I decided to do it; it was an inventive production with music especially written for it by Johnny Dankworth.

Michael Blakemore was our Sir Toby Belch. Those were the days before he became one of the best known and most respected directors on both sides of the Atlantic, but his success was to be expected; he was always a leader of men. I christened him 'The Colonel'.

When our tour of the provinces took us to Darlington, he sent us out on 'manoeuvres' to the schools to give tickets away to get people to come. (We'd been there over a week and hadn't sold a hundred pounds' worth of seats.) His strategy worked; we were sold out in our second week. There was an additional side tour to Portugal for the company, made memorable by a weekend on the beach at Estoril, where Michael, being Australian, taught me the finer points of bodysurfing. But the tour's highlight was in July 1964 when we performed at the Middle Temple, one of the Inns of Court, in the presence of the Queen Mother. She greeted the cast afterwards and was complimentary about my singing. 'It brought tears to my eyes,' she said to me, 'and the ... the ...' She pointed toward the roof. 'The acoustics?' I said, finishing her sentence for her – I was instantly appalled at myself for interrupting her – 'Yes, that's it!' she smiled. 'They were so perfect . . .'

Adza motored down to see me in Sheerness one evening when I was visiting Nan. It was in the middle of a postal strike and she wanted personally to deliver a play she had read that was to open in London at the New Arts Theatre. It was called *The Striplings*, and was a rather dark piece about the innocence of youth pitted against problems it is unequipped to meet, and an angry young man trying to adjust to life after the death of his mother. It wasn't exactly Chekhov, but I felt the role might have been written for me at that moment, so I agreed to do it.

The play had only a brief run at the New Arts, but it gave me some valuable clues to everything I didn't know about being an actor. I had a rather affecting speech near the end of the play, during which I condemned the world, a drunken youth railing against the heavens, unable to forgive the corruption of his sister. It didn't take long before I discovered that all the yelling was having a fairly disastrous effect on my throat; I developed nodules on my vocal chords and was forever coming down with laryngitis. In those days I was fairly smart-aleck in my approach to any kind of training, and I stupidly did nothing about learning voice control until some twelve years later when I was to star in the musical *Billy*. It was only then that I was finally placed in the capable hands of the finest of vocal teachers, Ian Adam, who undoubtedly saved me from doing more permanent damage.

Before we closed I heard the news that I had won a role in a new film to be made by Richard Lester, a man who was, by all accounts, Britain's newest, most creative director. I was cast in *The Knack . . . And How To Get It*. It was 1964, and for me the Swinging Sixties were really about to begin.

CHAPTER 10

RICHARD LESTER IS an absolute original, as brilliant and quirky as the decade that, cinematically at least, he came to symbolise. He is fast-talking and has a brain that travels at twice the speed of sound. He is ten years to the day older than I am, but when I first met him I was hard-pressed to gauge his age; he was a victim of early runaway baldness, and I thought him old enough to be my father. He has a monkish look about him. Whenever he consulted with anyone, he kept his hands folded in front of him, fingers entwined as if silently praying. His thin face was framed by a heavy fringe of sideburns, and he kept his naturally-tonsured skull shoved deep between hunched shoulders until he had something to say – then it popped up and moved about like the nodding head on one of those toy animals you sometimes see on a New York cabbie's dashboard.

His accent sounded Canadian to me but, in fact, he's American, born in Philadelphia. He began school there at age three and finished his studies at the University of Pennsylvania at nineteen (with a degree, I was awed to learn, in clinical psychology). By twenty-one Dick Lester was already well established in the infant industry of commercial television – an industry still so new that the television staff in his hometown had to use the radio station's studios in order to operate. It was Dick's background that fundamentally coloured the very idiosyncratic way he has with a camera.

By the time I met him in 1964, he had already been living in London for ten years. He decided to stay on when, after finishing a European tour, his professional experience landed him a job with the BBC at a time when no one in England knew that much about commercial television

Dick made his first big impact in Britain as the producer of a television comedy series (with bizarre show titles like 'A Show Called Fred' and 'Son of Fred') that attempted to achieve visually what Spike Milligan's 'Goon Show' had done on radio. He went into a project with Peter Sellers after that, directing a brilliant little film for him called *The Running, Jumping and Standing Still Film*. Eventually this and a few other 'small' films earned Dick a reputation as a director of cult classics. (A 'cult' director, Dick told one journalist, means you're unemployable.) It was his inspired lunatic brilliance with a camera, combining television-learned techniques with a kind of Keystone Cops visual humour, together with his incredible ability to work wonders on a small budget, that brought him to the attention of the Beatles' management.

They chose Dick to direct the first Beatles film, *A Hard Day's Night*. That film, which reviewers agreed 'captured the exuberant nonconformist spirit of the Beatles', gave Dick Lester the kind of full-blown success he deserved.

He had seen me in the Steve McQueen film *The War Lover* before he cast me in *The Knack*, a comedy adapted

from a successful West End play by the director/
playwright Ann Jellicoe. It was all about the problems of
an idealistic young lad, Colin, desperate to learn the
knack of getting the girls from another young fellow,
Tolan, who definitely had it. At the time the part of
Colin seemed to me entirely autobiographical. Ray
Brooks was cast in the part of Tolan, the London
Lothario with a success rate in female conquests that
would have given David Hemmings pause, and he was
superb. Donal Donnelly portrayed an Irish painter, a
cheery witness and sharp commentator on the scene. The
object of our hot pursuit was Rita Tushingham, a quiet,
charming girl, and a fine actress too, who had already
made a name for herself in an earlier film, *The Girl with
Green Eyes*. John Barry was brought in to write the film's
music score. It was a Lester family party from beginning
to end.

Like the other early Lester films, our budget was pretty
much a shoestring affair. This wasn't Hollywood; we
three men shared one caravan – no comparison to those
vast American recreational vehicles – and we had to be
damn careful about where we stood in it. There was no
special paraphernalia to keep the caravan standing level
as there is today, and if we happened to group at one end,
it would tip up completely and all the chairs, tables,
lights and make-up kits would fly from one end to the
other.

Much of the play's original dialogue was retained, but
with the help of his brilliant screenwriter, Charles Wood,
Dick Lester's surrealist camera opened up the story to the
whole of London, rather than keeping it stuck within the
closed confines of a flat as in the play. There is a sequence
in the film for which Dick is justly famous. He and his
camera followed Donal, Rita and me through chilly
London streets and alleys, over railways bridges, and

down the Thames on a raft as we pushed, pulled or rode on a massive iron bedstead that we picked up in a scrap yard – a bed the young hero hopes will bring him the knack he is so desperately hoping to acquire. It took about six days to shoot the scene, and it was incredibly hard work. The bed was ridiculously heavy. It took an Act of Parliament just to move it up and down the steps of the Royal Albert Hall. The scene was only sketchily laid out, and Dick would follow behind us with a hand-held camera so he could capture the spontaneous reactions of all the passers-by. People of all ages, classes and descriptions served as Dick Lester's wry chorus throughout the film, lamenting the decline and decadence of contemporary youth.

It was about this time that I had a child maintenance and breach of promise case brought against me. Both were settled and a court order was agreed to by both parties not to talk or reveal details. Without breaching that order I would just like to say that that child has grown into a very special young person who chooses privacy.

In the middle of shooting *The Knack* I took time off for an interview with the writer and director Ned Sherrin, fresh from his most recent success as the creator of the brilliantly innovative 'TW3' (*That Was The Week That Was*). Ned was one of the bright new voices in broadcasting in the sixties and, like Dick Lester, he was thoroughly grounded in television and keenly aware of all its powerful possibilities. Ned was working on a new series for BBC-TV, a kind of sequel to 'TW3' called *Not So Much a Programme, More a Way of Life* – or, as it was promoted, '. . . a way of looking at the world; one eye open wide; one eye closed; and between the two the picture gets composed'.

Ned claims he first saw me when I was still Michael Ingram in a radio play called *The Little Beggars*, which he had written with Caryl Brahms. Based on my work in *Come Blow Your Horn* and *Twelfth Night*, he cast me in the part of a cool Liverpudlian character he invented, working with two wonderful writers, Peter Lewis and Peter Dobereiner. As they envisioned it, the character would serve as a kind of teenage everyman, an observer of the human condition, like Holden Caulfield in J. D. Salinger's *The Catcher in the Rye*, telling stories and analysing the current social scene in a five-minute segment of the Sunday night programme.

The scheduling was absolutely ideal; I could continue filming *The Knack* during the rest of the week. More importantly, Ned's show was the perfect spot for me to wear my new tailored leather jacket and winkle-picker shoes; I even used my bike as an occasional prop. My accent sounded not unlike the Beatles' George Harrison, and after the amount of work I'd done trying to perfect it, I found it hard to lose. (I saw an old recording recently of an interview I did at the same time as myself – that accent was still there, and painfully embarrassing to listen to now.)

The writing was sharp, and even at this distance a little shocking; I remember a speech about motoring and waiting at the traffic light next to another car: 'There was a girl in the car, one of those debutantes. Y'know . . . she had an expression on her face as though she was thawin' out a packet of frozen peas between her legs.'

The audience absolutely adored it; it was as though all my previous years of work had never happened. Suddenly I had no past at all; I was just 'Byron' – the model 'Mr Cool', the young man with a sharp vocabulary who had only to say things like 'smashed to fragments' or describe a situation as 'turgid' for those words and phrases to become part of the 'in' vocabulary.

The reader may get a clearer picture of the character of Byron from the sample of a Dobereiner/Lewis monologue that follows. It was written for my appearance at a Royal Show before the Queen and other members of the royal family, but was never used.

> ... When I think what you have to go through [to attend one of the royal functions] really they ought to give you a Duke of Edinburgh's Award for it. I'm not surprised he's chickened out. Of course they [the royals] don't have to come out to go to the pictures, you know. They make their own. You've probably seen it. He's probably in their private cinema right now with his feet up waiting for that funny bit, sucking his orange juice through a straw and telling Charles to hurry up and pass the nuts. Still it's nice to have the rest of the family here. I mean, the management are pleased. It's the one time they can play the National Anthem without emptying the cinema ...

(Never used, I say, because nothing short of a firing squad could have persuaded me to stand before Queen and Country and deliver that speech.)

Byron Fan Clubs sprang up everywhere. I was even given my own column in *Fab* magazine 'with commentaries on the social scene by "Byron"'. I only played the role for nine weeks but the character was so strong, it would pigeonhole me for years. Any future problems, however, were far outweighed by the immediate benefits: 'Byron' was in professional demand.

When Dick wrapped up work on *The Knack*, I began rehearsals for a play called *Travelling Light*, to be directed by Ann Jellicoe, and produced by Michael Codron, co-starring Harry H. Corbett and Julia Foster. It was in this play that Harry was finally able to remind everyone what a fine comedian he was by escaping from his television image in *Steptoe and Son* – something that for some time to come was to elude Michael 'Byron' Crawford. Harry was a wonderful man. I never saw him when he wasn't carried away in some rush of enthusiasm about something or other, too excited to finish a single sentence or stand still, as if his mouth couldn't keep up and his madly flailing arms had to do the talking.

The production of *Travelling Light* was plagued by troubles from the very start of rehearsals, which were long and arduous, starting at eight-thirty in the morning some days and sometimes running past midnight into the early hours of the next morning.

We were set to open at the Prince of Wales Theatre, a difficult place to fill at best, and where, two years before, I'd been with *Come Blow Your Horn*. It holds somewhere between eleven and thirteen hundred people, depending upon the production, and is set very wide. It has a history of musical shows, and I've always thought of it as rather unsuitable for something billed as an 'intimate farce'. There was immediate friction between Ann Jellicoe and Harry Corbett, who didn't see eye-to-eye on the development of Harry's character. He simply didn't believe what his character was being asked to do, but she stood her ground. Both believed passionately in their point of view, but there was little compromise between them, and Ann Jellicoe eventually left the production to be replaced by Billy Chappell, a director with a background in musical comedy and dance.

Travelling Light was written by Leonard Kingston. He kept right on writing it, in fact – right up to the very first moments of our opening night. Harry was cast as a salesman of soap made by the blind and I played his flat-mate, a naïve young man who likes to meditate while folding himself in the lotus position. We could all see the show had more than a few story problems and we were constantly being given new scenes to memorise, sometimes on the afternoon of a matinée. I had lines written on tiny slips of paper inside my coat pockets; lines were stuck on the backs of chairs. There were lines written under suit lapels, on my cuffs, on my shirt, under my tie, everywhere. One day I actually found a new page of dialogue when I opened a suitcase in the first act.

In desperation, Harry and I developed a kind of choreographic routine to deal with all the changes. The sequence ran something like this: read lines written inside left-hand, then change to inside right-hand, then right-hand-to-left-wrist, then back-of-right-wrist-to-back-of-other-hand. (We'd do that by rubbing the hand underneath the nose, always a popular ploy; when you see somebody rubbing their hand under their nose on one of those chat shows, just check to be sure they're not reading a line written on the back of their hand – or when they pull on the ear lobe, watch out, you might see a line written inside the cuff.) All this carrying-on, mind you, was designed just to get us through the first scene in Act I.

Regrettably, on opening night at the Prince of Wales we went from Act I to the end of Act II to close the end of Act I – Harry had understandably forgotten some of the sequence in our routine. Fortunately, I was playing a complete simpleton so I would look just as stupid as I felt. I'd stare at him and say, 'Uh, what do we do now . . . ?' It got to be the running line that night – and rarely has a line held so much meaning! One reviewer, in fact, said the dialogue was 'beautifully written, full of comic invention and exactly tailored to fit the characters'. I can only assume he had mistakenly wandered into the wrong theatre at the interval.

Almost every night after the performance Harry and I would go for a drink at a place owned by the writer Wolf Mankowitz called the Pickwick Club, opposite the Arts Theatre in Great Newport Street. It was a favourite theatrical hangout. There seemed to be many more of such places in those days, where actors would mix with other theatre people for a pint, some music, and a good supper after a performance.

At that time I was still in the fog of turmoil and confusion into which I'd been thrown by the death of my mother. For the first time in twenty-one years I wasn't the most important person in someone's life.

But however unhappy I was, I'd always believed that one day I would find the love of my life.

Then I saw her. I felt just like Robert Taylor when he stood on Waterloo Bridge in the film of that name, and saw Vivien Leigh emerging from the fog – except that I was in a basement nightclub in Great Newport Street and she was emerging from a haze of Peter Stuyvesant cigarette smoke. The Pickwick used to boast good pop music along with the ale, and here was the girl who was evidently employed to play records. I could only see her from the waist up, because she was sitting in what looked like a converted confession box, but with the main grille taken out.

Unlike my dear, folically deprived priest, though, she had long, dark, shoulder-length hair and a pale, delicate beauty. She'd take a lazy drag of her cigarette, then the cigarette would be whisked away as her head was thrown back and she blew the smoke slowly downwards. It was heaven! She hardly ever looked outside the box, but I wouldn't have had the courage to meet her eye anyway.

When I sat with Harry, I made sure my back was to the wall so that I could watch her. I never had the nerve to go over and speak to her, but she knew I was interested; night after night after night, I sent over a request for her to play Donovan's 'Catch The Wind'.

I nagged at Harry about how I fancied her and that I'd like to invite her out but I didn't know how to do it. I drove him crazy for weeks. I was so excited I thought maybe I should send her over a bottle of Asti-Spumante? 'For Chris' sake,' he finally exploded, 'I'll go and sodding sort it out before you drive me completely round the sodding bend!'

'Ah, Harry,' I said (now that he was doing exactly what I hoped he'd do), 'that's very nice of you.'

'Oh, piss off,' he snorted. Harry walked over to the booth, and I could see him animatedly talking to the girl. She smiled at him, and peeked over his shoulder to take a look at me. I used that moment to duck. 'Look,' Harry was saying to her, 'there's a geezer over there with his head under the table who's driving me sodding mad about taking you out – and he hasn't got the bottle to come and ask you himself, so I've been sent over. For Chris' sake, go out with him before he drives me round the sodding bend!'

After such a charming introduction, how could she possibly refuse?

'Well,' she said, 'he doesn't look too keen . . .'

'That's because I've just kicked his arse for him,' Harry

told her. She still seemed reluctant, but eventually she joined us and, thanks to Harry, I was finally introduced to Gabrielle Mary Lewis.

'If you have a night off,' I said, hoping to impress, 'maybe you'd like to come and see our show?' Then maybe not, I thought; I was playing a retarded door-to-door salesman of soap made by the blind – hardly Richard Burton as Henry IV. Anyway she agreed to come and to have dinner with me afterwards. I couldn't think of anywhere to go, so I took her, with all the imagination of a potato, to her place of work, the Pickwick Club.

I believe I've always been guided to the right people. Gabrielle and I had an immediate rapport. She was very talkative, and seemed quite self-assured. She was an actress currently in a repertory company in Bromley and working as a disc jockey at night to pay the rent on her flat in Guthrie Street. Besotted, I sent her flowers when she appeared in one of her rep productions – a dozen roses with a card that read, 'Good luck, shy star!' We were seeing each other all the time. We were madly in love and our energy was endless. We were here, there and everywhere, as the Beatles so beautifully put it. At that time image was everything. Gabrielle had the Biba look, hair cut shorter now and very short skirts. When it came to high fashion, Harry Fenton was my weakness. We had great fun with clothes and style, which resulted in some memorable photo sessions with David Bailey et al.

Gabrielle and I could communicate across a room, exchange just a look or a glance and know what the other one was thinking. When we made love I never wanted it to end. I remember holding her so tightly. 'I hope we're doing this when we're sixty,' I said.

The day came, of course, when I was invited down for the weekend to meet her parents, who lived in Kent, in a charming cottage called 'The Roses'. Frankly, the prospect of a weekend with her parents frightened me, but they made it very easy. Her father, Ben Lewis, was a Naval Surgeon Captain. He had served in the Pacific, Malta, and in Tunis, at all the big Naval hospitals. He was an immensely popular doctor of the old school. No matter how busy he was, he always had time for everyone and I found him very easy to talk to. Gabrielle's mother proved to be a bit more daunting.

Molly Murless Lewis had to be a very strong lady, raising her four children pretty much alone while her husband was away on active duty. Gabrielle told me her mother had been a journalist before her marriage, working on various newspapers and ultimately landing a job as Editor of the *Nursing Times*. She's always been a great adventurer and boasts a pilot's licence. (A woman after my own heart!) I'm sure neither of the Lewises relished having their only daughter marry an actor, but they made me feel instantly and completely at home. Their lovely place in Kent brought back some wonderful memories for me of hot afternoons in Sheerness. I loved their garden – so much, in fact, that one day I went scrumping in the gooseberry bushes outside the kitchen window. Hearing the commotion outside, Mrs Lewis thought she had discovered a prowler and she ordered me out of the bushes at the end of a shotgun pointed directly at my backside. It took me a while to live that one down.

I lost my voice again during the run of *Travelling Light* and went to Norman Punt, throat specialist to the Queen and very popular with theatre people, who told me I would have to take a week or two off from the show, a piece of news that normally would have driven me up the wall. But this wasn't like having the flu, when the performer has at least a choice in the matter; no voice means no performance, and there wasn't much I could do about it except obey doctor's orders.

With the thought of two weeks' enforced vacation ahead of me, and not much else in my head, I had the brilliant idea of taking Gabrielle to the Cannes Film Festival, where *The Knack* was showing to rave reviews.

I can't go to work, I told her, and I've been invited to the Festival, so why not drive down there for a few days? Gabrielle thought it was a marvellous idea. So, in that careless, romantic state of mind that comprised our entire approach to life in those days, and with barely a word to anyone, including the theatre management or her parents, we took off in my prized little Austin 1100 and drove straight to Dover, travelled across on the hovercraft, and drove overnight to Nice and along the French Riviera to Cannes. We even found a flat to let in a beautiful little town called Eze-sur-Mer just outside Cannes; it was over a patisserie and cost us practically nothing. We arrived just in time for the festivities and met up with Dick Lester and *The Knack* producer, Oscar Lewenstein. I remember John Lennon was there at the time, and Rita Tushingham too. Cannes was one great big party.

Within forty-eight hours a photo crossed the news service wires to London showing my Cheshire grin wedged between the smiling faces of John Lennon and Richard Lester, all of us saying how delighted we were about the success of *The Knack*.

Michael Crawford? Isn't he the actor without a voice, the one who can't go on because he is under a doctor's care?

I have no idea how she managed it, but Adza tracked us down and was immediately on the phone: 'Dahhhlling, I think you've made a definite error of judgment here.' She sounded very theatrical. 'No, sweet one, you haven't actually done anything illeeeegal,' she said, 'but you could say that it is a bit of a cock-up!'

The engine of my Austin had barely cooled from the long journey to Cannes when I had to turn it round for the trip home. Tail between my legs, I returned to London, exceedingly defensive about the trip. 'Well, here I am back again. What do you want me to do? I can't go back on again, I've still got no voice . . .' 'Not surprising,' replied Michael Codron, 'after a day-and-night drive to France on half a bottle of Pro-Plus!' I was lucky I wasn't suspended, but Michael was easily the most tolerant producer I've ever worked for. One more lesson learned – as usual, the hard way.

Before the year was out I had received the Variety Club Award for 'best newcomer of 1965' for my work in *The Knack, Travelling Light* and as 'Byron'. And to top it off, I was nominated for *The Knack* by the British Film Academy as 'most promising newcomer' along with Judi Dench, Barbara Ferris and Michael Nardini.

The film awards gala was held at the Grosvenor House Hotel with all the elegance and excitement you would expect. The entire work force of the Granada Television Network was also in attendance to guarantee the event was given worldwide coverage. The evening's master of ceremonies was the debonair film star James Mason, whose job was to read out the name of each category nominee and the film they were in, then wait while the film clip was shown before he announced the name of the winner.

By any standard it had already been a long evening when 'the most promising newcomer' award rolled around. Mr Mason was beginning to look a bit frayed around the edges by this time; in fact there was a distinct impression throughout the room that someone had tampered with his water jug. Mind you, Mr Mason continued to be debonair – I'm convinced he emerged in that condition from his mother's womb – and was pursuing his duties in the best show-must-go-on tradition as he slowly began to read out the nominees for '1965's most promising newcomer'.

It was a nervous moment. This was only the second time I'd been up for any kind of prize since winning a bow and arrow at Oakfield School for coming first in the high jump with a wind-assisted jump of four feet six inches.

'And the winner is . . .' he announced, taking a hard squint at the television monitor, 'the winner is Michael, uh, Crawford for, uh, his performance in *The Knack* . . .' The applause rang out, and I went completely insane.

I am the first to admit it; I love winning awards of any kind. But there was something especially sweet in this one. The film had done very well in Europe and America, winning all kinds of honours abroad, yet it had met with resistance from the film establishment in England. *The Knack* won the best picture award at the Cannes Film Festival, but had been originally rejected by the British selection committee, and was only shown on the enthusiastic recommendation of the French cultural attaché in London. Thus I felt doubly overjoyed receiving this honour from the British industry for a film which it had previously snubbed.

I leaped to my feet and bounded up the stairs, three at a time, scarcely touching the richly carpeted floor on my way to the stage. Mr Mason looked at me with a slightly quizzical stare. He appeared to be trying to take in all the grinning Crawfords standing in front of him, as if he were trying to decide which one he should address. Then he was interrupted by Michael Scott, the compere. After an eternal moment of consultation and paper-rustling, Mr Mason apologised to both of me (and to the twenty million television viewers).

'Oh . . . well, I'm awfully sorry,' he said, 'but there's been a mistake . . .'

'I'm sorry . . . ?' I gasped.

'Michael, it doesn't appear that you actually have won . . .'

My face took on the sort of glow not seen there since the doctors slapped me around at birth. *Please, God*, I silently prayed, *if you'll just send a small earthquake to open the earth and swallow me up right now, I'll never ask another favour.*

'I'm so sorry,' he said.

Ever ready with a merry quip – and in an attempt to convince the audience I was taking all this in my stride – I said: 'Well, did I come in second . . . ?'

Silence.

Mr Mason just gave me a 'kindly leave the stage' look, and read out Judi Dench's name over my shoulder.

I left the stage, my eyes firmly fixed on the now hideous carpet design as I rushed back to my seat, bumping into tables and knocking glasses out of hands en route.

I'm older now and a bit more philosophical, and can accept the experience with relative calm as one of those things that happen in life – but, hopefully, never again to me in this lifetime.

CHAPTER 11

DICK LESTER HAD just finished another film with the Beatles called *Help!* and was embarking on a new project when he called me. He said he was off to Spain to direct the filming of the Stephen Sondheim musical *A Funny Thing Happened on the Way to the Forum*, a wild comedy set in ancient Rome. With Lester at the helm, I knew 'wild comedy' meant slapstick; Dick loved the golden age of silent comedy with all its pratfalls and stunts and chase scenes.

I was called in for the young romantic hero (he was even called Hero). The big question was my legs; what's he going to look like in a toga? *Forum* was a farce, so my legs were judged a smash – so much so, that Dick decided to exploit my knobbly pipe stems by having Hero known throughout the film as 'the fellow with the lovely legs'.

I was thrilled to discover that one of my silent-screen idols, Buster Keaton, had been signed for the film, along with Phil Silvers, Michael Hordern, Roy Kinnear and Zero Mostel, who had starred in *Forum* on Broadway. Sadly, this was to be Buster Keaton's last screen performance, but his work was still a joy to watch. In one scene he had to walk into a tree branch and do a pratfall, backwards. Throughout rehearsals and on the take, it was never less than perfect, and he was far from being a young man. He died of lung cancer two months later.

Zero Mostel and Phil Silvers were a law unto themselves; there was a great competition between the two of them to see who could make the most noise. On screen or off, they were always 'on'; it was a case of 'Can You Top This?' But their competition produced enough jokes to fill a week of stand-up comedy at the Palladium. Silvers was at the height of his *Sergeant Bilko* television fame at the time and he carried the role around with him; I was his 'Doberman', his stooge. 'Speak like this,' he'd say, 'when I tell you,' and whatever sound I made, he'd slap me around the mouth saying, 'Not like *that* ... [slap, slap] ... like this!' More often than not I was sorely tempted to slap him back – but that's not what a good stooge does.

There was always a special affinity between Dick and me when we worked together; we had similar ideas on the way things should be done, and it was marvellous to create a film character with him. And I learned an enormous amount from his ace stuntman on *Forum*, Bob Simmons. I had some ideas I wanted to try for my stunt sequence in the mad chase scene at the end of the picture. I wrote up every wacky idea I could think of involving a chase with a runaway chariot and presented my thoughts to Dick, who agreed to let me go out with my own camera crew and put it all together.

I think you'll find some semblance of those great screen comedy chases in every one of Dick Lester's early pictures. In *Forum* our big chase involved a horse becoming separated from our hero's chariot – the horse gallops off in one direction, but the chariot carrying the foolish Hero and his heroine rolls off in quite another. It was all absolute nonsense.

At one point I had to jump out of the moving chariot and run on ahead of it, climb a ladder to get over a wall and tip it so that, in a cantilevered effect, I'd be hurled over the wall straight into a great pile of wet cement. I staggered out of the mess, covered in chalky white dust, and continued my dash down the road, trying to clear the way for the runaway chariot which follows me, carrying our heroine who is frantically waving at me not to leave her behind. The chariot was kept in perpetual motion by the use of a concealed Yamaha outboard motor on the back. It made a noise like a continuous and enormous motorised fart; the sound was later obliterated from the track by our technicians.

The scene suddenly shifts to a barn; I run inside followed by the chariot, and there is a wild sequence of flying-feathered pandemonium and sounds of great internal commotion as panicky chickens, ducks and barnyard animals scramble out of the building.

Then I come flying out of the window at the top of the barn and slide down a long chute, landing on top of a rolling barrel. My head ached for days afterwards – not surprising in view of the fact I'd been using it as a jackhammer. It took eight takes before I managed to leap off the barrel and grab the chariot as it raced by. I hung onto the back with both hands while the chariot dragged me along the sandy ground in my short-skirted toga. My mother had always wanted a girl – if that scene had gone on much longer she would most certainly have had her wish.

Gabrielle and I were married after completing the shooting of *A Funny Thing Happened on the Way to the Forum*. I drove to Paris from Madrid with one of the film's editors, who came along to act as a witness.

Gabrielle met us there with her parents; Adza was there as well, and we were married by the British Consul in a scene right out of a Richard Lester film. Dick was my best man as well as our cameraman, and he filmed the entire ceremony as only he would, with a cranked camera that made it look like Mary Pickford marries a Keystone Cop. Ah, well, that's the way things were done in the sixties. (Dick may have been shrewder than I thought: when I watch it now and see what I wore for the occasion, I'm rather glad it all moves rather quickly. Oddly I've never been able to throw out the old corduroy suit I wore that day; I even had mildew twice removed from it during one extremely damp winter. Perhaps I should stuff it like a trophy – like Roy Rogers stuffed his dead horse Trigger, putting it on display in his home. I guess I'm sentimental about that suit – and besides I am the grandson of a secondhand clothes dealer.)

We didn't have time for a proper honeymoon. Television, theatre and movie projects were coming so thick and fast that there was often only a weekend to rest before starting something new.

Terry Kendall had decided to move to America to live with his daughter and he sold us his little Clapham flat. Gabrielle and I just had time to move in before I was called to start rehearsal on a new production of a hilarious black comedy called *The Anniversary*. It was to open at the Duke of York's Theatre, and was a first play by an actor called Bill MacIlwraith.

The play starred the marvellous Mona Washbourne as the kind of mother who gives Mother's Day a bad name. Mona was one of the great ladies of the theatre and a genuinely sweet and charming woman; it was a great privilege to work with her. There was such a still, calm centre about her when she was on stage, along with an enormous presence. There was never any kind of aggravation with Mona, no inquisitions about mistakes made during a performance. She wasn't one of those tyrannical ladies of the theatre who can and do scare the hell out of youngsters – I've worked with a few of those in the past. With her gentle face and twinkling eye she was like a loving mother and I for one adored her. Noël Coward was another of her great admirers. He came backstage on opening night, and I was thrilled when he told me he'd been keeping an eye on my career in the three years since *Come Blow Your Horn*, and that he thought my timing was improving with age. I was flattered beyond belief at his remarks, well remembering that if he didn't like something he wouldn't be shy about telling me that either.

The rest of the stellar *Anniversary* company included dear Sheila Hancock, June Ritchie, who I had known from my season at Nottingham Rep, and Jack Hedley (before his great success in the *Colditz* television series), with whom I shared a dressing room – an experience I'm sure he would rather forget. Jack is a rather sober, serious-minded soul, and I think the fact that we had to share a dressing room depressed him beyond belief. Not that I did much to improve living conditions: The Mamas and Papas were at their height then and I insisted on playing their music over and over and over again in our very confined quarters. (*California Dreeeeeeeeming . . . on such a winter's daaaaaay.*) Jack and I didn't exactly share the same taste in music, and I drove him mad with the song. When he came into the dressing room each evening, his characteristic expression of melancholy turned positively funereal in anticipation of yet another evening spent with the Mamas and Papas and me.

The run of *The Anniversary* marked a very special time for Gabrielle and me; she was pregnant and we were delightedly making arrangements for her to stay in a

London nursing home in Wigmore Street when the baby arrived. I kept practising driving the route from Clapham to Wigmore Street in our little British-racing-green Austin 1100. Both of us read all the baby books and had 'Dr Spock'd' ourselves to death. Everything I read served to reinforce my conviction that when the baby finally came, I'd have to get Gabrielle to the nursing home in double quick time.

One Monday night, Gabrielle picked me up at the theatre as she always did, but on the drive home she complained of feeling some discomfort.

We lay in bed that night . . . well, in those last days of her pregnancy, I didn't exactly lie beside her. Rather, I hung off the end of the bed because it just wasn't big enough for the three of us. I was almost asleep when I heard Gabrielle say, 'Darling, I think it's coming . . . I think I'm going to have it.'

'Right! Now, for God's sake, don't panic! Whatever you do, don't panic!' I then inexplicably leaped onto the bed. 'Are you sure? Are you absolutely sure you're having it?' Her expression ran the gamut from wonder and bemusement to sheer terror as she watched her maniac husband hovering over her, bouncing up and down on the bed like some crazed jack-in-the-box.

Finally convinced she was as sure as she could be – that this was indeed it – I ran into the bathroom, setting what I considered to be the proper example of complete calmness. I started to shave. What the hell am I shaving for, I thought, it's the middle of the night! I rushed out of the bathroom, still half-covered in shaving cream, and dressed in underwear and shoes. I looked like the sad remains of a Knickerbocker Glory.

Gabrielle tried to take command as best she could. 'Michael, for heaven's sake!' she pleaded. 'Please, just calm down, get dressed and take me to the hospital . . .'

'I am calm . . . I am totally calm,' I argued. Then remembering Dr Spock, I tried to soothe her. '*You must not panic.*' I was all sweet reason. 'You're panic-stricken at the moment, and I understand that. I understand your condition, and I've trained myself to deal with you . . .' It was as though I was taking someone down off the ledge of a very high building.

She started to laugh hysterically. 'Don't laugh,' I said, 'this is no laughing matter. Don't laugh now, because that will induce it . . .' I was very impressed by that word; God knows, I'd seen it often enough in Dr Spock. I was also aware she could dilate at any moment.

By dint of calm persuasion Gabrielle was able to get me dressed and into the car and we started the mad drive to the nursing home. I couldn't understand it; in just a few short hours I had completely forgotten the way. We drove in some raging fashion, going the wrong way down one-way streets and finding every cul-de-sac in Clapham.

Finally we found Central London.

Greatly relieved, I pulled up at the entrance of Westminster Hospital, totally the wrong place. Now really in a state of panic, I threw the gears and raced off again, trying to find the elusive Wigmore Street. (I made a silent vow to myself at that moment to make sure when we had our next baby, it would be born at Westminster Hospital; that way, I'd be sure to get it right the first time.)

I stayed with Gabrielle a while after we found the nursing home, but the staff sent me off saying she'd be alright and would sleep the night. 'If anything happens . . .' I said. 'Don't worry,' the nurse said, 'we'll call you . . . and we've notified her doctor . . .' (He was delighted, of course, to be called away from his dinner party.) 'He said he'd drop in later . . .' the nurse added.

Early the next morning I went to see Gabrielle; but

now there was no sign of the baby. Not a contraction in sight. It was apparent that nature was in no mood to be rushed. A disapproving nurse watched me narrowly as I explained that I was taking my wife home.

'Well, you've got to sign a proper release form to show that you're taking her away . . .' she said.

'Yes, I know,' I told her, 'But I'm entitled to her, she's my wife . . .

I drove her home, enthusiastically explaining all the while that what we'd saved on the nursing home could be used later on for the baby's education. Gabrielle didn't look convinced, and the chilling prospect of a repeat of that ride to the nursing home did nothing at all to improve her humour.

But late that evening her contractions began again and soon it was clear that all systems were absolutely go. The drive this time was decidedly less manic: I did my best to help the baby on its way by driving over the bumpy Vauxhall Bridge Road. Finally, on Friday afternoon, word came to the hall where I was rehearsing (a television play called *Three-Barrelled Shotgun*, with Donald Pleasance) that our daughter, Emma, had been born at 3:15 pm. They let me out of rehearsals, and I rushed straight to the hospital before I went to the theatre for the evening performance of *The Anniversary*.

Gabrielle became pregnant again a year or so later, and this time we planned that I would actually be present at the birth. The gynaecologist who attended Emma's birth declined to take our case this time, obviously deciding that he had had enough.

The new doctor didn't know me very well, and agreed in a rash moment to permit me in the delivery room at Westminster Hospital. He realised his mistake very early on, and for the next several months took on the added role of theatrical agent in his quest to get me into a job and out of town before the birth. I did have a new job by then (I can't remember what it was, only that it prompted me to grow a beard), but much to the doctor's despair, it was in London. Besides, no matter what he arranged, there was no way I was going to miss the experience.

I'm delighted to report there was much less time spent on the A22 for the birth of our second child, Lucy. (Remembering my instinctive knowledge of the route to Westminster Hospital, I kept the vow I made to myself and booked a room for Gabrielle there.) In the hospital that day I made myself useful as I sat with Gabrielle and helped her time the contractions. Her labour was much shorter this time.

Memory plays bizarre tricks; how odd to remember that we were watching the beginning of a new police series called *Softly, Softly* on television when the nurse came in. 'It's time to go down now, Mrs Crawford . . .' she said. I followed along, walking behind the rolling stretcher into the elevator and down to the delivery room. I held on to Gabrielle's ankle all the while, like a child holds its mother's hand, as much for my own support as to comfort her – not wanting to be intrusive, but knowing full well that I was.

I was stopped at the delivery room door. 'Would you go please and scrub up, Mr Crawford . . .' the nurse said.

'Well, I had a wash before I left,' I said, 'I'm really clean . . .'

'No, Mr Crawford,' she explained, handing me a surgical cover and mask. 'We *all* scrub up here, whether we've had a wash or not . . .'

'Oh, certainly, yes, of course . . .' I said. 'I understand the routine . . .' I nodded. 'Ten-four.'

A hospital scrub-up room is a place at least as unsettling and alien to the outsider as any Martian space ship might be to an earthling. Eyes peer at you from all corners of the room All conversation stopped when I entered; only the hiss of running water broke the silence. Out of the corner of my eye I saw the doctor standing next to me glance speculatively in my direction; he looked me up and down as I adjusted the mask over my bearded face, then he sighed in resignation. I caught a glimpse of myself in the mirror. With red whiskers poking through the mask at odd places, my face looked like a wasp's backside.

The doctors and nurses did much turning on and off of water taps with only the use of an elbow, an impressive feat in my mind. Of course when I tried it, I squirted my dirty soap all over the doctor standing next to me, who then, rather pointedly, proceeded to scrub up all over again.

The scrub-up over we entered the theatre. Gabrielle lay on the table, her legs resting in the uncomfortable-looking stirrups; she was surrounded by masked nurses. I gave her a confident everything's-under-control nod. (Good grief, what am I in for! Please let me get through this without fainting!)

'Would you like to stand by your wife's head, Mr Crawford?' the doctor asked. 'Yes,' I said, 'but isn't it going to happen down there!'

'Yes, Mr Crawford,' he signed, 'but it's best if you keep out of the way. Why don't you comfort your wife . . . just speak to her . . .'

'Hello darling,' I said to her. 'How are you?' I then ran out of conversation. I looked at the doctor: 'Is there anything in particular you'd like me to tell her?'

'Just comfort her!' he said. 'Hold her hand or something . . . !'

Gabrielle began to emit sounds of high hysteria, caught between the pain of contractions and laughter at the fiery whiskers that lopsidedly pierced a face mask, which I now began to realise was muffling my speech.

'Hi,' I said, 'are you alright?' I sounded as though my mouth had been stuffed with cotton.

'Pardon?' she asked. 'Pardon?'

I had to shout at her to make myself understood: 'Everything's okay, everything's fine!'

By the time the birth process was reaching its climax I was on top of the bed trying to see exactly what was going on down the busy end. When the baby finally appeared, I was shouting at the top of my voice: 'It's a boy, It's a boy!'

The doctor glared at me. 'It's a girl, Mr Crawford, it's a girl.'

'It's a girl?' I said. 'Well, what the hell is *that*?'

'*That*,' he said, 'is the umbilical cord.'

'Oh, thank heaven for that,' I said. 'I thought . . .'

'Could you leave now, Mr Crawford!' the doctor said quietly. He looked tired.

'I'd be happy to,' I said, much relieved. 'Oh, I'd be happy to, because I think I'm going to . . .'

'We know,' he said. 'Please leave!'

'Well done fellows,' I mumbled. 'It was great . . . good stuff . . .' I punched Gabrielle on the shoulder with a reassuring tap. 'Good girl . . . you were great.'

I found the Gents only just in time. When I tried to get my head over the sink bowl to douse it with cold water, my legs almost collapsed from under me.

I staggered back to the room where we started, still wearing the now completely soaked surgical mask. A sign hung on the door. 'Mrs Crawford – Engaged.' I crossed the word off and wrote 'Married' over the top of it, and went in. *Softly, Softly* was still on the television. I hadn't missed a thing.

In those forty-five minutes I'd been gone from the

room, I had experienced one of the most beautiful things that this life has allowed me. I tell embroidered tales of the delivery room doctors having more trouble dealing with me than they did with Gabrielle. But I shall be forever grateful to have been there, and more often than not, my recollections of that day, when our daughter Lucy was born, tend to make my eyes mist quite uncontrollably.

CHAPTER 12

THERE ARE SOME wonderful people in this world, great caricature figures, men and women who, no matter their profession, are quite larger than life. In the theatre, one expects that sort of thing, but even in this business there are people who would be high on anyone's list of unforgettable characters. High on my list is the film director Michael Winner.

Almost anyone who has worked with Michael has all kinds of war stories to tell about the experience and will happily cite daunting examples of his outrageous behaviour. I remember reading somewhere that in his early school reports, he was warned not to keep seeing gangster films or he would assuredly grow up to be a gangster. This advice was obviously either never heeded or came far too late. He can be rude, arrogant and outrageous, all of that – but I like him, and I like the way he gets things done.

I first met him in 1966 during the run of *The Anniversary*. We had a meeting to discuss a film he had written with Dick Clement and Ian La Frenais called *The Jokers*. We met at Michael Winner's London office, a beautifully appointed room filled with handsome antiques and a huge desk.

When he rises to speak, he stands quite round-shouldered, in the shape of a comma – a comma holding a big cigar. He puffs furiously, rocking back and forth on his heels while his hands constantly jingle whatever he happens to find in his pockets. When he's excited about something, he paces the room like a well-tailored wading bird – head pulled into hunched shoulders, his free hand placed palm-up and neatly folded behind him while a lead toe tentatively steps forward, daubing the carpet as if to test some sandy shoreline before his trailing leg and upper torso can be pulled forward to join the rest of him. He was pacing in this way as he told me about *The Jokers*. 'It's a maaahvellous story, my dear . . .' (Everyone is always his 'dear'.) 'All about two brothers who set about stealing the crown jewels from the Tower of London . . .' I had already read the script and loved it, so of course I asked him the obvious question: 'Who's going to play my brother?' 'Oliver Reed,' he said.

OLIVER REED?! (Enter here my second nomination for that list of unforgettable larger-than-life characters.)

Now, I have never been quite sure if Ollie was discovered by Michael Winner or if it was the other way round, but by the time I met them they had already done a film together called *The System* (which also starred Barbara Ferris, and my old friend David Hemmings), and each claimed credit for discovering the other.

A reporter once described Oliver Reed as being somewhere between 'a Hippie and a Minotaur'. Well maybe, but, with his heavy black brows lending a certain menacing quality to his looks, he was what the romance novels call 'broodingly handsome'. There was a tension about Oliver Reed, a certain aura of danger. On the one hand he'd come from one of the grandest and most establishment of theatrical families – his grandmother was an opera singer, his grandfather an actor, and his uncle the eminent film director Sir Carol Reed – and Ollie always retained something of the presence and the air of authority of the Victorian actor-manager.

On the other hand there was something inside him that rebelled against his background and all authority, and also against his natural advantages in life, including his talent. Part of him wanted to tear it all down, and perhaps this is what gave him the air of danger that made him stand out among English actors of his generation. Ollie once told a reporter that for him, going into the acting profession was 'an involuntary muscular action like going to the bathroom'. That's a fairly typical Reed response, designed to shock the listener – but I came to know first-hand how very seriously he took his work.

But Oliver Reed as my *brother*! I really dug my heels in on that one. There was absolutely no way I thought an audience would ever accept Oliver Reed and me as being even remotely related. Because of this I kept finding excuses not to do the film, questioning absolutely everything in the script. During a meeting with Ian La Frenais and Dick Clement in Winner's office, the writers irritably asked, who in hell does Michael Crawford think he is, asking all these questions – Jesus Christ? Michael Winner, with a beat replied, 'He might be, my dears, he might well be; keep writing just in case.' It was finally fixed that I should meet Ollie – and his brother was to be present as well. I'll never forget the shock when he turned up; his brother was fair and skinny; he could have been my double. There were no more arguments; I agreed to play the part, and I must say we had a ball doing the film.

For all his reputation as a night owl, Ollie was a thorough professional, and as good as gold to work with. However, depending upon how he was cast at the time,

I think it is fair to say there was always a certain amount of physical risk present when you worked with Oliver Reed. The problem was that he tended to live the part he was playing. I'm thankful he played my brother in *The Jokers*. I think it gave us a real bond. Whenever we walked about the set together, he always kept a fraternal arm around me and every now and again, he'd give me a brotherly squeeze, the kind of squeeze a fruit-extracting machine would give to a ripe orange.

The only sticky moment between us came during the filming of a scene where the script called for Ollie to half-strangle me. (In the story, his brother had supposedly betrayed him.) I was really dreading it, quite rightly, because as we shot the scene Oliver took my 'betrayal' as something entirely real and completely personal and suddenly my life wasn't worth tuppence. His ham-like hands were fastened so tightly round my neck, I felt the end of my life was imminent. It took four people to get him off me – and only two of them were scripted.

I was very saddened to hear of Oliver's death while filming in Malta in April of 1999, at the age of sixty-one, far too young.

Michael Winner ran a tight set on *The Jokers* and exercised a strong grip over cast and crew, whose mood alternated between hating him for his personal outbursts and admiring him for his technical flair. He was a hard taskmaster, but I rather thrive on that. I was still playing in *The Anniversary* during the production – the sixties marked an extraordinary point in my career when I worked nonstop for months at a time, day and night, on totally different projects – and Michael always accommodated me and looked after me, making sure I got off to the theatre in good time.

On the other hand he could be amazingly insensitive to members of the crew or some of the actors in lesser roles. 'Alright ... You, my dear,' he shouted at one unfortunate actress during an early morning lineup. 'Yes, you, the one with the big tits, come and stand in front.'

I cringed for the girl. 'Hey, Michael,' I yelled back at him, 'your girlfriend says you've got a little pecker, but we don't keep talking about it!' The crew hooted.

We were always concocting pranks to play on Michael; he was the perfect target. We painted the mouthpiece on his megaphone with shoe polish – it made him look as if he were Al Jolson about to break into a chorus of 'Swanee'.

And it didn't take much coaxing from Ollie to convince the crew to hoist Michael's car up on bricks one night. Michael had just returned from a location site. 'Alright,' he screamed at the departing company, 'I want a better day tomorrow than we had today ...'

'Yeah, yeah, yeah ...' everyone muttered. One technician gave the finger to his back as he climbed into his car. His driver prepared to drive off, but the wheels began to spin. The car didn't move. The engine stopped, the door swung open and Michael clambered out and into his bantam rooster walk, charging the crew. 'Who did this? Who the hell did this!' Everybody scattered.

Michael had a passion for chocolate and sweets and had the annoying habit of 'borrowing' them (never to be returned of course) from the rest of us. When he walked on the set in the morning, you could make book that his first question would be, 'What have we got to eat today, my dears?' It became a running joke. We were shooting on location in a discotheque somewhere in London late one afternoon when I heard Michael's slightly nasal drone directed at me. 'What have you got to eat, my dear?'

'Nothing, Michael, only some chocolate . . .'

'Oh, but I *love* chocolate!'

'Oh, go buy your own sweets!' someone mumbled. 'You've got more money than all of us put together!'

'But I don't want to buy my own, my dears,' and he sounded that police siren laugh of his as he bore down on me: 'I want some of *yours*!' I finally gave in, undid the chocolate, and gave him several pieces. It was almost four o'clock by then, and I went directly off to the theatre to work.

I called Michael at home after the curtain came down that night. 'Michael is that you?' I asked.

'Yes.' His reply was short, and clipped.

'Hi, how are you?' I asked. 'Are you well?'

'Yes.'

'Well, I'm just ringing up to check on how the rushes looked.'

'Very good.'

'Oh, were you pleased?' I asked.

'Yes, yes.' He was very abrupt.

'Okay, well, are you sure you're okay?' I asked again.

'Yes!' He barked.

That's very unlike Michael, I thought; if ever you've had words with him, once the air is cleared, that's that; there was never any sulking afterwards and he was instantly back to his old self. 'Right,' I said, 'well, I'll see you tomorrow morning . . .'

'YES!' CLICK.

The next morning, things seemed to have returned to normal on the set. 'Good morning, my dears!' I heard and turned to see Michael walking briskly through the set.

'Morning Michael,' I said. 'You were very short last night.'

'You baaaaassstard!' he roared. 'You little bastard!'

'Why, what d'you mean?' I asked, in wide-eyed wonder.

'I'll tell you what I mean! I was in the bathroom when you called – and I'd been in there for hours! What in Chris' name was in that chocolate?' I had given him laxative chocolate – and three squares to boot; even one can be dynamite. But of course I knew he wouldn't even bother to look at what I'd handed him. He had just pushed the chocolate in his mouth and started to chew as I knew he would, never dreaming of the bowl-hugging consequences. Michael receded into the woodwork over the next few days, and everyone agreed it might have been the most tranquil and genial time we ever spent on one of his sets.

The Jokers was a terrific success in England, and one of the few really successful British film exports at a time when the industry was rife with independent film makers who found it difficult to achieve even limited commercial success abroad. We had amazing reviews in America. Charles Champlin of the *Los Angeles Times* compared it favourably to the early Ealing comedies of Alec Guinness and Alastair Sim, and even so august a body as the *New York Times* called the film 'both stirring and disturbing, delightful and devastating . . .' I believe the film was an important stepping stone in all our careers; I know it was instrumental in completely changing my professional life.

The Anniversary continued its run for six months, perhaps not a major success by London standards but, to my mind, it was far from a failure. When other commitments forced some of the cast to leave, management in the person of dear Michael Codron decided to close the production rather than attempt to recast and duplicate what had been such a strong ensemble effort.

Later, some of the company played in a film based on

a revised version of the play in which I declined to take part. Our ensemble version was reworked to serve as a vehicle for its star, Bette Davis. That's the one thing about film that I find slightly depressing; so much of the time a stage property, or book, is revised to serve the interests of a particular star; and not with altogether the same pleasing results as the original. Film-making is much more a technical business, equally commendable of course, but usually the actor has far less input than in theatre, where he has the opportunity to build up a dialogue with his director, and the luxury of additional rehearsal time to create interplay between characters, because the actors have grown into their roles together. And to me, most importantly, you retain the control over the timing of your final delivery to the audience.

My last performance in *The Anniversary* was on August 13, 1966, and within nine days Gabrielle, Emma and our newly employed baby-minder Joanna were on our way to Hamburg in Germany, where I was to start work on Richard Lester's new film *How I Won the War*, a project very dear to his heart. Dick was terribly excited when he first told me about it; for the first time he was going to be his own producer as well as directing. He wanted to make the ultimate pacifist film, parodying and deglamorising other war films and showing the utter senselessness of combat – 'a tragedy of the absurd', as he called it. It was the most serious film he had done so far, and certainly the one most difficult to understand. I thought the best description of it was from Walter Matthau, who called it 'an anti-war poem'. It's still discussed today, having become something of a cult film. 'It's very complicated, isn't it?' someone always politely remarks, but the talk invariably centres around the fact that John Lennon was in the film playing his first straight part and minus the other Beatles.

By 1966 Beatlemania had been a worldwide phenomenon for three years, and when the group decided to take the time off from living in each other's pockets, it was agreed that each of them would go his own way for several months. According to what I've read, John Lennon joined the production of *How I Won the War* because he needed something to occupy his time until the Beatles reconvened and, as Hunter Davies reported in his authorised biography of the Beatles, John thought acting was 'the new thing' he was looking for. I know he had felt comfortable working with Dick Lester since *Help!* and *A Hard Day's Night*, and the small role of Gripweed fitted his scheduling needs perfectly.

Of course, everything John did for the film was probed, examined, dissected and intensely scrutinised by the media. I remember that when he had his long hair cut in favour of something more in keeping with the period, the press attention was overpowering. Reporters completely surrounded our hotel, sleeping in the bushes overnight to try and get shots of John getting his hair cut. In the end, I believe, exclusive coverage was given to a German newspaper, but every single paper reported it as breathlessly as when Elvis Presley had his hair cut for his induction into the United States Army.

All of us were dazzled at the prospect of working with John, but none of us knew quite what to expect. However, it was clear from the beginning that he was a complete professional, ready with his lines and always on time. He didn't pretend to be a great actor, but he had inventive suggestions to help his character, and he was very natural on the screen. It was his idea to wear little wire 'granny glasses' in the film and, of course, he created a worldwide craze for them. Apparently he completely abandoned wearing contact lenses for personal appearances after that. But the actual process of film-making didn't suit him at all, and, according to reports, he loathed the tedium of endlessly waiting around between scenes for the crew to set up the next shot. Well, on that score he wasn't so different from the rest of us. He could be very caustic and intolerant in his humour, but he was generous with all of us, and mixed freely with the actors and crew. No job was ever 'beneath' him, and he was treated like everyone else, down to the early morning starts and queuing for his meals at the canteen.

I first began to spend some time with John when we were on location at a site near Hamburg. It was there that I had a first-hand view of that unimaginable world fame that people speak about. We (Lennon; Neal Aspinall, the Beatles' road manager; Gabrielle and I, would make an occasional visit to a Hamburg store to buy jeans or a T-shirt. We drove in an ordinary Mercedes, but for most of the ride John was forced to lie out of sight on the car floor until we arrived. Then, in the kind of surreal marathon that Richard Lester would appreciate, we opened the door and John would dash into the store; he had a maximum of five minutes to look around, see something, try it, buy it, and get out of that store before his fans descended on him. One person would spot him and suddenly, out of nowhere, a mob of people would totally envelop our car. It is something we all read about and see in newsreels, but unless you actually experience it, you cannot imagine how frightening it can be. Thousands of hands reached out to touch him, and I was quite sure we were all going to be overrun and completely torn apart.

We later moved the production to the small coastal town of Almería in southeast Spain for a few months, at that time an isolated and difficult location. David Lean had used the area for some of the exteriors for *Lawrence of Arabia* – which will give you an idea of the climate – and although the area was fairly remote, the natives had become used to seeing movie companies come and go through their villages. Dick Lester remembers borrowing David Lean's Rolls-Royce with its blackened windows to ferry the actors around. John added a few touches of his own to the car; he had two enormous speakers wired underneath, from which Bob Dylan music blared while we drove along – John was mad about Dylan in those days – scaring the hell out of the cows.

Gabrielle and I (both of us passionate Beatles fans) took a villa with John and his wife, Cynthia, whom we both found to be very real and down-to-earth. Later on we were joined by Ringo Starr and his wife, Maureen, who both stayed for six weeks, and Neil Aspinall, who also came along. The area was policed, of course, and so John felt it was safe to wander around at the end of a day's shooting.

I lived with John for months within that 'family unit', but I can honestly say that I hardly got to know him. It might have been because he was in the midst of world fame on a scale beyond our ken; or that he'd reached a point where he had nothing to give any more, outside of the songs he continued to write and the friendship he shared within the tiny circle of people he knew well and trusted. That is all entirely possible, but I am in no position to analyse him and I can only tell what I knew of him then.

Cricket was the favourite outdoor pastime, and John became quite a good bowler. The only time he had a little trouble was when I was batting, and he couldn't tell which were the wickets and which were my legs. Ringo's favourite breakfast was spam wrapped in batter, and Gabrielle used to cook it for him every morning – it may be the only thing she ever did learn to cook! We had some great parties in spite of the electricity failing most evenings and leaving us without hot water. Some evenings we'd all play Risk or Monopoly, and as there was a piano we sometimes also had jam sessions. To listen to John compose was fantastic. I remember one day we were just lying on the beach, taking photos of each other, and he picked up his guitar. Thirty minutes later he had half-composed 'Strawberry Fields'. It was a thrill to hear him go over and over those few chords. He'd suddenly interrupt himself: 'Naaahh, I don't like that much . . .' and he'd look up at us sitting there wide-eyed.

'Ah no, it's great John,' I'd say, pretending to understand everything. 'What do you mean by "the firemen"?' I asked him one night, when I plucked up the courage. 'That wasn't me, was it?'

'You?' he said.

'Oh well . . . It's just that . . . it's someone in a uniform . . . I thought, well . . . with me being in a uniform in the film . . . you know . . .'

'No, Michael.'

'Right, sorry, John.'

Anyone who was around in the late sixties will remember that in those days, when people were beginning to smoke dope, being cool at parties meant sitting around saying nothing. Here I was, sharing a house with the coolest person in the world – the king of counter-culture. I would bounce around, heart on sleeve and unable to keep my mouth shut, eager to please people who didn't want to be pleased; mostly they just wanted to brood.

John Lennon never said anything that wasn't deeply serious, even his jokes were philosophically meaningful.

When he spoke to you in that deep, nasal whine, it was always as if he were speaking from somewhere far off in his head – except the time I 'doctored' one of his gigantic, hand-rolled cigarettes by removing some of the tobacco and filling the gap with a mini-explosive, purchased at Pedro's Joke Shop. I handed him the cigarette early one morning; he lit it and *phhhffft!* I thought my exploding cigarette was hilarious. John just stared at me impassively. It was as if I'd just confirmed all his existential anxieties about the futility of existence. 'Piss off!' he grunted.

Watching John compose is the kind of memory I want to hold on to in light of everything that has happened since those days. I can't say he was an 'ordinary person'. I wouldn't know how to define 'ordinary' in that context. I thought of him as a very special working-class poet – and it was putting his poetry to music – together with Paul's gift for melody – that made the Beatles great. I have no idea what happened to John in later years. I think the man I lived with in Spain would have been the first to say of that 'other' John, 'He's gone missing from his head!' and then he would have written a song about it.

How I Won the War had no conventional plot. The screenplay was written by Charles Wood (who had worked with Dick on *The Knack*), from a book by Patrick Ryan. It was based on the reminiscences of a young officer who, having been taken prisoner while crossing the Rhine, relates everything that has happened to him since he joined the Army. I played this officer: he was an idiot, one of those dangerously obedient innocents who might follow orders to go behind enemy lines to lay an advance cricket pitch, and so lead an anonymous group of men into slaughter. John Lennon was my batman – a very astute bit of casting by Dick, because John was ten times cleverer than I, as batmen are so often far cleverer than the officers they serve.

The story sounds simple, but there was enough obscure imagery in the film to puzzle even the most passionate Lester fan; there were also switches of time and place, with real and imagined events thrown in; the scenes of genuine battles were filmed in monochrome – Dunkirk was green, Dieppe was pink, Arnhem blue – and when a man in the regiment died, he continued through the rest of the film completely covered in the colour of the battle in which he was killed.

When filming started, it was the usual grand Lester party for all of us, but it was a tiring, gruelling, complicated film to make, and I think the dual role of producer/director more than took its toll on Dick. Beyond the heat of our desert-dry location, there was the never-ending problem of having to beg, borrow or steal military hardware for the venture. The military establishment was reluctant to help without seeing the script, and, if they had seen it, they most certainly wouldn't have helped at all.

By the end of the shoot the party atmosphere had disappeared, and a tense climate of exhaustion prevailed. The previous week I'd had an unpleasant surprise when I did a stunt that required me to be blown up in an explosion and thrown back through the air, landing in a sand dune which had been covered in about a ton of oatmeal to soften my fall. I found myself buried headfirst in sand, oatmeal and thousands of maggots that had hitched a ride with it.

The heat didn't help, and on a day near the end of filming, I reached a point where I simply couldn't remember my lines after God-knows-how-many takes. I began to argue with Dick about the scene we were shooting; I didn't understand what the scene was about or what he was after. Dick completely lost patience with me as well – unheard of in our previous collaboration. I think we were all relieved when shooting was finally completed, and we could all leave for London and home.

In the end, the film didn't receive the reaction we had hoped for; instead, it provoked hostility and strong controversy wherever it was shown, especially in England. Some critics expressed great shock at the sight of death and destruction held up to ridicule; the sight of John Lennon sitting on the ground with a bloody hole in his stomach made one critic feel 'as though he had been kicked in the teeth'. Others objected to the film's cynical vision of such heroic war figures as Winston Churchill and General Omar Bradley; one critic wrote threateningly, 'When Mr Lester crosses the road, he should look to the right and to the left and to the right . . .' There were problems, too, because two major British film distributors refused to give it a general showing.

To this day Dick, however, echoes something he said a long time ago, 'If I were run over by a bus tomorrow, I would like to be remembered and judged by *How I Won the War*.' Dick never compromised. He always stood by what he believed in, even if it made him unpopular.

The film marked the last time I worked with Dick Lester, which makes me very sad, because for me they were great years. I loved working with him.

CHAPTER 13

THE RIGOURS OF that Spanish location were scarcely behind us when I was called for a play scheduled to open on Broadway in February 1967. I'm fairly certain the success of *The Jokers* in New York was instrumental in bringing my name into the casting discussion. Peter Shaffer, surely one of Britain's greatest playwrights, had written a one-act piece for the National Theatre's 1966 season at Chichester called *Black Comedy*; it was his first attempt at broad farce and a great success. The play later enjoyed a very successful run in London as part of a double bill, and now a Broadway production was being planned.

Certainly I wanted to go to America. I had always dreamed of making my mark on the Broadway stage, but I boarded the plane for New York with very mixed feelings: I hated the thought of being away from Gabrielle and missing Emma's first Christmas. We had scarcely left London air space before I was miserably homesick for my family. I simply couldn't afford to bring them with me at that point, and Gabrielle and I had agreed they'd come out to join me once I'd moved into an apartment in New York. Before that, however, we were scheduled to take the play to Boston for the pre-Broadway try-out, which meant a separation of a few weeks; it was a really dismal thought.

Lynn Redgrave was with me on that flight; she was to co-star along with Peter Bull and the American actress Geraldine Page. Already a great favourite in New York, Lynn had only just returned from a promotional tour of the States for *Georgy Girl*, the film which made her a star, and *Black Comedy* marked her Broadway debut.

Nothing had quite prepared me for my first glimpse of Manhattan. I stared mesmerised as our plane briefly followed the winding ribbon-path of the Hudson River, then flew directly over that island of flamboyant skyscrapers that winked back at us, jewel-like, in the bright afternoon sun.

Lynn and I were met at the airport by the show's American producer, a human dynamo by the name of Alexander Cohen. Alex, along with his wife Hildy, was arguably the most successful producer on Broadway in 1967. He had *At the Drop of a Hat*, the witty Flanders and Swann review, and Jules Feiffer's *Little Murders* already running successfully and was about to open Pinter's *The Homecoming* with Ian Holm and Vivien Merchant, while a new Peter Ustinov play was in the works. Alex immediately made us feel very important by rushing us through customs and carrying us off in a limousine to the Algonquin Hotel in the centre of New York's theatre district. It was a favourite place for theatre people on both sides of the Atlantic in those days; someone told me Olivier used to stay there, and Gielgud as well.

Whenever I think of the Algonquin, I always hear the whine of fire sirens and the roar of mid-town traffic that used to filter through my window at night. (They say New York never sleeps, and the city seems determinedly bent on making sure that every one of its residents stays awake all night to keep it company.) I can't remember what I thought my first experiences of New York were going to be like. I'm sure I believed that because we shared a common language with the Americans and I had seen all their films, that somehow I'd feel more at home there and much less alien. It never occurred to me that America might be a totally different culture. The food was my first clue: they've never heard of Marmite, or mint sauce, digestive biscuits, or Branston Pickle, Ribena or custard creams. And if you ask for trifle sponges, you'll be led to the bath mop department. Mind you, I would never complain: Americans serve the most enormous portions at mealtimes – 'more bang for the buck', as they put it – but nevertheless I felt an unremitting longing for England and all things English.

In those first few weeks away from home, my best friend was the Algonquin switchboard operator who placed at least a hundred calls for me to England. The lowest point came on the freezing Christmas evening in 1966 when I sat in the Algonquin lobby under the watchful eyes of the hotel porters. Feeling lonely and awash with self-pity, I poured my heart out to Gabrielle in a long, very long letter, telling her, between bites on my giant turkey sandwich, how much I missed her.

Life improved as soon as we started rehearsals at the old Edison Hotel across the street from the theatre. In his *Black Comedy*, Peter Shaffer employed a device (hilariously staged by our director, John Dexter) used by the ancient Chinese in their theatre; all the play's characters behaved as though they were in a pitch dark room, blindly bumbling around and crashing into furniture, but all the while the stage lights were actually on, giving the audience a full view of the action.

The setup was simple enough; the curtain goes up, the

scene is dark. (Everything is reversed, you see.) I am an artist, Lynn is my fiancée and we're both waiting for her father (Peter Bull) to arrive with an art dealer who we hope will buy one of my dreadful paintings. A fuse blows, the lights go out, but on stage they actually light up, and for the rest of the evening, we stumble about in supposed total darkness. The staging was dotted with some wonderful visual gags, such as when I had to figure out a way to give my seat (in the dark) to the lady next door (Camilla Ashland). First I sat down, then I cajoled her into sitting on my lap; then I undulated my lap out from under her, leaving her sitting on a chair. Split-second timing was required, and John's staging was brilliantly served by all the company.

I had a particular piece of business where I had to attempt to grope my way blindly across the stage, one foot at a time, feeling my way to a platform some six inches off the floor. When I reached the platform, I climbed on it but accidentally stood on a carefully placed telephone which slid across the platform, carrying me with it and resulting in a spectacular pratfall. My body flattened out on the platform. Just to put the lid on it, a doorbell rings, and I quickly and blindly walk towards the door, hitting the door jamb straight in the middle of my forehead and bouncing off it a full five yards. There was a cushioned foam inset that my head hit, so it was not quite as painful as it sounds. Still, I managed to concuss myself a couple of times.

After weeks of rehearsals we flew to Boston, a terrific place (the critics were unanimous in their praise there, which will always endear a city to an actor), and Gabrielle was finally able to join me for the opening night. For me, the only negative thing about our Boston run was that it marked the beginning of my arguments with John Dexter.

I felt that John had been rude on a number of occasions to the dear actress Camilla Ashland, who played the elderly visitor from next door. In my view, this was causing terrific tension within the company, and I took it upon myself to confront him. Not a good move, as it turned out. Camilla was saved, Michael was doomed.

In staging *Black Comedy* John Dexter had created a marvellously rough sort of ballet for the eight artists on stage and, much like a dance captain, he'd give us notes on the performance every single night. It's a common theatre practice and I think it's one of the best ways a company can maintain its highest standards.

I am fervent in my belief that the audience is entitled to see the same high-energy first-night performance every night of the week. The problem was that John stopped giving us our nightly notes even before the end of the Boston run, and so again I challenged him: 'There must be something you want to say about the performance . . .'

He wasn't thrilled with the tenor of the conversation, and became visibly irritated. 'Well, what can I tell *you*, Michael,' he said. 'You've read your review, you're wonderful . . .'

This was certainly not what I wanted to hear. 'What the hell does that mean?' I questioned. 'There must be a million things I'm doing wrong.' The argument escalated and my last memory of the encounter was my attempt to hang John on my dressing-room coat hook before I left the theatre. Given my big mouth and passionate convictions and John Dexter's reputation in some quarters for being sarcastic and difficult with actors, I suppose our confrontation was entirely predictable.

Tempers were soothed, if not smoothed, in time for

our New York opening night, but a thick blizzard of snow forced us to cancel the Broadway opening, and a new date was set for a few days later. Despite the increased jitters caused by the delay, we had an absolutely thrilling first night. Afterwards we went back to Pat Kingsley's apartment (the show's press representative) and waited for the reviews to appear; then we went on to the party at the Rainbow Room for a noisy, happy public reading of Walter Kerr's review in the *New York Times*. Because it was very complimentary, we could expect a good run.

Gabrielle and I spent the next few days in a state of euphoria, but were soon jolted back to earth.

Within days of settling into our new apartment, Emma became dangerously ill with a stomach virus, followed by almost fatal dehydration. I was at the theatre when Gabrielle called; she had tried to send for an ambulance but we ended up getting a taxi to take us to the nearest hospital. Holding our wretchedly ill baby in my lap, it seemed we drove miles, although Gabrielle has reminded me since that it was only a matter of five blocks. By the time we arrived Emma was unconscious, but the hospital refused to take her in because we didn't have the proper insurance and couldn't prove we could pay the bill!

In desperation I contacted Alex Cohen, who was an enormous help. He called the hospital immediately to guarantee payment. Gabrielle stayed there while I went to do the evening performance. When I returned to pick her up afterwards, I was horrified at the sight of little Em's condition; she was strapped into her crib and was being fed intravenously. The nurse had been unable to find a 'proper' vein in her arm or foot, and had ended up inserting the needle into a head vein near her temple. Gabrielle and I were in a terrible state, but Emma seemed to have settled down and eventually the hospital staff persuaded us to leave for the night

When we returned the next morning, it was apparent she hadn't been checked at all; the needle had partially worked its way out of her head vein and her face was covered in fluid. We called for the nurse and demanded that she get the surgeon, but she told us he was in a meeting and unavailable. 'Take the needle out of her head . . .' I yelled. 'Just take it out . . .!' She did as she was told and put a plaster on Emma's little head. Then I picked her up and, despite the staff's attempts to restrain us, we left the hospital.

In a state bordering on total panic we nevertheless somehow managed to find another cab and drove to another nearby hospital. This time they were wonderful; later on, the doctors told us that if we hadn't done what we had, Emma might have died. It was a terrible way to begin our stay as a family in New York.

Gabrielle hated being on her own after that. We had rented an apartment overlooking Central Park for the duration of the Broadway run. It was perfectly safe, but quite a distance from the theatre, and she found it frightening and lonely to be by herself in the evenings while I was performing. She came to rely for company on some of the wonderful friends we made in New York – people like Angela Lansbury, Joel Grey, Carole Bayer-Sager and Anthony Perkins and, of course, Roddy McDowall, who was so very kind to her. He'd been at the first night of *Black Comedy* and when we found we were neighbours, he told her, it's mad, you being by yourself, insisting she come for dinner or to watch a film in the evenings, and generally taking her under his wing. Another great friend, Patric Walker, the astrologer, also lived nearby and was a great friend and companion.

It didn't take long to discover that New York reveres

those it sees as winners. *Black Comedy* was a hit and, consequently, Gabrielle and I were overwhelmed with invitations to every conceivable kind of social function. As a surprise my agent, who was a close friend of Vincent Sardi's, organised a special night at Sardi's restaurant, a name synonymous with Broadway opening-night glamour. The maitre d' seated us at a table right by the door to be seen by all who came in – a 'hot table'. The service was great, and there were seven gigantic shrimps in Gabrielle's seafood cocktail. Three nights later, flushed with the success of our first visit, I stupidly booked reservations without the assistance of my agent, expecting the maitre d' to remember me. On arrival he greeted us with 'Right this way, Sir,' and ushered us past 'hot tables' number one, two, three, four . . . by the time we reached table seven, I saw we were ending up at a definitely not-so-hot table – right beside the kitchen. There was a minimum wait of twenty minutes for a drink or a menu, and there were only five tiny shrimps in Gabrielle's cocktail. When I pointed this out to the waiter, he threatened us with a table upstairs, tantamount to purgatory. So, Gabrielle and I made the decision to quit while we were still ahead and that in future we'd be better off at somewhere slightly downmarket. Downey's Irish Pub became our favourite.

(In fairness, I should tell you that Vincent Sardi sent a lovely letter of apology afterwards. And years later, they hung a caricature of me on their famous wall of celebrity – a double caricature in fact, one of me as myself and one of me as the Phantom. It was right next to the kitchen door.)

Now much of my work was in America I needed an international agency and, sadly, that meant moving on from Adza, though we remained loving friends. Milton Goldman, my New York agent, held some of the world's best parties on Sunday afternoons in his apartment. People vied for invitations to Milton's. He was one of the founders of International Famous Agency (later ICM) and his client list read like an international who's who of the theatre: Olivier, Gielgud, Redgrave, Richardson. Everybody, but everybody, showed up at his parties – in London as well as New York. Milton and his longtime companion Arnold Weisberger used to arrive at the Savoy for six weeks every year to host a series of glamorous galas for his clients. Milton was a wonderful character in his own right: a total charmer, always impeccably dressed, an Anglophile of the first water and a bit of a snob too: I remember he was always terribly impressed by a title.

It was at one of Milton's New York Sunday parties that we first ran into George Brown (then Britain's very controversial Foreign Secretary). George was a great fan of *Black Comedy*, and he used to meet us at Downey's once or twice a week after the theatre. He'd come lurching in, usually held upright between two plainclothes security officers, who would dutifully guide him into a chair at our table, then park themselves discreetly behind us for the rest of the evening. They would monitor the evening's conversation – I'm sure just in case diplomatic secrets were spilled – but the truth was that George's stories would usually run along the lines of how Moishe Dayan lost his eye or how many tissues it took for General de Gaulle to blow his nose. At the end of the evening, George would be gently lifted from his chair by his escort and they would then lower him into his limousine.

George took us on our first visit to the United Nations. Gabrielle and I sat in the gallery and watched in awe as the delegates debated the Six Day War in the Middle East. Our second visit to the United Nations came a few months later when Gabrielle was pregnant with Lucy and beginning to show it. (Lucy was conceived in New York in the middle of a hot Monopoly game; somewhere between the Waterworks and Liverpool Street Station.)

Gabrielle remembers the UN Gala because she had nothing to wear that fitted properly and opted for a little flowered smock that was, in fact, her night dress. The highlight of that evening for me was having my picture taken with Secretary General U Thant. The caption in my scrapbook reads 'Me and U'.

At the other end of the New York social scale, we met a man who shall remain nameless, a fabulous 'Guys and Dolls' type character who puffed on a big black Havana cigar and wore dark glasses. He saw *Black Comedy* one evening and came round after the show to invite Gabrielle and me for a drink. We really took to him. He never said what he did for a living but we had our suspicions. In the middle of a meal once, he suddenly got up. 'I gotta go out . . .' he said. 'I'll be back in about an hour' – adding ominously, 'Don't ask where I'm goin' . . .'

Of course I said, 'Where *are* you going?'

'You shouldna asked me dat . . .' he cautioned. 'Just a little business to attend to . . .'

When we ended our New York run, he threw us a goodbye party at the old Park Sheraton Hotel on Broadway. We didn't know a soul. They seemed to arrive in shifts, twenty or thirty of the toughest tomatoes imaginable, stuffed into that room to say goodbye. The air was thick with the smell of cigars, and it was 'Hey, Mikeeeee' (to me) and 'Hi, doll' (to Gabrielle) all night long. I don't suppose they had the slightest idea who we were; they were there simply because they'd been ordered to show up.

We thought we had seen the last of him after New York, but he came to see us in Los Angeles when I was working on *Hello Dolly!* the following year. I remember his visit because I was teaching Emma how to swim at the time. She was only eighteen months, but I was forced into it because again and again while we were cooking supper in the evening, we'd hear a great splash which meant that Emma had shot out of her bedroom, straight across the lawn and into the pool. She didn't know how to swim, but that didn't hold her back; she loved being in the water. When our friend arrived from New York he watched me throw a delighted Emma into the pool.

'Don' do dat to de kid!' he suddenly yelled.

'Don't worry about it,' I said to him, 'she loves it . . .'

'I don' wanna have to tell ya again . . .' he warned me. And to underscore his words, he shoved his hand inside the breast of his jacket.

'Hey, whatever you say,' I quickly assured him. 'I'll never do dat again! Even if she likes it – I'm gonna deprive her! It'll do her good!'

Years went by. Then out of a clear blue sky, he sent a very old-fashioned tape recorder in a battered briefcase (still reeking of tobacco) to the Majestic Theater in New York where I was playing in *The Phantom of the Opera*. Inside were two Frank Sinatra cassettes and another by Fats Domino. There was a little fan letter from him as well – no address of course. I've kept all of it as a kind of souvenir; the old machine runs very slowly, but I wouldn't dream of using anything else for my vocal warm-up tape.

As I've said, *Black Comedy* is written as a precision

instrument. If one of the cast arrives a little late on stage or speaks a little early, then, like a Swiss watch, the whole won't work. And indeed after a few months without the benefit of John Dexter's expert eye, the play's original timing did get out of kilter. I don't think the company saw John Dexter again after our opening night in New York; to all intents and purposes he had disappeared entirely. And while the audience reaction was generally fine, they were not seeing the original picture John had painted on our opening night, and we weren't getting the same degree of laughter.

I took my problems to Alex Cohen, who was very sympathetic when I asked if we could have John Dexter return for a look at the show. Apparently John was unavailable so Peter Shaffer, who was living in New York at the time, kindly answered the call and took over direction duties for a while.

The run in New York might have ended on a calmer note if only I hadn't vented my frustrations to a reporter friend of ours who was only too delighted to include in an interview my comments about the less-than-professional direction the play had taken. I looked into his sympathetic eyes and opened my big mouth – and I learned another bitter lesson. The production may have had its problems, but it was hardly buoying to morale to see our difficulties spelled out in the Sunday newspaper: the company refused to speak to me for days.

I've always regretted discussing the production and the fact that I may have embarrassed Peter Shaffer in an unthinking moment. Even after a span of some thirty years, I trust there is no such thing as a statute of limitations on an apology.

CHAPTER 14

BEFORE I LEFT *Black Comedy* I had the pleasure of meeting a gracious immensely talented Texan named Roger Edens, who came backstage one night to introduce himself and talk about his latest project. Roger had begun his career as a musician and become a major producer at MGM, collaborating with the likes of Judy Garland, Fred Astaire and Gene Kelly. He told me he'd just been named associate producer for the 20th Century-Fox film production of *Hello Dolly!* It was Roger who arranged for me to audition with *Dolly*'s director, Gene Kelly, which completely changed my life.

I was asked to go with Dick Lester to San Francisco to promote *How I Won the War*, which had been selected to open the 1967 San Francisco Film Festival, and it was arranged that I should meet Gene Kelly during my three-day stay in California. The words look so matter-of-fact as I write them: Gene Kelly! But let me tell you, just the anticipation of meeting that great American dancer was enough to tie me in knots.

The flight from London arrived in San Francisco late at night and the jet lag was excruciating, but there was absolutely no way I could sleep. I felt turned completely upside down and inside out. When I arrived at the hotel there was a message waiting for me: 'Gene Kelly called, will call later.' I've still got that piece of paper. My God, how could I ever just throw it away? GENE KELLY CALLED ME! I was doing mental handsprings! It was all I could think about. Gene Kelly called ME! THE Gene Kelly called me, Michael Crawford! The fact of it, the very sound of it was delicious. I kept phoning down to the operators to ask them to repeat my messages. They thought me mad. 'Sir, are you sure you don't want these messages sent to your room?'

'You can if you like,' I said. 'But I'd still like you to keep a copy so you can repeat those words to me . . . By the way,' I asked, playing my little game again, 'who called?'

And they would answer, 'Gene Kelly.'

'Oh,' I said, '*that* Gene Kelly.'

His representative eventually called to say Mr Kelly would meet me at the hotel at ten in the morning. Fine, fine, fine: ten in the morning. Of course I'm up at six. I have a long bath to try and kill some time. I figure that will take an hour if I wash my hair and have a shave. Alright, all done. I get dressed. It's ten past seven.

I need a project, I think, something to do. I know, maybe another bath – but this time I'll try it in slow motion! I undress and start the process again and slowly wash my hair (please God, anything to pass the time!) and then try to keep my mind on the early-morning local television programmes. Quarter-past eight. Nervous hysteria begins its steady march across my brain; the mind never stops and operates only in exclamatory sentences.

Still hours to go! Bugger it! I can't have another bath! I'll look like a skinned prune! I've already turned my shaking hand to yet another shaving attempt – with decidedly mixed results. The bad news; all the tiny daubs of toilet paper that cover my chin and neck. The good news? I've removed at least three layers from the map of freckles that covered my face.

Grasping for any project to keep my mind off the time, I change clothes again and think, no, this isn't smart enough for Gene Kelly. I change again, then change back. I only have three sets of clothes. In those Mod days, everything was different stripes and patterns, outrageous stuff. I am still changing as the doorbell rings, standing in checked jacket, floral shirt and striped trousers, nothing going with anything. I open the door and see that famous genial Irish grin. Gene Kelly stands there.

'Ohhh . . . Ohhh . . .' I croaked.

That was his first sight and sound of me. I added another 'Ahhhhh!' and apologised for my bizarre get-up.

'What?' he said.

I stumbled on: 'Oh, nothing. S-s-sir. Would you like to come in?'

He walked into my room and never took his eyes off me. I think he thought I was going to pull a knife on him. Not that it would have bothered him – he was obviously in much better condition than the pipe cleaner in pants who stood before him.

'Do . . . do . . . do sit down,' I stuttered. He was already sitting.

'Right,' I said, 'I will too.'

'Let's cut the small talk,' he said. I hadn't said anything yet. He apparently wasn't going to waste time asking if I'd had a good trip or if I'd arrived in one piece. He obviously knew I'd arrived – whether I was all there mentally was the question in his mind.

'Can you dance?' he asked.

'Well, actually . . .' I tried to relax and nonchalantly threw one arm round the back of the couch. It missed, and my elbow bounced off my knee. 'Well, I've done some in the bath, ha, haaaah.'

'What?'

'Oh, it's just a little humour, Mr Kelly. Ah.' (Pause.) 'Well, you know how you sing in the bath? I just said I'd danced in the bath.'

How in hell can I tell him I haven't danced a step in my life?

There was an odd look on his face – What have I got here? I've travelled all the way from Los Angeles to see *this*!

'Actually, Mr Kelly, I'm not known for my dancing!'

'Well, what *are* you known for?' he said.

'Well, nothing really.'

Then he said, 'Well, listen, can you try something . . . maybe give me a few steps?'

'What now? Immediately?'

'Well, yes,' he said, 'just get up and do something.'

'But I haven't had breakfast yet. And I've got jet lag. It's affected my legs, and especially my feet.'

He kept staring at me. 'Try this,' he said. He cleared the coffee table, got up on it, and did a couple of tap steps.

'Oh, that!' I said, now truly panicked. 'Right.' I got up, and bumbled around, talking to my legs, vainly asking them to go places they had never dreamed of going.

His compassionate eyes were glued to the human rubber band who helplessly flailed away in front of him – until I finally came to a pathetic halt. 'I'm afraid . . . the flight . . .' I said. 'Not doing too well, am I? Uh, looks as though . . .'

'Now, listen,' he said.

'I'm listening . . .'

'Siddown,' he said.

'Right, I'm siddown,' I said.

'What we're looking for here,' he said, 'is for someone to play Cornelius Hackl . . . He's an attractive idiot.' He paused. 'Now, my wife . . . well, she thinks you're attractive. And I . . . think you're an idiot. So between us,' he said, 'I think you could be exactly right for this film. What I want you to do is go back to England and make a test. I want you to sing, "It Only Takes a Moment". I'll find someone to teach you to dance. Do some steps, sing the songs, and send it back. We'll show it to the producers and I can have a look at you.'

'Oh, thank you so very much!' I leaped at him and shook his hand almost off the end of his arm. When he finally managed to extricate himself, he walked out the door and down the corridor. I swear I heard him talking to himself.

I called out after him: 'Thank you, Mr Kelly. D'you know I've never missed anything with you and Ginger Rogers.'

I reminded Gene of this story later on. 'I've read that story,' he said. 'It would be funny if it were true, but you never said that to me.' He winked. 'You wouldn't have lived to talk about it.'

When I got back to London, I worked for weeks with a powerhouse of a dancer named Leo Caribbean who had been a member of the original *West Side Story* company. Leo taught me some of the basic choreography Gene wanted to see, and we put together a half-hour test for 20th Century-Fox that combined the song and dance for four *Dolly* numbers. After that, all we could do was wait.

You've all seen the hundreds of clichéd scenarios that

show the actor when he gets THE BIG CALL. He's been hounding his agent every fifteen minutes for weeks: Have you heard anything? Then Hollywood calls. Wildly embracing anyone and anything in sight, the actor goes completely insane. This is *it*! He's going to be a star! It wasn't any different for me; when the call came I went completely crazy. At that moment, it meant absolutely everything.

I was signed to a contract to make three pictures for 20th Century-Fox Studios and now, incredibly, Gabrielle and I would have some money. We were still living in the tiny flat in Clapham that I had bought from Terry Kendall. Another baby was due soon, the only place left for Emma to sleep – she'd outgrown the chest of drawers – would be the bathtub. My contract with Fox meant that we could let the flat go, and just before we left for Los Angeles we were able to take a mortgage on our first home. We finally had a house of our own to return to.

What I couldn't possibly have known at the time was that all that glow of a new career ahead was simply the reflection of the sun setting on a Hollywood era of lush, expensive movie musicals. The era of the great movie studios and their moguls was coming to an end – and 20th Century-Fox and its Chairman, Darryl F. Zanuck, along with it.

At the time, *The Sound of Music* appeared to be 20th Century-Fox's golden goose, but in hindsight it's perhaps more accurate to say it became that studio's undoing. In 1968, several years after the release of that film, the studio was still attempting to duplicate its extraordinary profits and produced some very expensive (for the time) films like *Star!* with my favourite, Julie Andrews, and *Dr Dolittle*, but neither film was able to recoup the original costs.

Swallowing those costs in 1968 and 1969 left 20th Century-Fox with a bad case of corporate indigestion: the studio was in terrible financial condition and in deep debt.

Desperately hoping to regain those *Sound of Music* glory days, the studio was determined to go ahead with *Hello Dolly!* After all, it was one of the great successes in American theatre history, so how could it miss? The rights were bought for over two million dollars from its Broadway producer, David Merrick, and a contract signed which stipulated that the completed film would not be shown to the public until after the Broadway production had closed. (How could anyone have guessed at the time that the show would continue to run for another several years? We finished filming in 1968, but the film wasn't released until almost two years later – and then, only after a large cash settlement had been made with Merrick.)

All the stops were pulled out and the studio press department trumpeted daily releases, building up great public anticipation. No expense was spared on costumes and huge sets. Over two million dollars was spent turning the studio's main street set into a New York City street, and thousands more to turn the little town of Garrison, New York, into a perfect turn-of-the-century village – three thousand miles from the studio sets. And when Barbra Streisand was signed for the lead role, it was done with all possible fanfare. The rest of the company included Walter Matthau, Louis Armstrong and Tommy Tune, and a marvellous ensemble of young dancers and singers. For one gargantuan parade scene, over four thousand extras were hired.

Barbra Streisand's character, Dolly Levi, was a

'marriage broker' with romantic designs on Walter Matthau, the 'richest man in Yonkers'. Cornelius Hackl was his clerk, a wonderfully innocent young man who has never found love and is stuck working in Yonkers with his friend Barnaby (Danny Lockin), wanting only to break out to find adventure and meet a girl. I could relate to Cornelius in every way. He was like my younger self. Of course, Dolly introduces him to Irene Molloy, the lady of his dreams, and everyone lives happily every after.

For the part of Irene, my leading lady, Gene had cast an actress named Marianne McAndrew, a beautiful and charming woman. She didn't actually sing and was partially dubbed through the film. But Gene thought her look was perfect; she had enormous style and class.

Walter Matthau was a bit cautious about me in the beginning. I seemed to have arrived out of nowhere; he had never heard of me, and he was surprised to be sharing top billing with me (no more surprised than I was!), but we soon began to work well together. And how could it not be exciting to work with a legend like Barbra Streisand? There were stories about how difficult Barbra was, but I found her to be nothing less than thoroughly professional. She was always prepared, she had always done her homework, she was always well rehearsed. There were stories that Barbra was uncomfortable in the role of Dolly – in the past it had always been played by much older actresses – but I think she simply always thought of it as a challenge.

The only time I had words with Barbra – and they were friendly words, I might add, said with great good humour – was during a scene where I was standing opposite her when she entered. 'Gene,' she called, 'I need to move Michael around here' (opposite to where I was standing).

'But,' I argued, 'I haven't got the music to get me that far before the gag . . .'

'Well, we gotta do it,' she said. The reality of the situation was she didn't want the camera to shoot from that side.

'Barbra,' I said, 'I need to stand where I am . . .'

'No, I can't do it,' she said, 'I can't . . .

'I don't know what you're worried about,' I said, 'You're just as ugly on the other side!'

'Whadda mouth!' she said. 'He looks so innocent, he looks so goddamn innocent. Whadda mouth he's got! Do you eat with that mouth?'

I sorted her out in the end. We came to a compromise. I stood exactly where she wanted me to.

But as far as I'm concerned there was never a problem with Barbra. Indeed, I'm not at all sure that the studios aren't themselves responsible for encouraging artists to be 'difficult'.

As an example, the front office would ask Barbra, what would you like? You want a trailer, right? So, we'll get you a trailer, Barbra. What would you like, a 30-foot trailer, 20-foot, 10-foot? Barbra, not being stupid said, 'Oh, sure, I'd love a 30-foot trailer.' Fine.

Well, Barbra, how would you like it? A little Victorian? Edwardian? Just something simple? And she'd say, 'Oh, no, I'll have Victoriana. I love it, all the reds, blues, I want the drapes, the tassels on the toilets . . .' So Barbra got a 30-foot trailer with air-conditioning, beautiful bed, chaises-longues, the works: she had three hairdressers in there as well. (How can three people work on one head?)

Then the studio brass went to Walter Matthau. Would you like a 20-foot trailer, 10-foot? What do you want? So Walter – no fool he – said, 'I'll take the 20-foot trailer.' And how do you want it? Do you want different colours, the chaises-longues, a telephone, air-conditioning? Fine.

I had third billing and no choice. I got the 10-foot trailer and they put mine at the end of the 30-foot trailer so that I got the benefit of the cool air blowing out of Barbra's air-conditioner through my windows. How would I like my trailer decorated? Red or green? I was difficult: I said I'd like it pale blue. So they painted it pale blue, and I got a couch and a mirror with lights around it.

My proper dressing room was on the *Peyton Place* lot inside the town hospital. The TV series, which starred Ryan O'Neal, was being shot adjacent to the *Dolly* set. There were days when I was held prisoner inside my dressing room because the *Peyton Place* crew were filming just outside my door. When I got my set call one such day, I decided not to wait: I put on my straw hat and marched through the middle of *Peyton Place*, nattily dressed in the turn-of-the-century wear, smiling, with a jaunty 'Good morning, doctors!' (I still get residuals from that little walk through.)

In Los Angeles, a city that's essentially built around the use of the automobile, having the right car has always been something of a status symbol. I'd rented a red convertible Mustang during our stay, and I loved that car; I was enormously proud of it and adored driving to and from home with the top down, often in costume, a rather distinctive old-fashioned grey tweed woollen suit, with a stiff-collared shirt, braces and a straw boater. The studio supplied eight copies of the same outfit for everyday and emergency use. Normally I'd keep a spare at home, get into it in the morning, and always bring a clean one home to replace it. It was just laziness; it saved going to the dressing room and changing. With the jacket off I was never terribly conspicuous, but with it on I looked the picture of a proper dandy driving my flashy red convertible.

I drove in costume to work one morning to be met by an overly-efficient security guard. 'Name?' he asked. 'Crufferd,' I said. I still say: I'm 'Mike Crufferd' in the States when they ask – that is how they pronounce it if they remember it at all. ('Michael Cranford' appeared on my dressing-room door in Los Angeles when I did *Phantom of the Opera*, a reminder of my first stint on Broadway for *Black Comedy*. The New York crew never could remember my name: I was always 'Cranford'. At the end of the run I took them all out to supper between shows and they presented me with a briefcase beautifully inscribed, 'Michael Cranford'.)

But back to that 20th Century-Fox gate: 'Name?'

'Crufferd.'

'Crufferd?' he said. 'What are you on?'

At that moment there was only one film in production on the lot. And to give him an added clue, I was sitting there in a straw boater, a woollen suit and a stiff high-collared shirt – and the sweat was beginning to pour. (Being typically English and determined to wring out that last drop of the sun's rays, I had the convertible top down in temperatures exceeding one hundred degrees.) I simply sighed and said *Dolly*.

'*Dolly*? No, I haven't got you down here . . .'

'Well,' I explained, 'it's third billing, it goes Streisand, Matthau, and Crufferd . . .'

'Oh, I gotcha . . . Here you go . . . Nope, he's already gone in . . .'

'Oh, well, fine,' I said. 'I guess we've taken this one about as far as we can go . . . if Gene Kelly happens to call to the gate and asks if Mike Crufferd has arrived yet, tell him I did come but you wouldn't let me in, so I went home again.' And I left. But I had to call the studio to ask them to inform the gate when that guy 'Crufferd' arrives in a Mustang, wearing a woollen suit and a straw boater, it's okay to let him on the set.

When I returned to Los Angeles some twenty years later to do *Phantom of the Opera*, I went driving with Emma and Lucy, nostalgically trying to find the Fox lot. Bit by bit, the land has almost been sold off to the developers and now the area has ballooned into the sleek skyscrapers of Century City. Totally lost, I drove round in circles until I finally found the sole remaining studio entrance near what used to be the back lot. 'There it is, there it is!' I yelped, finally recognising some of the area. Parking the car outside, we got out and the girls took a couple of photographs of me looking the total tourist, grinning delightedly while I pointed at the gate. Almost immediately a security guard came out barking, 'Hey you, get outta here!'

'But I used to be in *Hello Dolly!* . . .' I tried to explain.

'Yeah, and I'm Louis Armstrong,' he yelled. 'Get outta here!' And we were thrown off the lot. Some things never change.

Gabrielle and I found a house in a section of Los Angeles called Bel Air, one of those amazingly manicured areas high in the hills overlooking the city. Elvis Presley owned the house directly below us and, hoping to catch a glimpse of the great man, I used to get up early in the morning and walk on the ledge of a small ornamental wall built around our home that banked straight down an ivy-covered hill directly into the Presley garden, and there, on that wall, I practised at the top of my lungs one of my *Dolly* songs, 'Put on your Sunday clothes, there's lots of world out there . . .' About three days later, a For Sale sign was put up in front of his home – and he moved.

As a family we had a marvellous, sunny time of it. As the song says, 'It never rains in Southern California . . .' Gabrielle and I were like a couple of sunburned, star-struck, greenhorn children teaching our own babies to swim, playing tennis with athletes like Dino Martin and Pancho Segura's son, Spencer, and meeting legendary film stars like Gregory Peck. It was a dream life – slightly unreal, but dazzling, lush and enormously seductive.

It was eight months of hard work for the company, and an emotional time as well. While we were filming in New York in June 1968, Robert Kennedy was assassinated in Los Angeles. He embodied an era of grand possibilities for many Americans and we all mourned his loss. Gene was crushed; he'd been a friend of the Kennedy family. Barbra and Walter were shattered by the news as well. The set was closed down the day after the tragedy. No one could even think of working, and when production started up again in the California summer heat, the mood was bleak for cast and crew. Yet Gene Kelly was able to handle it all with great equanimity. He was enormously understanding and empathetic to his artists.

Gene believed in a lot of rehearsal, more than I'd ever experienced before, but I knew right away that I loved it and it's the way I've worked ever since. I spent countless hours rehearsing with Roger Edens, who worked with the artists on musical arrangements. I owe Roger a great debt: he gave me a confidence in my voice that I'd never had before, encouraging me in the easier, more 'natural' way I had of singing, rather than in the use of the somewhat stagey delivery (what I call back-of-the-throat tenor) that had long been favoured by juvenile leads in the theatre.

The romantic 'It Only Takes a Moment' was my big song in *Dolly*, and one of the loveliest in the show's dazzling Jerry Herman score. Under Roger's guidance I played the scene with as much honest emotional intensity as I knew how, intently focusing on the song's lyrics. I'm a young man who finds himself in a park at midnight with a beautiful girl, a young man who's hardly ever spoken to a girl before. Suddenly I can feel the palpitations, every nerve ending in my body seems to stand on end, and I start to sing a true love song. I looked up at Gene when I finished and saw he was in tears. He came over and put his arm around me. 'That's my boy!' he said. I think the scene worked well, but I couldn't have done it without the support and constant encouragement of Roger Edens.

Hello Dolly! finished production at the close of summer in 1968, but it never had the kind of success we had all hoped for. It was a lovely, old-fashioned valentine of a musical, but it was hampered by the bad timing of its release and the new economics of Hollywood. It proved to be the very last of the big budget musicals and the end of a Hollywood era. But I'll always be grateful for the chance to have been involved in it and the learning experience of working with the very best people in the industry.

In the year that followed I was asked to do the second of my three contract films for the studio. Called *The Games*, it happily reunited me with Michael Winner. The film centred on the lives of four marathon contestants who have come from all over the world to compete at the Rome Olympiad. The film seemed to have everything going for it. A fine Euro-American cast, led by Ryan O'Neal, Stanley Baker, Jeremy Kemp and Charles

Aznavour, and a script written by a 'hot' writer, Erich Segal – the Yale University professor of classics who had written the amazingly successful book and film, *Love Story*, that made a star of Ali McGraw. Additionally, we could boast of extravagant scenic locations in Vienna and London, Australia, Italy and Japan.

Everybody agreed I was the perfect physical specimen for the role of the young runner from Britain, a milkman, an English 'skinny mouse'. I based my character loosely on a true life English marathon runner named Jim Peters who, while competing in the 1954 Empire Games in Vancouver, became totally dehydrated after running twenty-six miles and, in a state of delirium, ran the wrong way on the last lap of his race. It is against competition rules to touch a runner in such a condition, and all horrified officials could do was scream directions and give arm-signals, and hope to God they could somehow halt the poor man's tragic course. I remember seeing the newsreels of the race when I was a child: it was not something one could easily forget. That's how I ended up in the film, like Jim Peters, running the wrong way around the track, and I now can't help but see this as a symbol of the way my film career was heading at the time.

I was determined to make sure that my running looked authentic. Before we started to film, I trained for three months with the great British Olympic runner Gordon Pirie, who had once set world records in the three and five thousand metres. Gordon took me training every single morning. First, he'd run from his home in Surrey, which was ten miles away from our house in Wimbledon, then he'd take me for a fifteen-mile training run, and after he finished with me, he'd run home again! This guy will do anything to avoid paying a bus fare, I thought.

He had a favourite maxim as far as my training was concerned: 'You've always got to eat a bit of breakfast before you go' – something I immediately decided to forget about. I'd throw up as I ran. However, Gordon practised what he preached. I know he ate a hearty breakfast before we met for practice because he was constantly breaking wind as we ran. I'd found in the past it was easier for me to run behind someone in training – but not, believe me, when running behind Gordon Pirie!

But that, I swear, was his training technique: he would pass wind. 'Oh, *Gordon*!' I'd bitterly complain, as I huffed and puffed behind him. 'Go, go, GO!' he'd scream. I would run to get upwind of him, and all of that turned me into a four-minute, twenty-second miler. Anyway, all that training certainly sparks one's physical well-being. My body was in great shape, I was a totally different man. Gabrielle would purposely not get out of bed in the morning till after I got home from my run.

She also did her best to help and took me out to train in the evenings, driving in the car to pace me. One night she turned the car left as I ran straight on and, without knowing it, ran over my foot. It was at least ten minutes before she even noticed that I wasn't running behind her, because she had the radio blaring the Beatles' 'Michelle, Ma Belle'. She eventually came back and saw me lying within the range of her headlamps. 'You silly bitch,' I yelled. 'You've broken my foot!' (She hadn't.) But doubled-up and helpless with laughter, she was absolutely no help at all.

I think it was Michael Winner's ingenious handling of the entire production, not to mention the budget, that made *The Games* much more than just a filmed sporting event. I'm convinced that only Michael, with his enormous drive and his arrogant refusal to accept anything less than his will, could have done what he did.

The climactic scene was set in the stadium in Rome. But how does one employ thousands of extras to fill the stadium on a less-than-epic budget? Simple, you don't. Instead Michael employed thousands of plastic dummies (on a ratio of three dummies for every live extra). The Italian extras union was, of course, ready for warfare, but Michael would hear none of it and barked at them all through his megaphone. We ended up employing between five and ten thousand frantically waving extras, flailing about amid many thousands more dummies.

Gabrielle and I shared a house in Rome with co-star Stanley Baker and his wife, Ellen, for the duration of filming. Stanley, later to become Sir Stanley Baker, was a great Welshman, a favourite character actor who excelled in the kind of stalwart roles that usually required wearing a uniform or a sword. He died just a few years after making *The Games*, tragically young, and much beloved by the industry.

Stanley Baker, I found, took his work at least as seriously as Oliver Reed. In *The Games* he was cast as my rather embittered trainer and, taking the role to heart, did his best to inspire me both on and off the set by placing some pretty steep bets on my speed, and whether or not I could actually reach the top of the hill on which I was training. He even bet, one day, that I couldn't carry him up that hill. Of course, like a damn fool, I couldn't resist the challenge. 'Get on!' I yelled, and the two-hundred-pound Stanley climbed onto my one-hundred-and-twenty-pound frame. I ran up the hill to prove my point, Stanley lost his bet and I ended up half an inch shorter.

One night, we all returned from dinner to our house

at the end of the Appian Way and found the place in a shambles. We had been burgled, most of our valuables were gone, and poor Ellen Baker in particular had lost a considerable amount of jewellery. We lost very little, having little there in the first place – only Gabrielle's fur coat. (I had hidden my per diem money, which didn't amount to much, in some socks hanging in the cupboard.) They had evidently loaded all their booty in our American Tourister suitcase.

We later discussed insurance and, after listening to Stanley's explanation of his fairly substantial claims, I loftily remarked in my best one-upmanship manner, 'Oh, well, that's much the same as ours.'

'What!' He swung round. 'Why you little bastard,' he laughed, 'you haven't got bugger-all near that! You came away with a pair of jeans and some sneakers, and that's how you travel!'

'Well, my wife lost her fur coat!' I replied, sounding absurdly defensive.

'You call *that* a fur coat!' he scoffed. 'It wasn't fur, it was skunk! We've got the room next door – I know it was skunk! And,' he added, 'it hasn't long been dead! Who would buy his wife a skunk coat?' (He was absolutely right, it was skunk. I wanted my wife to have a fur coat, but with limited money to pay for one, we didn't have much choice in the matter. Gabrielle always told people it was rabbit because it sounded better than skunk. But I thought she looked terrific in it.)

'Well,' I retorted frostily, 'I hope to remedy that when the insurance claim comes through!' From that day on Stanley was convinced we were putting in false insurance claims and he decided to teach me a lesson.

We checked with the police constantly for news of our belongings until one day while waiting on the set, I looked up and saw Stanley walking slowly towards me from a distance of four hundred yards, the length of the home straight. He was grinning from ear to ear with a look of glorious victory on his face as he savoured the moment. He was carrying our American Tourister suitcase and was accompanied by an Italian gentleman of rather formidable build.

Stanley spent the next tense moments almost convincing me that his companion was an insurance assessor come to arrest me for filing false claims. Actually he was a policeman, intercepted by Stanley as he'd come to return my suitcase, which had been found floating empty three miles out to sea off Naples. I've still got that suitcase; the lining is loose from its water adventures, something that provokes Customs officials to poke it about, loosening it even more. But I wouldn't give it away for anything.

Gabrielle got a new fur coat in the end. When the insurance claim was paid she was upmarketed – to wolf. For myself, I preferred the old coat. At least it never gave her the trouble of the new model, which came with a zippered extension so that the fur could be lengthened to her ankles for appearances at more formal occasions. At the premiere of *Hello Dolly!* in New York, she looked quite as resplendent as any movie star. She was escorted by our friend Patric Walker, who was looking after her until I could meet up with them after a photo session with Barbra Streisand and Louis Armstrong. As my wife walked up the stairs through a battery of flashing press cameras, she suddenly heard the sound of Patric's horrified 'Oh, my God!' behind her. 'Come along, Patric,' she said, but then turned to see him standing stock still at the bottom of the stairway gazing at the now completely unzipped extension trailing in her wake like a long furry train. While all the flashbulbs popped, she hopped about in a frantic re-zipping effort. Patric understandably abandoned his escort responsibilities on the spot and disowned her completely.

It took some time before she forgave me for my purchase of a faulty fur extension. But I think my judgment has been vindicated: I mean, it never would have happened with the skunk.

We had just completed *The Games* and were headed back to London when word came that the great man himself, Darryl Zanuck, had asked for me to do his next film, a love story called *Hello and Goodbye*. Because he had headed the studio and had apparently specifically requested me for the film, I felt very flattered that he wanted me.

Producer Darryl F. Zanuck's career had spanned an era of remarkable creativity in American cinema. Some of the finest of American classics – films such as *The Grapes of Wrath*, *All About Eve* and *Gentlemen's Agreement* had been produced under his guidance. Shirley Temple, James Cagney, Tyrone Power, Gregory Peck, and a multitude of other screen notables were started or helped on the road to stardom under Zanuck's reign. And a reign is exactly what it was. He ruled as one of the last of the Hollywood titans you read about, with an absolute authority over his kingdom at Fox. In photographs he was a wiry, dynamic, and very fit man, with a trim moustache and an expensive cigar. Complicated, driven, and fiercely competitive, Zanuck was also an enormously creative film-maker. He'd written dozens of screenplays in the early part of his career under three assumed names, and he was a complete master of the art of film editing as well as studio administration.

I was totally unsophisticated in my view of the studio and the workings of the Hollywood scene. I felt euphoria: the bigwigs in the front office actually knew I was alive! That, and the fact that Ronald Neame, fresh from his directing triumph with *The Prime of Miss Jean Brodie*, had been signed to direct this not-so-terrific script, was all I knew or really cared about. Ronald Neame was, to my mind, a cinema legend. In partnership with director David Lean, he'd produced some of the greatest films of what I've always thought of as the golden age of British cinema – *Brief Encounter* and *Great Expectations* among them; later, he'd directed Alec Guinness in *The Horse's Mouth* and *Tunes of Glory*. It meant I'd be working with the very best people – my movie-making prospects began to appear awfully good again.

I hadn't the faintest idea, of course, that when Zanuck made the decision to produce *Hello and Goodbye*, he was doing it against the advice of the Fox front office, and solely as a vehicle for his latest girlfriend, a twenty-three-year-old French woman named Geneviève Gilles whom Zanuck was determined to make a star.

After seemingly endless negotiations with agents and agents and more agents, I was summoned – there's really no other word for it – to meet the Great Man himself, who had set up digs at the Byblos Hotel, an opulently beautiful complex of apartments and hotel overlooking the bay of St Tropez. It was arranged that I meet Zanuck for supper along with his protégée. I was very nervous, but also intrigued. But I was disappointed in the physical Zanuck: he wasn't what I expected at all. He was a little man, five-feet five-inches, far too short to match the vision I had of such an enormous Hollywood legend. He sat behind a large desk, puffing away on his giant cigar, and spoke very enthusiastically about the project and the script. I didn't think it was exactly Academy Award material myself, but I thought with the kind of direction

Ronald Neame was certain to provide, it might prove to be a pleasant romantic comedy.

Sometime during the initial conversation, Zanuck finally got around to introducing me to my co-star, who was sitting quietly in a corner on the other side of the room. There was a bland prettiness to her face, surrounded as it was by a great deal of very expensive jewellery. I don't think I paid much attention to her until she briefly echoed Zanuck's enthusiasm for the project in what I was soon to realise was the limited amount of English at her command: 'Allo . . . Aye sink zis be grrrreat movie . . . !'

I don't believe there is an actor alive, once he becomes involved in a project, who doesn't say to himself and believe to his heart's core: this is it, this is the big one, this will be the best movie (or play or poetry reading or even commercial) ever done. The dream is always that somehow, no matter what the signs to the contrary, everything will turn out in the end! My dream was about to be tested to the limit on the set of *Hello and Goodbye*.

From the beginning, none of us was ever in doubt that Mr Zanuck was completely obsessed with Mademoiselle Gilles. He made sure he was on the set whenever she was scheduled for a scene. He coached her, checked on her; he cheered and cajoled her, and studied her every movement.

There were only a few occasions that Mademoiselle Gilles and I found ourselves able to rehearse without Zanuck hovering beside us. We were doing some scenes in a car, and I was attempting to coach her a bit. Before we had time to accomplish anything, Zanuck would lean through the car window with that enormous cigar. 'How'd it go?' he'd say suspiciously. 'Everything okay . . .?'

Then there was our other co-star on the film, the

German actor Curt Jurgens. For some reason I only remember him as always playing a U-boat commander. He certainly looked just right for that kind of role: he was well into his fifties by this time, but still extraordinarily handsome – tall and blonde with a rather elegant military bearing. He had been described to me as 'a star of the old school in the vein of Von Stroheim'. Having worked with what I had thought were the 'old-school stars' like the disciplined Gene Kelly, I was not quite prepared to deal with Mr Jurgens. He came to the studio in a different Rolls for every other day of the week. Along with his retinue, he would not so much arrive as *descend* on the set, sometimes with what seemed to me to be little more than a Deutschmark's worth of memorised lines in his head – a fact that irritated me beyond belief.

Finally, one day, when I couldn't stand it anymore, I got completely carried away, and in a loud speech I managed to combine a criticism of his professionalism with a tirade involving a complete replay of World War II. I knew I hadn't done a damn thing to help matters, of course, but at least I felt a lot better.

We were barely weeks into shooting when Ronnie Neame left the production. I recall we were sitting in my caravan, parked beside a dock on the Marseilles waterfront, when he told me of his decision. He was very apologetic because he knew how much I'd wanted to work with him, but he explained that he simply couldn't continue, given the problems he was experiencing with Zanuck. He left the picture the very next day, and most of my hopes went with him.

Ronnie was replaced by an old croquet-playing chum of Zanuck's, Jean Negulesco, who had directed the very popular *Three Coins in the Fountain* for Fox back in 1954. Conditions really began to deteriorate after that because Negulesco was ineffectual, afraid to argue with Zanuck about anything at all to do with our leading lady. In his own frustration he would have moments of Romanian temperament with me, which only made me resent him; I would fly home to London almost every weekend just to get away from the set.

Everything started to go wrong after that, even the stunt work. The script called for me to drive a Rolls-Royce into a swimming pool. The whole scene had to be done in one take – I did a speech, then drove the Rolls out of a garage through some open gates, under an archway, and right into the pool. (It wasn't quite as simple as that, of course: in reality, a ramp had been built at the pool's edge so that once the front wheels had gone up the ramp it would put the car at the right angle of attack to hydroplane onto the pool. A small explosive was placed under the ramp and when it blew, it upended the front of the car which otherwise would have gone in nose-first, and I might have drowned. I practised driving up the ramp for days, hitting it at precisely the right speed.) There was a camera on the roof of the car, inside the car, on the gates, on the side of the pool, twelve cameras in all, but when we looked at the rushes the next day we found that only two cameras had actually been working.

If I had to point to one small incident to sum up the production, it would be the day when we shot a rather silly scene at the pond in the countryside outside of Cannes. I stood by the water's edge watching Genevieve swim about. The rather tepid joke of the scene had me pointing to a sign that said *Défense de Pêcher* and telling the lady that the sign meant the water was poisoned – whereupon she walks naked out of the water saying, 'Défense de pêcher ees no feeshing!'

Mademoiselle Gilles was clearly upset about something even before the scene started. I never quite understood what her problems were because she only used French when she shouted at Zanuck. But that morning we were made to understand that she wasn't sure how deep the water was, and this clearly upset her. 'Let me take care of it,' Zanuck told her in English.

Without another word Mr Zanuck, fully clothed in his shirt and safari shorts, his cigar firmly clamped between his teeth, strode into the water to test the depths and calm her doubts. 'Nah, it's fine,' he hollered at her, 'it's not porous . . . it's all solid here.' We could only stand there and stare at this industry giant as he waded fully-clothed about the pond, desperate to please his young girlfriend. It all seemed so sad.

Zanuck had more or less taken over the direction from Negulesco, and we were doing take after take after take. We were way over budget, and there was grumbling in Hollywood about the amount of money being spent on Mademoiselle Gilles' clothes. There were new clothes for every new location – and everything was Dior or Chanel.

The consequences of the whole venture, a dismal failure for the studio, were disastrous for Zanuck. Shortly after the film's release, to head off a stockholders' rebellion, the Fox Board of Directors stripped him of the last vestiges of his power and voted him off the Board and out of the studio he had founded. *Hello and Goodbye* was to be the last film he ever made. Ms Gilles' star faded quickly thereafter, except for the spotlight she shared as one of the principals in a convoluted law suit after Zanuck's death.

I was greatly relieved when the picture ended and I could finally return to London. The experience put me off even thinking of doing films again for many years.

CHAPTER 15

No one who knows me would dispute that my knowledge of high finance couldn't fill a gnat's navel, which is why I had a conversation with John Barry about business investments. John had done very well in the intervening years since he'd composed the score for *The Knack*. His music for the James Bond films in particular had made him Britain's top composer for the cinema. So when Gabrielle and I began to think about investing some of my 20th Century-Fox earnings, John seemed to be one of the logical people to talk to; he was a good friend – and he looked very prosperous indeed.

It was in 1970 – not long after I limped back to London, still bloodied from the *Hello and Goodbye* wars – that Gabrielle and I decided to set up a plan to include trust funds for the children, and John gave me the name of his personal banker who had apparently done very well for his clients in the past.

John was an enigmatic man, but had tremendous good taste in fashionable clothes, food and wine, and drove a beautiful white E-type Jaguar. He had started out as a projectionist in one of his father's cinemas in York, and always seemed to have a smile on his face, as if enjoying some private joke with himself.

'What are you smiling for?' I'd say.

'I'm not bloody smiling,' he'd reply, in his down-to-earth Bradford accent; 'it's just that you look so bloody miserable.'

On this particular evening I had something to be miserable about. I'd set up a meeting with the gentleman who proposed a plan specifically designed for my family's needs, saying he could guarantee an earning of twelve per cent on our investment. It was all completely above board, he told me, all perfectly legitimate, and he talked on and on about things like offshore companies and the like – exactly the sort of conversation that makes my eyes glaze over. (The only thing I paid attention to was the bit about guaranteed earnings.)

In order to explain what followed in the simplest terms, I can only say that I placed all the money I had earned from my Fox deal into the hands of a fast-talking little man from Brighton to deal with in what he called a 'pyramid' investment. The base of the 'pyramid', he explained, would be solid in unit trusts, with only a small percentage of my own money risked at the 'top of the investment pyramid'. 'We'll only risk a bit here and there,' he said, 'but rest assured, Mr Crawford, we absolutely guarantee we'll make twelve per cent.' He also advised me to enjoy some of the money I'd earned from *Dolly*. 'Spend some of your money, Michael enjoy it!', and so I bought a secondhand Rolls-Royce, which cost a cool twenty thousand pounds.

Gabrielle and I joined John Barry and his wife for a night out in London several months later when John's guest – his *new* financial advisor, recently hired to investigate some of John's current business affairs – made a brief announcement to the party at large that the old advisor had pooled John's money and mine (along with that of other clients) and in the process, lost most of our funds in a series of questionable investments.

This time I heard phrases like 'he invested in companies already going bad' and 'the money he invested, he got back for himself'. (I still don't understand the whole scam.) It was the part about our quarter-of-a-million-pound investment being gone that really grabbed my attention.

Gabrielle and I just sat there in a state of shock and listened. I felt numb and embarrassingly stupid, unable to take in what was being said. Neither one of us could think of a proper response. I just kept repeating, 'We have nothing? Nothing at all?'

As you might suspect, this news put a slight damper on the evening and our party quickly ran out of steam. Gabrielle and I left the restaurant and walked outside to our Rolls-Royce, the last opulent souvenir of all the Hollywood hoopla. 'I suppose this is the last time we'll drive home in this,' I said. (Almost, but not quite true. The first thing I did next morning was make phone calls to sell that car and quickly discovered that it's a damn sight easier to buy a Rolls than it is to sell one.) All the way home we sang the words from the old song, 'Pick yourself up, dust yourself off, and start all over again.'

Well, why not? We were young, we'd be fine. I simply had to hustle a little more and keep working. But it didn't take long to find out that the kind of work I was looking for wasn't out there for me, and the work that was being offered always seemed to be totally wrong.

I admit that much of this was my own fault, but the experience of doing *Hello and Goodbye* had annihilated me. I had known what I was in for early on, yet because this was the last film in my three-film contract with the studio, I had had no choice but to stay on the project. Now I swore to myself that I would never again take work that I couldn't entirely justify in my own mind, and the only way to do that, as far as I could see, was to return to my roots in the theatre. There, at least I knew I would have some control over what I did. So I concentrated all my efforts on finding a play. But having once been burned, I became ultra-shy about any new project; I felt paralysed, terrified to make a wrong move and, of course, by the time I finished turning things down, nothing more was being offered.

That was a long, tortuous eighteen months. I had been used to working constantly over the past ten years, sometimes with as little rest as a long weekend between major projects. Now there was nothing. It was purgatory being unable to ply my craft, as it is for any actor. I was tetchy and withdrawn and non-communicative, and I made it a miserable time for Gabrielle as well. The constant stress of never knowing how to pay the next bill only compounded our problems. Gabrielle has her own hardy brand of determination and pluck, and she threw herself into a venture based on an idea of her brother, Roger, the gypsy in her family. At the time he was making a living stuffing cushions made from inexpensive fabrics; this was the time of the Maharishi and sitting on cushions was becoming rather chic. It was Gabrielle who thought of bringing in luxurious fabrics from places like Afghanistan and India, and establishing an up-market shop featuring enormous floor cushions. We located a small shop in Chelsea and called it 'Absolute Elsewhere'. (That idea also came from Roger, who can best be described as a son of the Age of Aquarius.) The shop very quickly became a rather 'in' place. (Both Terence Conran and the John Lewis chain bought from us but later started to manufacture their own; you can't patent a cushion. You can still find some of our cushions in Annabel's in London.)

Gabrielle did everything from designing to promoting and selling, as well as running the shop – from which I was more or less banned. I was completely useless with the customers. All one of them had to do was express an opinion – 'Oh I don't like that' – and I'd pounce.

'You don't like it! What's wrong with it?! How can you not like that?' I'd say. 'We brought it all the way from Afghanistan!'

Suddenly from the back of the store I'd hear, 'Michhhaaaeeelll! Leave the shop!!'

So it was agreed that I could instead concentrate my energies on outside duties, and I coordinated getting the linings made by the Wadings, a dear couple who owned a dressmaking shop in Battersea. My loyal friend and film stand-in, Steve Corrie, helped me stuff those enormous floor pillows with small pieces of sponge in our 'factory', a warehouse room at the back of the Chelsea Football Grounds in Fulham. The initial deliveries were made in our Rolls (to the bemusement of some of our customers) until the car was finally sold and I bought a Ford Escort van for the enterprise. We had 'Florra's' (our name for our floor cushions) painted on it; I refused to drive a van with 'Absolute Elsewhere' scrawled on the side.

The success of the venture was largely a tribute to Gabrielle's efforts. She had come into her own as a businesswoman and the shop got us through the year and far beyond. We were also blessed with wonderful friends who helped us through the darker moments, people like Jackie Collins and her husband, Oscar Lehrmann, who were extraordinarily generous and insisted on taking us out to Tramp for dinner every week. It made us feel less isolated. Things like that one never forgets; they were very caring people and their attitude towards us didn't change when we were down on our luck.

It was at the point that I began to believe the manufacture of floor pillows was certain to become my life's work, when I was offered the lead in a new play by Anthony Marriott and Alastair Foot. It was a typically English sex farce – a rather slim piece – but it contained some wildly imaginative moments.

Most of our friends knew I had already turned down all kinds of other, apparently more serious, opportunities, and they were hard-pressed to understand why something with a title like *No Sex Please, We're British* could inspire my return to the theatre. The play was all about a young, newly married bank manager who discovers there is pornography being delivered to his bank branch because of a mistaken address. Everything is further complicated by the imminent visit of a bank inspector, the appearance of a disapproving mother-in-law, and a couple of nearly-naked girls arriving for some sort of sex convention. The manager assigns his weedy, awkward junior clerk the job of disposing of the porn, and . . . well, you can imagine the rest.

I spoke to John Gale, the producer, and suggested that instead of playing the bank manager, I would far rather play the bank clerk; I thought I could do more with the part which, to my mind, combined some wonderful elements of pathos with grand opportunities for knockdown slapstick comedy. I saw something in that character that opened up quite another avenue for me as an actor; I felt it offered a kind of independence, a chance to experiment and, hopefully, to leave behind the romantic juvenile roles which had been developing since I had dipped a first tentative toe into Hollywood's cinematic waters.

We started long, complicated rehearsals, blessed with an absolutely first-rate company: Anthony Valentine was cast as the bank manager, Linda Thorson as his wife, and that grand and wonderful English theatrical institution, Evelyn Laye, as the grande-dame mother-in-law. I was Brian Runnicles, the neurotically nervous, bumbling junior clerk. The script wasn't terribly strong so rehearsals became, of necessity, an imaginatively creative time. Alan Davis, our director, left us pretty much to our own devices. Tony Valentine and I spent hours together, improvising and shaping physical bits to add to the evening. For instance, there were piles of huge books positioned on the stage, so we invented all sorts of sight gags using the books as props, with me staggering under their weight, or balancing and juggling great stacks of them on my knees while I attempted to answer a telephone. And I did lots of jumps and leaps through the hatch of a tiny on-stage kitchenette.

I enjoyed a particular piece of business in one scene when I was chased into the bathroom by two half-naked girls. (Not a bad way to earn a quid!) Shortly thereafter I re-emerged, clad only in my shorts, and appearing completely comatose as I was carried across the stage, sitting on the shoulders of a large, luscious lady. My arms were held high over my head in a kind of stupefied pose.

In rehearsals, when the actress carrying me reached the door, we both realised my body was positioned too high to go through it. To solve the problem I had a picture solidly bolted to the wall above the door; she could walk through it – but I was left hanging by both hands from the picture over the archway. Then, still seeming to be totally unconscious, I let one hand drop down while the rest of my body, hanging by one arm from the picture, swung at a snail's pace round to face the audience. It used to bring the house down.

We were scheduled to open in Scotland: what a place, I thought, to take an English farce on opening night! It's part of theatrical folklore that English comedies and comedians go to Glasgow to die. Every music hall comic I've met can tell alarming tales of being pelted with rotten vegetables by an unappreciative audience of Scotsmen. I was dreading the opening, only hoping that the men of Edinburgh would be of a gentler disposition than their Glaswegian compatriots. We had toiled so hard and long that by the time we reached Edinburgh, we were beginning to be fairly pleased with our efforts and the look of the production.

In fact, we need not have worried at all: the Edinburgh audiences were warmly receptive. Sadly Alastair Foot didn't live to see the opening night and hear the audience's laughter. He was always very enthusiastic about our inventiveness – not the usual case among playwrights. The audiences were totally delighted, and their word-of-mouth kept us in full houses.

The show moved on to Manchester, to the Opera House there – much too large a theatre for such a farce – and we didn't do as well. But Tony and Linda and I spent every waking hour at the theatre, devising, improvising and sharpening new business for our opening night in London. By the time the curtain went up at the Strand Theatre in June of 1971, our ensemble playing was honed to as near comic perfection as we could make it.

Gabrielle and I went out to dinner after the opening, and later drove on to the West London Air Terminal for the early editions of the papers. The reviews for the play itself were fairly reserved, but praise for our company was unanimous, and a few days later, the eminent theatre critic for the *Sunday Times*, Harold Hobson, wrote a review that I shall always treasure, calling my characterisation 'a creation of innocent beauty, and also of athletic skill, which makes one proud of the theatre' – difficult to believe that that review was written just a few months after I'd spent more than a year stuffing floor pillows for a living. The vicissitudes of a life in the theatre never cease to stagger me.

Creating a character on stage is partly a matter of growing into that imaginary person's natural rhythm. Where in a sentence does that emphatic nod come? When, during an aggressive confrontation, does that characteristic twitch of the leg betray the seething nerves under the calm exterior? In comedy generally – and particularly on screen – much of it can be almost subliminal, but in on-stage farce you need to make every inch of your body work for you. Farce, you'll often find, is based on a highly dramatic situation and as that drama unfolds it's possible to allow your body to be wracked by the turmoil of each moment, as if moving ever more out of your control, fuses going off down one part of the body after another.

A lot of people playing farce make the mistake of sacrificing character to timing. I don't think that that works. If you don't believe in the truth of a character, you won't laugh or cry with them – and surely this applies to all forms of drama?

I have a memory from when I was very small of Nan and Mont struggling to carry a wardrobe downstairs. Mum offered to help, but 'Don't interfere,' said Mont, 'we know what we're doing. We work as a team.' Mum and I gave each other a look. Inevitably the weight of the wardrobe proved too much for Nan, who sat down heavily on the stairs, letting go of the wardrobe so that the whole burden fell on Mont, who was supporting it from below. Now he, too, fell backwards, the wardrobe slid down the stairs – revealing Nan's legs akimbo and the never-seen bloomers that dwelt underneath – and, as the back of Mont's head hit the hall carpet, the door of the wardrobe swung open and a plaster statue of the Virgin Mary with child shot out, sailed through the air, and hit Mont right between the eyes. With a little 'clink' the baby Jesus' head fell off. Later we glued it back on, but it was forever afterwards a bit askew, the baby's head embedded in Mary's bosom, which is maybe why we kept it in the cupboard under the stairs after that . . .

If I were trying to re-create this scene on stage, there would be two things I'd emphasise: firstly the pomposity of Nan and Mont, so that their comeuppance is funny; and secondly how the consequences of this initial pomposity accelerate out of control.

I got a call from John Barry not long after the opening of *No Sex Please*, asking if I would be interested in playing the role of the White Rabbit in a musical film of *Alice in Wonderland* for which he was writing the score. I told him that as long as he didn't want me to invest any money, I was charmed by the whole idea. And having been out of work for so long, I decided not to miss out on anything worthwhile that came along.

Bill Sterling, the director, assured me that my scenes would be shot early in the day, allowing plenty of time to return to the theatre at night, but the schedule turned out to be far more gruelling than anything I could have imagined; worse still, it left very little time for a home life. The extraordinarily complicated process of doing the make-up required me to be at the studio by six in the morning. We'd shoot all day and then I'd race to the theatre in early evening, finish the performance, and arrive home about midnight. I went six weeks with less than five hours of sleep a night, ending the film in a state of near-collapse. By then the physical stress of exhaustion and my continuing absence from home had begun to add to the strains on our marriage.

In the years following my meeting and falling in love with Gabrielle, I began for the first time to get a lot of recognition, particularly from the opposite sex. I'd never had this attention before – now, suddenly, I had choices. My ridiculous male ego was enormously flattered.

How does a man's mind work so that he believes that an infidelity won't interfere with the love that stands at the centre of his life? Of all the mistakes one can make, this one ranks right up there with the worst. But then I'm afraid I compounded all the hurt: I told Gabrielle what I'd done.

As a Catholic you think of confession in terms of doing penance and receiving absolution. You think you can lay it off, be forgiven, and stop feeling so bad about it. But Gabrielle never trusted me completely again. I'm sure I would have been exactly the same if it had been the other way round.

So each of us began to pursue our own lonely path, pulling at one another in ways we never imagined. I thought I needed to do as much work as possible, to take on everything worthwhile that came along and somehow make up for all the long months I had been unable to practise my craft. She wanted me at home more and, however much I wasn't there, I still wanted her to be there when I came home. With me out at work and both our energies depleted, the weaknesses in our relationship were exposed – and always in the background was the memory of my infidelity.

Arguments gave way to long periods of resentful silence, terrible weeks for both of us with little or no communication. I didn't help matters by continually escaping to the refuge of the theatre where I could shut out the problems at home, sometimes arriving in the afternoon for an eight o'clock curtain. Gabrielle began to spend more time with her family, and with friends unconnected with the theatre. The resentment and friction put unbearable stress on the mechanisms that made our marriage work until everything seemed to rip apart at once.

I took a brief vacation in the Caribbean when *Alice in Wonderland* was completed, hoping that the separation would serve to clear the air. But little changed after my return until the weekend Gabrielle took the children home to her parents for a visit and didn't return, and we began a 'trial separation' and all the unpleasant business of having one's life placed in the hands of the legal establishment. There was also the additional pressure of keeping up appearances to keep our separation secret and out of the newspapers – and there, at least, we were amazingly successful; it wasn't until eighteen months after the fact that our problems became public knowledge.

I moved out of our Wimbledon home in November 1972. But we had gone our separate roads months before we ever parted, and it was fairly clear in Gabrielle's mind that our marriage was over, although, at the time, I adamantly refused to admit it to myself. Later on a friendship developed for Gabrielle which gave her the strength to face the realities of our own relationship. I had always been a passionate football fan and loved going to the matches, but the whole thing rather bored Gabrielle. I used to keep at her about it: 'Look if we've got to get ourselves together,' I told her, 'we have to be part of things for each other, so why don't you come to the football games . . .' This kind of argument went on for months until she finally relented and came to a Chelsea match with me. Ironically, she ended up living with the centre forward for Chelsea, and had two children by him. I hate to say I told you so – but I knew she would enjoy herself once she'd actually been to a match.

However much I loved Gabrielle I don't think I loved her enough, but at the same time I don't think I could have loved her more; perhaps if we'd met later on, when I was more mature, it would have lasted.

When you have destroyed a love like we had, one danger is that you will never forgive yourself. Another is that nothing that comes after will ever live up to it. In many ways it won't. But the way I look at it is: how lucky I was to know that love. Every time I see our daughters, Emma and Lucy, I'm reminded of it. Since my break-up with Gabrielle, of course I've loved again, but I haven't reached the point of feeling confident enough to re-marry.

Our friends were supportive and helpful to a man. Patric Walker and his friend Martyn Thomas suggested I come out and stay with them in their vacation home in Spain – an invitation they lived to regret. The minute I got off the plane, my first words were 'Do you think I've done the right thing by coming here . . . ?' and from that moment I proceeded to drive them absolutely crazy; all I really wanted to do was go home. Patric was particularly patient; he drove me to the airport almost every day. Halfway there, I'd decide not to go and he'd have to drive me back to the house again.

In the evenings Patric and Martyn used to watch me from the terrace as I mournfully prowled the beach below. Then I'd sit near the water's edge half the night.

(You could always tell where I'd been: the site was marked by the clutter of Guinness bottles I'd left behind.)

The day came when I decided it was time to go. No more indecision. I even booked myself on the afternoon flight to London. This time, rather than risk another two-hour drive to the airport, Patric and Martyn put me in a taxi and waved me off with a heartfelt 'It's been lovely having you', in the joyful realisation they wouldn't have to put up with me for another day. They watched the car until it disappeared from sight and then they breathed a collective sigh of relief.

Patric had a dinner party that evening, although not, he swears, to celebrate my departure. His guests sat on the terrace enjoying the sunset when someone noticed a taxi pull up to the top of a nearby overhanging cliff. 'Oh God, no,' Patric said. 'it can't be.' It was. My flight had been cancelled. 'Why didn't you just sleep at the airport?' Patric asked me. 'I mean, did you have to come back? I mean, well, it's not that we didn't want you . . .'

I left for good the next morning. I'm sure there was dancing in the streets.

My football-playing friends came through in a big way too. Dave Webb, another Chelsea player, was a particular pal of mine and he and his wife, Jackie, were kind enough to invite me to stay with them after the separation. But I was so unhappy at the time, I knew I would have driven them mad, just as I had Patric and Martyn. I needed to be on my own more than anything, so Dave found a little council flat for me in Russell Gardens Mews at the back of the Olympia railway cuttings.

Mike Summerbee, who played football for both Manchester City and England, was another great friend: we'd met one night when we were both guests on one of those fast-talking television game shows (my first and last). Both of us made fools of ourselves during the quiz, each of us coming over as a complete ignoramus. (When Mike was asked 'What race goes under several bridges on the Thames in the spring of each year?' I think he answered, 'the roller derby'. And when I was asked how many wives Henry VIII had, I said 'eight'. It was the last number I heard, and the only one I remembered.) Of course, Mike and I became friends on the spot.

He called me that first Christmas after Gabrielle and I separated, urging me to spend the holiday with him, his wife Tina, and their children Rachael and Nicholas. I was feeling completely miserable, not the least for having contracted chicken pox a few days before, a condition that hardly seemed to bother Mike. 'The kids have got to get chicken pox sometime,' he insisted. 'They might as well get it all at once. Just get yourself in a car and get up here.' When I arrived on Christmas Eve, Mike and Tina took me in hand and sent me straight to bed, feeding me copious quantities of sweet rum punch. They had been hoping to go to a party so I volunteered to be the baby sitter, which worked fine until Nicholas woke up about ten pm and I had to go into their room. I must have looked like Swamp Man and it scared the hell out of the pair of them. They were still screaming when Mike and Tina got home at midnight.

By Christmas Day, I was a good deal worse and ran a high fever. No doctor would come out on that holiday morning, of course, so Mike and Tina called in the next best thing – their local veterinarian. He was obviously pleased he was about to do battle with something other than the hind side of a horse. He came equipped with a needle the size of a milkshake drill and gave me a shot that put me to sleep for two days. It couldn't have been much of a holiday for Mike and Tina worrying about their patient upstairs, but their kindness made that Christmas a very welcoming time for me.

I might even have welcomed having the chicken pox that holiday weekend had I known I was carrying with me a Christmas present of unimagined proportions, a script for a new television programme called *Some Mothers Do 'Ave 'Em*.

For those who have never seen the show (or its lead character Frank Spencer), let me simply define it as one of those miracles that have periodically visited my professional life – almost always at the point when someone is asking whatever happened to Michael Crawford? Their astonishing frequency has me quite convinced that somebody up there is watching out for me.

CHAPTER 16

THE GREATEST SUCCESSES of my acting career have always been the result of close collaboration with others and, as a consequence, there isn't a moment now when I'm not aware of how much I owe them. I have found it vital to have the support and understanding of these very special people on my creative journeys, and some of these working partnerships have felt akin to love affairs in their intensity. This was especially true in the case of *Some Mothers Do 'Ave 'Em.*

I'd been playing in *No Sex Please* for a few months when I was sent the script for *Some Mothers* by BBC Television. It was, I understood, only after Norman Wisdom and Ronnie Barker had both turned down the role of Frank Spencer that anyone even thought of offering it to me. I was very interested, and arranged to meet Duncan Wood, the head of comedy for BBC's Light Entertainment Group, and also the show's producer, Michael Mills. Michael was exactly the right man for such a project. He was a former Navy man, aggressive and bossy, but extremely competent and creative – very much a doer – and I love that kind of attitude. Michael was a great one for adventure, willing to try absolutely anything. He could be brusque and even domineering, but without him and his kind of drive, I doubt *Some Mothers* would ever have worked.

Because of the break-up with Gabrielle my emotional state was fairly shaky at the beginning of the series – half the time I found it hard enough just getting out of bed in the mornings – and I excused myself from some early planning sessions. But as work progressed I became increasingly caught up in Michael's enthusiasm and drive. He would have liked to work on the show twenty-four hours a day, and encouraged me to work with him during the pre-production period so we could agree on the way the series was developing.

Some Mothers was an outrageous farce, built around the kind of stunts and situations one used to see in the old silent films. In Frank Spencer we attempted to create a modern-day silent film character, an amalgam of some of my heroes from those early days such as Harold Lloyd, Buster Keaton and Laurel and Hardy.

I've always felt that the reason the show worked so well was because Frank was portrayed truthfully, as a real human being, rather than just a figure of fun. Indeed, I believe that the warm, positive qualities of Frank Spencer really do exist in the form of Raymond Allen, the young man who wrote *Some Mothers*. Raymond was a kind, very gentle person, the innocent baby-faced boy next door. For the life of me I can't imagine how he ever found his way into the fiercely competitive world of television where, in order to survive, you need ego, arrogance and an armoury of assorted defence mechanisms. He and Michael Mills were an odd couple, but perhaps it was those very differences that made them such a successful team.

Michael, Raymond and I set about creating Frank's character. We made him a study in physical (and mental) anarchy – hilariously accident-prone, the ultimate klutz and eternal underdog. His voice sounded like that of a nasal ten-year-old, and his every sentence seemed to end on a note of shocked disbelief. He was a walking Malaprop too. ('I don't know to what you are alluring . . .') The final physical touches were provided by our costume designer, Michael Robbie, who dressed Frank in an odd assortment of mismatched jumpers, a shabby raincoat and, in an inspired stroke, an old beret which became the Spencer trademark. We even gave Frank his own complete (and silly) personal history:

He was born, prematurely, in a cinema:

Frank:	The Spencers haven't been on time for five generations – My grandfather was three weeks premature, my mother was early and I was very immature myself . . . She was watching a John Wayne film.
Betty:	What happened?
Frank:	I don't remember . . . Oh, I think he got killed in the end . . .

After two attempts to have the hospital take him back, his father had deserted him in Paddington Station, where he suffered a mishap in his knickers – Frank was wearing a dress at the time:

Frank: A gypsy woman told my mother
                she was going to have a little girl,
                and she went out and bought all
                the things . . . I had to keep the
                clothes and wear them – and the
                dolly too – until the head fell
                off . . .

Other details were added as we went along. We made Frank a committed Catholic who goes to confession every day and drives his parish priest crazy (not unlike the twenty-one-year-old Crawford); and we even gave him a brief (one-day) military career (in the RAF, of course).

Frank was a bachelor in our first few scripts, but I thought it was crucial to make him a married man, and of course he'd need a wife who was extraordinarily caring, patient and understanding – a complete understatement for anyone who has seen the show. His wife had to be the steady anchor in his life, someone who believed in him absolutely, no matter how wacky his behaviour, otherwise he would appear too bizarre to be credible.

The role of Frank's long-suffering wife, Betty, finally went to the fine dramatic actress Michele Dotrice, daughter of the distinguished actor Roy Dotrice. It was extraordinary: the moment she walked in, we knew she was the right person; the chemistry was absolutely perfect. She was a natural comedienne and the series owed a lot of its success to her talent.

Beyond that, Michele's support and care for both Michael Crawford and Frank Spencer were such that she became a key part of my success and my life; no other person could have given me what she gave me. Michele was the sister I never had, and her kindness helped to guide me through one of the most painful periods of my life. She made me, quite literally, feel whole again.

Michele is a joy to play opposite; she has pluck and generosity and great humour, and I don't believe we ever stopped laughing. Whenever we rehearsed together she'd make sure we did it somewhere near the loo. I love to tell of one Christmas episode in which Frank and Betty participate in a Christmas pageant. Michele played the Virgin Mary, and I was dressed up as an angel of the Lord, complete with wings and a wire halo.

The script required that I be pulled up by one of the crew to dangle high over the audience in a harness. On the day of filming our technician (who'd been having his own private Christmas party) practically cut me in half when he hoisted me up on the wire. Then he abruptly let the wire go and dropped me – but recovered just in time to catch me before I actually hit the floor. I had just enough wind left in me to bleat an ad-lib – 'Well, that's ruined my Christmas!' – and the entire studio exploded in laughter. I bounced on my wire in uncontrollable laughter, bobbing about just inches off the floor, and when I glanced over at Michele in her Virgin Mary costume, I could see that, in addition to collapsing in hysterics, she had also very obviously wet her light blue cassock.

In the midst of all this pandemonium, Michael Mills swooped down from the production booth, pouncing on both the cast and the audience like a teacher scolding his pupils. He reminded us that television was a damn serious business and warned the audience that their howling response would only encourage more such pranks. In the retake the audience, having been thoroughly chastened, didn't make a peep, no laughs, nothing. Michael dashed out of the booth again pulling out his beard. 'When I said television was serious, that's not what I meant!' On the third take, both cast and audience finally got it right.

The episodes surrounding the arrival of Betty and Frank's baby were among the highest-rated in BBC history. Some of the material was loosely based on the birth of my own daughters. Those episodes marked a reunion with John D. Collins, my roommate from Nottingham Rep days, in the role of the young Dr Boyd, who is unwillingly roped into delivering Frank and Betty's baby. John laughed so much during rehearsal that he told me on the day of the recording he'd actually gone to church the night before to pray he wouldn't break up during the show.

I remember a particular line of John's – his face was inches from mine when he said it – 'I've been to see your wife and she's been telling me you don't come as often as you ought to!' I didn't answer. I just looked at him mystified, my mouth pursed in an aggrieved 'O', then I looked away, then back again. I must have done a minute's worth of business, looking up at him, looking at him sideways, nose-to-nose all the while. There were beads of perspiration breaking through on his brow. He wasn't going to last much longer. I finally said, 'But I've had a bit of trouble . . .'

'You've had some trouble?' he asked.

'Yes . . .' I answered him, 'But I can . . .' BEEP . . . (his doctor's beeper just millimetres from my face went off) '. . . Ooooooooooooooohh!'

I've no idea how we managed to get through the scene without completely doubling up. It was great fun, like being kids again in Nottingham.

*

Rehearsal and constant practice are the rules I work by. I did some fairly wild stunts in *Some Mothers*, but whether I'm roller skating under a lorry, being dragged by a train, or bouncing down a flight of stairs inside a wardrobe, success is all in the planning, the control, and knowing how to hang on like grim death!

But there were a few moments no one could have anticipated.

I had enormous trust in and respect for our wonderful team of stunt advisors – Derek Ware, Stuart Fell, Marc Boyle and Val Musetti – and we were meticulous in the way we rehearsed our stunts for the show. There was, however, one notable exception when a crucial part of a stunt had to be done without the benefit of any rehearsal.

The idea was to have Frank Spencer in training to be a window cleaner. I was lowered over the top and down the side of a building, along with Derek Ware, our top stuntman, who was playing my trainer. We stood in one of those window-cleaner cradles, a steel container approximately seven feet long and three feet in depth. It had a rail about three feet off the base which you held onto as you leant in to clean the windows. The cradle slid up and down the building, operated by a series of push-buttons in a metal box in the middle of the hand rail.

The visual joke had a very nervous Frank, who is afraid of heights, starting to clean a window, then glancing over his shoulder to see just how high he is – we were about two hundred feet off the ground. Frank's nerves get the better of him and he jumps back in fright, getting his foot caught in the water bucket. Frank's foot then shoots up in the air, flipping the bucket over the edge of the window-cleaner cradle to the car park below, where it smashes through the windscreen of the boss's car.

Now absolutely terrified, he starts to struggle with the other window cleaner. 'I wanna get out,' he cries, 'I'm afraid of heights, I wanna get out.' With that, the script called for me to fall over the edge of the cradle and hang onto the outside, pulling the other man with me so that we both end up hanging twenty storeys above the street.

A rope with a wire inside had been attached to me, allowing for a fall of about five feet below the cradle. Then Derek, who was wired independently of me, would land on my shoulders when he fell. We had never actually been able to rehearse in the cradle high above the street, and on the day of filming when we went into our falls our combined weight pulled the cradle down, making it tip and wedge itself into the runners on the building wall. We were completely stuck – it couldn't go up or down – and so we hung, helpless, on the outside of the cradle – two hundred feet above London's North Circular Road.

There was an awful silence: it was as if we were floating. The only sound was the creak of the wires as they twisted, first one way, then the other. Hardly daring to whisper, I said, 'Get them to get on the radio and pull us up.' I didn't want even to move my jaw. I was terrified that the slightest movement would send us plunging to our deaths. In the distance I could see Wembley Stadium, Willesden, Harlesden, and beyond that Marble Arch. And then we'd slowly twist back again: Marble Arch, Harlesden, Willesden and Wembley.

I glanced down and saw our cameraman looking up at me through the eye of his camera while he panned the whole scene. Oh my God, I thought, he's trying to get this for *News at Ten*! He was actually waiting and focusing in case I fell. I became aware my shoulders were soaking – I hung there with a damp stuntman on top of me. We were both pouring sweat. I thought, I'm about to lose my bottle. Well, if I do, I hope that bloody cameraman is standing directly below me!

After what seemed an endless twenty minutes, the crew managed to lower someone down in an attempt to pull us back into the cradle, but the rescue was only partially successful. The stuntman was brought up off my shoulders, but now, with the rescuing party, there were too many people in the cradle. So I had to continue to hang on the side of the building for another twenty minutes. Perhaps that doesn't sound such a very long time but – trust me – it was a very long time!

The real-life adventure of one of our crew members was used as the basis for a very popular episode. An amateur rugby player sent in the true story of how he and his team had been driving along a cliff road one rainy day when they discovered one of our editors stranded precariously on the edge of the cliff. He'd been having a picnic in his car and, during the rainstorm, the back wheels of the vehicle had slipped over the side of the cliff – miraculously, his front wheels maintaining a tentative hold on the top. Thankfully, the rugby team reached him in the nick of time. It made for a perfect Frank Spencer story.

This is how it appeared in the episode. Frank and Betty are caught in a sudden rainstorm on the cliffs and Frank exclaims, 'I think we're stuck. Don't look down, we're over the edge of the cliff. I'll get out, and climb on the roof, and get the manure out of the car . . .' (He's a manure salesman at the moment, and has sacks and sacks of the stuff in the boot.) For the stunt gag I had to get onto the roof of the car, then slide headfirst into a somersault over the boot and wind up hanging onto the bumper, over the side of the cliff. Then with one hand, I opened the boot and pulled the bags of manure out, which of course covered me, as they fell down into the sea below.

We found a fabulous location at Swanage, on a cliff hundreds of feet above the English Channel. A Mini-Minor was rigged to the edge for the sequence. Railway sleepers were built into the cliff edge and joints were welded onto the bottom of the car to act as hinges. The crew had complete control over the car's movements. I was wired to the back fender. Michele was up on the car roof with me: she was as game as the best stuntman. (I've always admired her pluck in doing this stunt hundreds of feet above the coast, but her mother vowed never to speak to me again for getting her involved in it.)

It was a complicated scene to film: there were cameras stationed everywhere – under the cliff, on top of the cliff – we even had a camera equipped with a zoom lens set on a boat far out to sea. (The coastguard had all kinds of calls that day from other ships reporting a car on the edge of the cliff with someone dangling from it.)

Michael Mills was on a safety wire too, standing at the edge of the cliff, bawling instructions to the crew. 'Are we ready, chaps?!' I imagine it reminded him of his old Navy days when he used to give orders from a ship's bridge. 'C'mon chaps, are we ready?' he called again. 'Let's go!'

'HOLD IT!' hollered one of the crew. He had suddenly noticed that someone had apparently undone Michael's safety wire. Everything stopped.

'Who's the bastard who did this?' Michael bellowed.

I think they heard his fulminations as far as Brighton. His wire restored, we were finally able to finish filming the scene, and it remains one of my all-time favourites.

The success of *Some Mothers* in the UK was instantaneous and extraordinary. Initially I had only agreed to do one season – a total of seven episodes. Every actor dreams of creating a character as substantial and effective as Frank Spencer, but with that comes the nightmare of 'how do I get rid of him?' The role had a huge impact on my life – my career was completely reborn – but it also carried the double-edged sword of public recognition and what proved to be an almost indelible public image of me as a disaster-prone nincompoop.

I don't mean to sound ungrateful but that kind of recognition has negative as well as positive effects. The role took over my professional and personal life, and my family's as well.

The girls were teased mercilessly at school, and apparently it was impossible for Gabrielle to find workmen willing to fix anything in the house at Wimbledon (where the neighbours had taken to calling her 'Betty'). I remember she had problems with the boiler and called for a repairman. I was visiting at the time and later walked into the room where Gabrielle was explaining to him about the boiler. He took one look at me and said, 'I'm not fixing that!' and left the house. It was amusing the first few times, but the family grew to resent the attention the show brought them.

I found life starting to imitate art – it seemed there was no escape from Frank Spencer! I had driven to Birmingham to appear on a television show called *What's My Line*. Afterwards, in an absolutely blinding rainstorm, I drove home via 'Spaghetti Junction', the network of crisscrossed roads leading back onto the motorway. I had just reached the top of the motorway when the car broke down.

The rain was torrential and certain to ruin my suit. Those were still relatively lean days for me, and to be truthful, I owned only one suit. So I crawled into the back seat to find my suitcase; I pulled out my pyjamas, took the suit off and got into them. Then I climbed back out of the car and began trying to get it started again. There I was, bent under the bonnet in my pyjamas, when a police car pulled alongside. The policeman got out and walked towards me, waving his torchlight over me as he looked me up and down.

'Excuse me, sir,' he said. 'Might I ask what you're doing on the motorway in your pyjamas?'

'Well,' I said, 'it's raining!'

'It's raining?' he repeated.

'Well,' I exclaimed, in exasperation, 'you can see that it's raining!'

'Ahhh, yes, of course, it's raining,' he said, as though the clear logic of it all had suddenly just hit him. 'Yes, well ... Thank you very much sir. Good night.' He turned, and without another word or any offer to help, he got back into his car and sped away.

Two years later, I told this story on a radio show and a listener called in to say he had been that policeman. He said, 'I knew it must be Frank Spencer. I couldn't believe what he'd said to me! That's why I left him there because there was just no answer I could give. I mean, I knew it was bloody raining, but why in hell was he in his pyjamas? He didn't explain that he only had one suit and he didn't want to get his suit wet! He just said, "Well, it's raining."'

Some time later, when I bought some plants from a nursery in the country and filled the car with them, I drove along the motorway with every conceivable form of greenery – there were even some palm trees – poking through each opened window. The only human thing visible inside my car was my head. It must have looked disembodied, perched on the steering wheel, while the rest of me was hidden by a forest of greenery.

Very soon I had the paranoid feeling that I was being circled by other cars. As I drove in the middle lane, a row of cars would overtake me, slow down, get in the inside lane, watch me as I passed, then overtake and go round again. A bit like Apaches circling a wagon. Every now and then one of the drivers would give a gleeful thumbs-up sign as he passed. He was sure he'd caught Frank Spencer with his plants down! (Sorry.)

Then, of course, the inevitable happened: it started to rain, and my windscreen wipers were broken. I had no choice. I broke off a longish palm frond, rolled up my sleeve, stuck my arm out the window, and moved the palm leaf back and forth to keep the view clear.

There must have been fifty people who phoned in during my next radio appearance to say, 'We saw Frank Spencer! We couldn't believe it! There he was on the motorway, and he had all these palm trees with him. He was using a branch as a windscreen wiper!'

'But it was raining . . .'

There was at least one man who ran around England who thought he really was Frank Spencer. I met him.

It was late one evening outside the stage door at the Drury Lane where I was appearing in *Billy*. I was very tired and I wanted to go home.

'Excuse me . . . Excuse me . . .'

I heard a familiar nasal whine behind me and turned to see a man following close on my heels up the road. When I hear children imitate Frank Spencer, I laugh; but when I hear it from a grown man late at night on a dark empty street, I am unnerved.

'Yes?' I asked, tentatively.

'Can you do anything for me?' he said, still using that ridiculous Frank Spencer voice.

'I'm sorry?'

'Can you do anything for me?'

Mike 'the Mod' Byron in the BBC's *No. So Much a Programme, More a Way of Life*.

MC and Buster Keaton in *Forum* – Wow!

Wedding day in Paris (*left to right*): Adza, Dick Lester counting the daisies on Gabrielle's head.

Gabrielle, Emma and me in New York, 1967.

The Games: Michael Winner showing me how to be a milkman.

Brothers, brothers.. there were never such devoted brothers. Oliver Reed and MC in *The Jokers*.

How I Won the War – John Lennon and MC.

(*Left to right*) MC, Gabrielle and John – lunchtime, *How I Won the War*.

MC, Barbra, Marianne McAndrew in *Hello Dolly!*

The Games, Rome 1969.

(Left to right) MC, Curt Jurgens, Genevieve Gilles in *Hello and Goodbye* – the jacket is for sale.

On the set of *Hello and Goodbye* with Daryl Zanuck.

Emma teaching Daddy to dance.

Alice's Adventures in Wonderland: on the set, Lucy and Emma.

'Oooh, this is a nice wide road.'

Michele and I teetering on the brink.

Trying to join the RAF: with Fulton Mackay.

'I don't know what you mean,' I said.

'Don't you know what I mean?'

'Please,' I said, 'I'm really tired.' (Just what I need, a candidate for the rubber room.) I tried to pretend he wasn't there, thinking he might just go away.

'Don't you know what I mean?' That voice again.

'Well,' I said, 'not really . . . I must go, I'm in a bit of a rush.' But he stayed glued to my heels.

I finally got to my car but then I couldn't find the keys. Oh God, please get me in this car and out of here.

But he wouldn't move out of the way and he kept rattling on in that awful voice. 'I mean,' he said, 'do you ever need a stand-in?'

'No.'

'Well, do you need a double?'

'No,' I said, 'I do my own stunts.'

'Does that mean . . .'

'Look,' I said, 'I think I should point out, I only play this as a character, it's not me. It's nothing like me.'

'Does that mean you don't need me?' he said.

'Yes, I'm afraid that does mean I don't need you.' (Better go slow here, he may have some kind of weapon.) 'You see, we have professional people to help with stunts. I never use a double.' I looked down at him. 'And I think there is a slight height difference between us.'

'Well, don't you know anyone who could do something for me?'

I squashed the temptation to say a good doctor might be useful, and I was finally able to get into my car and flee. As I turned the corner, I could still see him in my rear-view mirror standing where I left him, staring at the back of my car.

A year or so later, I read a newspaper story of a man involved in an accident, who had been thrown through the windscreen of a car. He sued the driver and the insurance company for loss of earnings that he would have earned as a Frank Spencer double. I sometimes wonder if it might have been that same little man, and he made an extortionate amount of money – about four times as much as I had made from the original character.

I thought I'd got rid of him until very recently, when I received a letter from a fan. It read: 'You may not remember us, but we met you on the Costa del Sol. I'm enclosing a photo of you signing our album covers outside your time-share office. It's always good to have a second string to the bow! You're very shrewd – and also a bit shorter than I imagined.'

CHAPTER 17

ROSALIND RUSSELL ONCE defined acting rather wonderfully as 'being on a stage naked and turning around very slowly'. I suppose I've grown used to the being 'naked' part – it's all the 'turning around very slowly' that causes me problems.

I am in the paradoxical position of being in a profession that I love and find very rewarding but which, by its very nature, continually forces me to confront my worst nightmare – making a fool of myself in public. Again and again I've stripped myself of my inhibitions and summoned up the courage to face my fears head-on – and made a fool of myself a million times over.

Many's the time when my name has appeared in print coupled with 'perfectionist' as if that were some dirty word. Perfection is, of course, an unobtainable state, but although one will never achieve the heights one aims for, in my view the mistake would be to stop trying. And anyway, the *real* reason I train and rehearse for weeks and weeks before a production is that it helps me at least *appear* to know what I'm doing when I finally join the company.

It was 1973. I had just finished doing *Some Mothers Do 'Ave 'Em* and was living on my own in the small council flat in Olympia. *Some Mothers* hadn't paid much, but it had given me professional success and more public recognition than I'd ever imagined possible, even during the years of making Hollywood films. Not a day went by that I didn't turn on the television to see myself being parodied as Frank Spencer; it's a bizarre feeling to see yourself as someone else sees you, but once the strangeness had worn off, I loved it. My career had suddenly taken off. After months of depression I was being lifted to the skies. I may still have been struggling in my private life, but professionally . . . well, I felt as if I were flying.

One day I met up with John Barry, who played me some songs he'd just composed for a new musical he wanted to do called *Billy*. He told me he'd written it with me in mind for the leading role. Of course I was incredibly flattered. It was such an honour to think that someone of John Barry's formidable reputation would have actually tailored a show for me. John, who had a group during the fifties called the John Barry Seven, is an extraordinary musician, and has been everything from a rock trumpeter to the composer of Academy-Award-winning scores for such films as *Born Free*, *The Lion in Winter*, *Out of Africa* and *Dances with Wolves*.

Months before, John had been discussing possible future projects with Peter Witt, a well-known American agent. Peter had suggested a musical based either on *Alfie* or on *Billy Liar*, the film versions of which had starred Michael Caine and Tom Courtenay respectively. John rejected the idea of *Alfie* (it already had its own song) but was intrigued by the idea of *Billy*.

Billy Liar is a north country lad working in an undertaker's establishment who lives two very different lives, the mundane existence he shares at home with his nagging parents, and the fantasy world he dreams about – life as he would like it to be. Don Black, who had previously collaborated with John on one of the Bond films and *Born Free*, agreed to do the lyrics for the show. The book, by Keith Waterhouse and Willis Hall, was adapted for the stage by Ian La Frenais and Dick Clements, whom I'd worked with on *The Jokers*.

I remember sitting in John's flat at Alembic House on the Embankment, as he and Peter Witt pitched the show to me like barkers at a carnival, overlapping each other in their excitement as they juggled exclamatory sentences: 'We want you to be Fred Astaire! . . . We want you to be Gene Kelly!'

I got home, lay down on my bed and thought about the project. Then the nightmare demons took hold of me: 'Shiiiittt! I can't do that . . . I can't *dance!*'

After *Hello Dolly!* I knew I could sing well enough to get by in a film. But my voice wasn't strong enough to sustain a live show. All the press accounts of my 'early classical training' have sounded so impressive that I've always been reluctant to admit the truth. I had a pleasant enough child's soprano voice, and I managed to hold my own in those early Britten works, but I was later kept on by management because, as Colin Graham explained it, I was 'a damned good little actor'. But I couldn't read music then, and I can barely read it now.

But a musical – on stage! I wasn't trained for it and as much as I wanted to do it, the thought of it absolutely terrified me.

In what must be considered an amazing show of blind faith, John and Peter set out to prove that I *could* do the part – a little training was all that was needed. John sent me to voice coach Ian Adam; though to call him merely a voice coach cannot possibly do justice to his talents or to the musical gifts he bestows upon his pupils. A gentle, mild-mannered Scot, Ian has a low-key professionalism and, in just the first few minutes of our meeting, he made me feel at home in his small studio.

'Now,' he said, 'sing something for me.' I didn't know what to sing: Ian said I chose 'Danny Boy'. Perhaps I did. Whatever it was, I remember I sang it gently, very gently. There was someone else in the room, the pianist, whom I hadn't met or spoken to beyond a brief how-do-you-do. All my attention was suddenly directed at this man playing the piano, and I was grim-faced at the thought of making a fool of myself in front of this stranger. In my mind the pianist was every bit as formidable and frightening as any audience of three thousand that fills the Theatre Royal, Drury Lane.

So I started to sing, stopping to apologise every now and again, and yet again at the end. 'I'm sorry, it's not very good . . .'

Ian paid no attention to my apologies, but murmured instead in that soft Scots burr of his, 'Och, Michael, it's a beautiful voice!' He smiled. 'Now, there may be a little bit lacking on the top . . .' And his lilting words moved up the scale a bit as if to emphasise a tiny problem. 'And we may have to go on a wee journey down below . . .' His voice dropped ever so slightly. 'But it's there, it's there . . . and now we have to go to work.' Glorious words of encouragement. I would have gladly walked on hot coals for him.

Of course, the voice doesn't develop as quickly as the body does – even if you run the vocal equivalent of the fifteen or twenty miles a day I trained for *The Games*. Body muscles develop fairly rapidly, but the voice changes more slowly – indeed painfully slowly, and the process has to be approached with great patience – never my dominant characteristic. However, under Ian Adam's careful guidance the voice did begin to improve and gained strength and assurance. Twenty-six years later I'm working on it still; I expect I'll be working on it always.

I was lucky with *Billy*. I got an enormous amount from my involvement with the creative process, being almost at John Barry's elbow as he composed each song, beginning to learn, beginning to sing, beginning to stitch Billy's character together. John's arrangements were brilliant. He had the idea of using only brass and percussion, like a colliery band from the north. We worked on my Yorkshire accent as well, keeping it middle ground. Too much, and the Americans don't understand a thing you say or sing.

Learning to dance was another story entirely.

The experience of making *Hello Dolly!*, and working with the unquestioned king of the trade and the people who practically invented the genre, was my first real primer on the art of the musical. Michael Kidd (a feisty Brooklyn boy, whose 'Nooo Yaawk' accent tickled my British ears) had been our choreographer. He had an established Broadway career and was one of the finest choreographers in film; his dance sequences for *Seven Brides for Seven Brothers* alone would have qualified him for any Dance Hall of Fame. He and Gene Kelly were old comrades and had danced together in a film called *It's Always Fair Weather* back in 1955.

Michael Kidd taught me how to move in *Dolly*, and the result of his and Gene's combined efforts and encouragement gave me some of the confidence (translation: courage) I needed to use my body as a dancer would; for the first time in my life I had felt as if I had really started to move as the character I was playing. I had learned to walk within the confines of the role; all the movement Michael taught me belonged to the character that was Cornelius Hackl – an awkward, gauche young hick from the sticks – who moved as clumsily as he spoke. Michael choreographed steps that were always slightly eccentric, and totally fitted the character. So I had 'danced' a bit in *Dolly*.

But if he had given me those steps to do as Michael Crawford, I couldn't have done them. I danced as Cornelius Hackl. And Cornelius Hackl was not Billy Liar. Billy Liar was going to have to be a real smoothie, and a real seducer at times. More than that, Billy was going to have to look like a master of dance and movement in a Fred Astaire and Gene Kelly pastiche. (And he was going to have to be bloody fit as well! That particular dance number went on for fourteen minutes, and then I had to sing a number to close the act. My heart has never pumped so hard.)

Then somebody had the inspired thought of bringing in Onna White, described as 'a poised, organised drill sergeant', and one of the best choreographers in the business. Onna had once danced with the San Francisco ballet, and later worked as Michael Kidd's assistant on various projects. Her reputation on Broadway had been assured with the bouncingly cheerful choreography she created for *The Music Man*. Later she did *Half a Sixpence* with Tommy Steele in London, and eventually won an Academy Award for her work on *Oliver!*

Single-handedly, that lady saved my life.

Onna sent orders from the States that, before I did anything else, I had to start learning to tap dance. Someone suggested that I go along to see a young choreographer, Gillian Gregory, whose later credits would include Ken Russell's *The Boyfriend* and *Me and My Girl*. Gillian, along with Larry Oaks, Onna's London assistant, became my first teacher. She worked with me on the basics for the two or three months before Onna arrived in London.

Gillian's lessons were a complete revelation. She was the first person to introduce me to the intense discipline of dance – stretching every day, learning to count to the music, tapping for hours to develop flexibility in my ankles. You have to do it constantly, like a drummer: day-de-dah-de-dah-de-dah. Other foot: day-de-dah-de-dah-de-dah. That foot's stronger than the other; work on the weak foot, do twice as much on that foot now . . . do four on the right, eight on the left . . . until it's stronger, stronger.

I improvised a system to help me, writing down all the step-hops and toe-slaps on charts and graphs, pasting them across my kitchen wall, practising up to five hours a day in my little flat. It was fortunate that the kitchen was over a small garage which was only used for storage, otherwise I would have driven my neighbours mad. I'd carpeted all of my flat except for the kitchen, so I needed its bare wooden floor for practice – I had to *hear* what I was doing, the sound of that tap-tapping. It all had to look so easy and unthinking and each tap had to sound crisp and clear. There were, as I recall, four step-ball changes to the cooker. Eight step-ball changes to the washing machine. And ten changes to the fridge – if the door was closed. When I became more comfortable with what I was doing, I opened the fridge door and pretended the eight Guinness bottles inside were the audience.

I was absolutely flat broke when I first moved into Russell Gardens Mews, and had no furniture at all to speak of. So I painted it white, built some low-level platforms for a sofa and a bed, and made the platforms comfortable using some large cushions. (I knew enough about cushions by this time to fill a home decorating manual.) That was it really – a far cry from the house in Wimbledon, but I was rather proud of what I had done on my own.

Nan was very distressed about the divorce, but she and Gabrielle remained close, and of course Nan never lost touch with the children. Now that I was alone she would come and stay with me occasionally, just to keep an eye on me, she said, and make certain that I was 'All right'. She was well into her eighties by this time, and my minimalist approach to flat decor didn't exactly suit her needs. She looked a comical sight, half-sitting or – more accurately – horizontally reclining on a cushioned platform by the window, her feet barely able to reach the floor. She used to watch me for hours through the open kitchen door while she fingered her beads, murmuring countless decades of the rosary, praying for a miracle to help me learn to dance.

'Hail Mary, full of grace . . .'
'Shuffle-hop-tap-step . . . Now I'm at the cooker.'
'the Lord is with thee . . .'
'Shuffle-hop-tap-step . . . Now I'm at the fridge.'
'Blessed art thou . . .'
'Three steps back, my bum is on the hob.'
'Holy Mary, Mother . . .'
'Three steps forward, try not to hit that knob.'
'Amen.'

'I never thought,' she marvelled later on, 'that he'd ever learn. I'd see him dancing in there and there was no way, no matter how many rosaries I was saying, he was ever going to get those feet together. But when I saw the show, I understood what the power of prayer could do!'

As we got closer to the start of rehearsals, Onna's dance assistant, Marty Allen, joined us from America and worked with Gillian on training me. Marty looked surprisingly heavy-set for a dancer, but he was wonderfully graceful. He used to watch me like a hawk, his eyes often rolling to heaven for guidance. It took months, but with incredible persistence and a great deal of toil and sweat, Gillian, Larry and Marty managed to fashion a dancer of sorts out of some very rough material. I prayed I would be competent enough not to totally embarrass myself when I faced Onna and the company at the beginning of rehearsals.

It was an exciting company. Diana Quick would play the role that Julie Christie had played in the film version. Bryan Pringle was my father, the wonderful Avis Bunnage my mother, and newcomer Elaine Paige, played my tarty girlfriend and lit up the production from the moment she stepped on stage. Rehearsals began at the YWCA in Great Russell Street at the back of the Dominion Theatre. Later on, we moved to Alford House, a place nicknamed by Marty as 'Awful House', where I felt that the living conditions had all the charm of a Victorian workhouse. Those responsible appeared to me to be of the opinion that suffering was good for actors. It was unbelievably cold in winter; most of the windows were punctured by cracks and holes, the result of stray footballs kicked through by neighbourhood kids.

Now at last I began working with Onna White herself. By the time I joined rehearsals I had already been taught the style and pattern of the 'Astaire and Kelly' number, and Billy's basic walk and movements for the first song, 'Some of Us Belong to the Stars'.

Despite having logged hundreds of hours learning the fundamentals, I was still light-years behind the other dancers when we started rehearsals. I don't know what I would have done without Onna's constant help and patience. She is an innately kind person – tough, but very loving, and she filled me with confidence. A good choreographer will give you that kind of belief in yourself. 'Ah, darling,' she'd soothe, 'you're gonna be great, you're gonna be my Billy . . .'

She used to stand with our director, Patrick Garland, and watch me, silently absorbing the eccentricities that became part and parcel of a Crawford dance rehearsal: I always had more trouble with the left foot than the right – and I would shout in frustration at the left foot to do what the right foot did so easily. I couldn't understand why if one foot could do something, the other couldn't. Patrick observed my bizarre behaviour quite mesmerised by the maniacal one-sided yelling match I carried on with my feet. 'I've heard him shouting at other people when they're not doing the kind of work he thinks they should be doing,' he told someone later. 'Then he is definitely not a happy man. But when you catch him shouting at his own feet, you know he's dedicated.'

I will work on a character's movement for hours. And I won't progress beyond those movements until I see a reason for every step and gesture. How does he stand? How does he walk? That's how the character is created – by inches. Details can lend an amazing depth to a characterisation or a performance. Think of the attention that Astaire and Kelly put into their musical numbers, or the tiny touches that embellished a performance by Margaret Rutherford or Alastair Sim. Rutherford and Sim created indelible characters, never caricatures: you could practically smell the person. (I'm sure Margaret Rutherford wore a lavender scent whenever she played Miss Marple.) The comic genius Buster Keaton was also a study in technical perfection, working out every movement in advance until it became a second skin. I've developed a regard for even such small particulars as buttons on a waistcoat, the scuff or shine on a shoe – all such things help to paint the three-dimensional person.

That tap-dance routine, the Gene-Kelly-Fred-Astaire pastiche I keep referring to (perhaps because it nearly killed me), was at the end of Act I, lasted nearly fourteen minutes (including costume changes) and ended with me singing a song and finally being carried off horizontally to the dressing room. I was dressed casually at the start, in a sweatshirt and slacks, dancing a soft-shoe shuffle as a fantasy Gene Kelly. Onna designed a far more elaborate affair for the Fred Astaire number that followed.

Wearing white tie, top hat and tails (what else?) and twirling a cane, I was surrounded by a chorus of Ginger Rogerses, all of them wearing a version of the famous 'feathered dress' she wore in that wonderfully languorous 'Cheek to Cheek' number in *Top Hat*.

Ginger Rogers was a great friend of Onna's, and she actually called me to wish me luck. I told her about my difficulty in dealing with all the feathers – my problem being that they tended to shoot back between my legs so that it looked as if I had a tail. Fred had had the same complaint, she told me. He'd said that the feathers kept shedding all over his clothes, getting into his eyes and mouth, and had appealed to the studio for a change in her costume. But Ginger had designed the dress herself, and both she and her mother (who was, according to Onna, the real power in the Rogers family) loved it. So Ginger's mother fought the good fight and prevailed, and in this case she may have been right. Of all the glamorous clothes Ginger Rogers wore in those classic films, I think that white satin dress covered in ostrich feathers remains the most memorable.

Dancing with the cane created many more problems.

Being left-handed, it was important to learn to carry and twirl the cane in my right hand because I knew Astaire was right-handed, and I was convinced that someone, somewhere in the audience, would surely pick up on it. (The audience notices absolutely everything.)

Onna brought a new dance concept with her, a rock and roll number she called 'The Bump'. It was a variation on a discovery she'd made when she and Marty Allen had done some work in Canada. They went along to a gay dance club one night, but when they arrived Onna was told she had to stay outside as it was strictly men only. Undaunted, she stuck around anyway and spent the rest of the evening peering through the window, watching some of the sexiest behind-grinding in North America. Perfect, she thought, for the Elvis Presley number she needed for *Billy*, the ideal sexy show-stopper.

For 'The Bump' number, Onna chose a bubbly, curly-headed bundle of fire, Jo-Anne Robinson, to partner me. I was slightly awestruck by the girl's abilities: the music would start and Jo-Anne could immediately, instinctively melt right into the character she was dancing; she was wonderfully raunchy too and could grind with the best of 'em. A total delight to watch, she was so far ahead of me that I would often double-up with laughter as I helplessly bumbled about. It took hours of rehearsal to rev up my rear enough to keep up with Jo-Anne. But she was as patient as she was talented and by opening night I was suitably swivel-hipped.

I was still in pain in my personal life, but on the day when my divorce was decreed final, Jo-Anne made me laugh. I had teased her in rehearsals, and her reaction was to go out and cover my car with shaving foam. From that moment I thought we'd get on very well together, and we started seeing each other.

The first preview of *Billy* was scheduled for late March 1974 in Manchester. Elaine Paige and I drove up there a few days earlier to appear at a press conference for the local media. Wearing the highest platform heels imaginable, her tiny frame decked out in a miniskirt the size of a postage stamp, Elaine dazzled the press. Her appearance alone practically guaranteed a run on the box office!

It was great to see my old drinking partner, Mike Summerbee, at the press conference too. Mike seemed to be everywhere at once: this was his town after all. He was still playing football for Manchester, and ran a shirt-manufacturing firm there besides. With Mike around, the company was immediately a favourite with all the finest restaurants in town; the best tables were always ready and reserved for us. He had shirts made up for every member of the cast, and put together a custom-made job for me to wear in 'The Bump' number. It was bright red, complete with frills. Not exactly Savile Row, mind you – more like something you'd find on the streets of downtown Havana.

The day before our first preview I came down with laryngitis – my voice was useless, and we had to postpone the opening for four nights. I was immediately bundled off to a throat specialist who, after every test imaginable, solemnly informed me that there was absolutely nothing wrong at all. Completely psychosomatic, he said, it's all in your head. I refused to believe it; I could barely whisper a word, for God's sake. But in my heart I knew there was some truth in what he said. All the old demon fears had knocked me out again; I was ashamed and scared – terrified I couldn't do the job, and scared to death of the responsibility for the company.

But if I felt laid low, you can just imagine Peter Witt's state of mind when he was forced to cancel our sold-out first preview of his one-hundred-and-fifty-thousand-pound investment!

A few days later we all breathed easier. The voice had returned, the legs were itching to move, and *Billy* finally opened. It was a sold-out performance, a glittering gala night sponsored by a local charity.

My first entrance had been designed to be terrifically theatrical. I was hauled up into the flies about fifteen minutes before the show started and hung there listening to the audience being seated, staying put until the curtain went up, when the crew lowered me straight down onto the stage as if I had just arrived by parachute, the silks gathering on the floor around my feet as I landed.

I couldn't hear much of anything up there – only the commotion of the opening preview audience and an occasional police siren from the street. I was totally preoccupied anyway. All the dialogue in the first scene had been changed and I was going over it again and again, as well as running through the lyrics of the first song which had only been finished minutes before. After a delay of almost thirty minutes, however, the thought penetrated even my thick skull that something was very much amiss below. (God, *now* what!)

'Hellooooo! . . .' I called out plaintively, imagining untold disasters. (Good lord, things couldn't have gone that badly, I haven't even been on yet!) Silence, except for my pathetic echo:

'Hellooooo! . . . Is anybody there . . . ?!'

To cut a long story short, there had been a bomb scare in the theatre – hardly an auspicious omen for the show. The police had cleared the building for about thirty minutes, then let everyone back in again. The bomb squad said they found nothing – obviously *I* didn't count.

I was eventually discovered dangling like a puppet

high in the wings. The crew had forgotten me in their rush to get to the street – which doesn't say much for my impact on the company. After being strung up for all that time, I could barely walk through the show's first twenty minutes: mind you, I'm not complaining. It had done my tenor voice a power of good!

Despite all the delays our reviews were fine, and box-office business was 'Boffo' by American *Variety* standards the next day. Every single show was sold out to the roof. Then, just as we looked forward to the London opening, another problem materialised.

In Manchester we were using a smaller version of the massive set we were to use in London. Our resident designer genius, Ralph Koltai, had designed a set made up almost entirely of scaffolding and planks – not unlike the shell of a building site. One afternoon during a matinée performance, I slipped and lost my grip while leaning too far over the first landing of the scaffold structure. I plunged down head-first and fell ten feet to the stage, landing on my wrist.

The excruciating pain sent a very definite signal to the rest of my body that something was terribly wrong. But I convinced myself that it was simply a dislocation, and continued with the performance. Starting to sing, I gave my wrist a sudden tug, jerking it very hard, thinking I could put it back into place . . . It didn't work.

Almost sick with pain, I continued to sing a slow mournful song. I pulled the wrist again trying to manipulate it. I have no idea how I got through the number, but at the end of it I staggered into the wings and called to the crew.

'Please, I can't go on again . . .' I told them, 'I think I need to go to hospital.' And then, so I am assured, I told the stage manager to ask the audience to wait while I attended to my arm. 'As soon as they put my wrist back in position, I'll be back to finish the show,' I said. 'Just tell them to wait . . .' Well, it sounds like something I might say: but on this last quote I plead, not arrogance, but acute delirium.

Later, when theatre management called to check on my condition, I assured them I'd be fine. 'I'll be back tonight.' There's just one difference, I added, I'll be wearing a plaster cast. No need to mention I'd be encased for eight weeks – better to face one problem at a time. We still had weeks of previews to do and the London opening to get through. (A small irony here: I had broken my 'good' arm, the left one. But by insisting on learning to do all the risky business using my right hand, the way Fred Astaire would have done it, I was able to continue doing the show, broken arm and all, with only minimal adjustments.)

I suggested that an announcement be made every night prior to the performance, informing the audience that the cast I was wearing was the result of an accident and had nothing to do with the character or the show. I knew the white plaster cuff would be spotted right away and would remain an obvious distraction to the audience. Let them in on what's happened, I thought: let them know what's going on and very shortly the cast will be forgotten. It worked, I'll swear it did.

Billy opened in London on May 2, 1974 and the reviews were uniformly wonderful. The British musical was finally coming into its own and our show was the first home-grown musical to succeed in the Drury Lane Theatre. 'Crawford the Conqueror Storms Drury Lane!' shouted the headline above James Green's review in the *Evening News*. (Awfully stuck on himself, you say. Sorry, but there are some reviews an actor commits to lifetime memory.) But Herbert Kretzmer in the *Daily Express* was much nearer the mark when he said, 'If Michael Crawford is the hero, Onna White is the heroine . . .' And no matter how great the temptation for swell-headed behaviour, my Nan was always around to set me straight.

Nan had a totally rigid code of standards. When she came to see *Billy* at a matinée shortly after the opening, I got her a seat in the Royal Box where she sat in grand style, along with Emma and Lucy and surrounded by her friends. All went well until the moment we reached a scene when, for reasons it would require a reprint of the entire script to explain, I had to say the line: 'Ah, piss off the lot of yer . . .'

A very audible and imperious voice was suddenly heard from the depths of that cavernous theatre: 'Michael!' it said, 'I've never heard you use language like that before . . .'

Peering into the darkness, I could vaguely see Nan standing in the Royal Box, fairly quivering in outraged shock, with Emma and Lucy tugging at her dress. For a moment the performance came to a screeching halt while everyone on the stage, in a kind of slow motion double-take, turned first to the audience, then back to me with a collective 'What-was-*that*!' expression written across their startled faces.

I think the best I managed was a cough to fill the very pregnant pause that followed. Then the company's bewilderment turned to hilarity and an uncontrolled fit of silent laughter swept the stage. For a second I thought we were all about to lose it, but somehow sanity was restored. I'm not certain what happened next, but I gather someone unceremoniously grabbed Nan from behind and sat her firmly down in her seat again.

When she came backstage later I was very cross with

her and said, 'For heaven's sake, Nan, you just can't do things like that . . .' She was quite unmoved, and made several comments along the lines of 'If your mother had heard you . . .'

'But, Nan,' I said, 'it's only a play . . .'

'Well, there's no need . . .' she harrumphed. 'Can't you exchange that word for something else, like "oh, go away".'

'But, Naaaaannn,' I argued, 'it doesn't have the same effect!'

'It means the same thing!' she retorted. 'What do you mean it doesn't have the same effect . . . !' Given the opportunity, I'm sure she would have washed my mouth out with soap.

With *Billy* I began a brand-new career in musical comedy. All the hard work had been worthwhile and the personal satisfactions were enormous.

For all of us one of the highlights was when Gene Kelly attended a performance and came round to the dressing room afterwards. 'So that was me, was it,' he said, 'this bit?' And step for step he danced most of the routine I had done on stage to imitate him, and which had taken me four months to learn.

He laughed at the expression on my face: 'Don't worry, kid,' he said, 'you're doing great.' Of course, it was obvious he was never going to have to lose sleep over my dancing skills.

Billy had enabled me to develop a decidedly new public image as well – if being the romantic focus of some assorted weird and wonderful fans was any indication, like the girls the company dubbed 'Meals on Wheels', two fourteen-year-olds who sent me three meals a week.

Of the weird variety, one of the more memorable was the woman who showed up backstage with a group of well-wishers; she pretended to leave with the group, but apparently hid backstage somewhere and crept back into my dressing room when everyone was gone. She scared the pants off me – obviously her intention – because she closed the door behind her and proceeded to pull her own clothes off.

In the middle of all this, one of the chorus boys pounded on my door. 'Come in! Come in! Come in!' I cried (blessed sound: rescue's at hand!).

He walked in. 'Michael, there's been a fire in . . .' then stopped dead. 'Whoops, sorry, didn't mean to interrupt!' And both his hands flew over his eyes.

'No, no,' I yelled, 'don't go!'

'Oh my, no,' he said, 'this isn't quite my scene!'

'This is not what you think!' I protested. 'Will you take this woman away – really, she was just leaving!'

'Oh, Michael,' he said. 'You're so cool, so hard . . .'

'Do me a favour and have someone come round,' I said through clenched teeth. 'We have a little problem here.'

He finally took note of the murderous look in my eye and returned a few minutes later with a fireman who was carrying an axe. 'No, no, I don't think we need to go that far,' I said, 'but this lady really must go now . . .'

The fireman cocked an eyebrow. 'Oh, you finished . . . ?' he asked.

'I haven't even started!' I howled.

By this time a small crowd had gathered outside my dressing room, and the scantily clad woman was escorted out of the stage door: she finished dressing herself in the street. Everyone could see the poor soul was not well, but the company never let me forget about my reputation as a heartbreaker.

Still, with the success of *Billy*, I began to cherish thoughts of laying to rest the spectre of Frank Spencer that followed me everywhere. Onna said that when she and Marty Allen came to Manchester for the opening previews, they wandered into a small antique shop near the theatre one day, and started chatting to the owner. 'You're Americans, aren't you?' he asked. 'What brings you to Manchester?' 'We're working round the corner on *Billy*,' she told him. 'With Michael Crawford.' Onna reported the poor man went ashen. 'Oh, God,' he said, deadly serious, 'don't let him in here! He'll break everything in my shop!' It seemed that no matter where I was or what I was doing at the time, the Frank Spencer image would remain alive and lingering.

While I was doing *Billy*, I was invited to do a radio telephone interview for Australia. *Some Mothers* had begun on television there and had taken off immediately. Richie, the Aussie interviewer, set up the call from Sydney:

'Hal-low, Moichael Croarferd.' Richie's voice crackled over the phone lines, and echoed the same words two seconds later. 'We're going to be coming through to you . . . (echo: *'to you'* . . . *'to you'*) and I shall just say, "Hal-low Moichael" (*'Moichael'* . . . *'Moichael'*) and you should just say, "Hal-low Richie" (*'Richie'* . . . *'Richie'*) and we'll be off into the conversation . . . (echo: *'. . . sation'* *'. . . sation'*)'

'Right,' I said, 'that's fine.'

A few minutes later, right on cue, I heard his voice again:

'Hal-low, Moichael' (*'Moichael'* . . . *'Moichael'*) he said. 'Yes, we're speaking to Moichael Croarferd who's in England (*'England'* . . . *'England'*). G'day, Moichael, thanks for being with us. (*'with us'* . . . *'with us'*)'

'Hello, Richie,' I shouted enthusiastically.

'Now,' he continued, '*Some Mother* is a great success here ('*here*' . . . '*here*'). It's number one in the ratings; everybody's watching it and what's more – all the girls love ya! They think you're a wow! ('*wow*' . . . '*wow*') And that's a bit strange, don't you think, because you're a bit of a woofter, aren't ya? ('*aren't ya*' . . . '*aren't ya*')'

I couldn't believe my ears. 'Sorry . . . What did you say?'

'Woofter,' he shouted, 'woofter . . ('*Woofter*' . . . '*Woofter*')'

'Okay, I heard you.' I spluttered. 'But I think what you meant to say was that the character could be construed as being slightly effeminate . . .'

'Well, to say the least, mate,' he said ('*least, mate*' . . . '*mate*').

'Yes,' I interrupted him, 'but, me, personally . . . well, I have a wife and two children . . . I mean, well, I don't at the moment because I'm in the process of a divorce. But if I wasn't going through the divorce, I certainly would be after a remark like that . . .'

I didn't wait for his answer. I pretended we'd been cut off and fled from the studio before anyone could say a word.

I was invited to participate in a Royal Variety Performance at the London Palladium shortly after we opened *Billy*. The compere that night was Bruce Forsyth, who had always been a great favourite of mine; he was terrific fun to work with.

Once Bruce had finished his opening speech he announced the first act. 'And now, Your Majesty . . . ladies and gentlemen . . . Welcome to the show . . . the first act this evening . . . !' And with that the curtain opened, but the stage was bare. (All a set-up of course.)

Looking suitably mystified, Bruce exclaimed, 'Oh my God, it's not ready, is it? What the hell's happening here . . .'

Suddenly, an apparition appeared from high up in the flies: dressed in beret and blue overalls, and swinging by one foot from a rope across the stage passing directly in front of Bruce, was Frank Spencer as bumbling stage hand:

'Oooohh, I'm sorry, Your Majesty. I'm so sorry.'

(It was a great-looking piece of business actually. The stunt co-ordinator made a perch up in the flies that I could jump off, swinging straight across the stage. It made for a wonderful effect and, as far as I know, it had never been tried before.)

A running gag had been worked out in which Frank Spencer would keep popping up throughout the evening to annoy Bruce. On one occasion I was arguing with him about something that happened on stage; I stuck my head through the curtain and closed it around me.

'And another thing,' I said to him, 'I don't like your attitude. You shout at everyone . . .'

He yelled back at me, 'I do not shout at everyone . . .'

'See,' I said, 'you're shouting now . . .'

Lowering his voice, Bruce replied: 'I'm not shouting . . . And now, ladies and gentlemen, may I present the world famous juggler . . .'

Frank interrupts again: 'I still don't like you . . .' And with that the curtain went up – and my head (and the rest of me) went right up with it – straight to the flies.

It's a stunt I had always wanted to do. While I was shouting at Bruce through the curtain, I was being attached to a device that looked like a cross between a rope cradle and a seat on a swing, so that when the curtain went up I was carried along with it. I spent the rest of the act hidden up in the flies waiting for the juggler to finish, and when the curtain came down, so did I. I simply walked through the curtain and walked off (as Frank Spencer) apologising all the while: 'I'm sorry we're having all this trouble . . .' bowing in the direction of what Frank thinks is the Royal Box (which, of course, was on the opposite side of the theatre).

We did the big fourteen-minute dance number from *Billy* to end the first act and received a grand reception. The next day, the review in one of the papers read, 'Billy the Kid Steals the Show.'

I left *Billy* in 1976. It's always painful to say goodbye to a character like that and to a company which over the years you inevitably grow close to.

It also marked the end of my special three-year collaboration with John Barry, whose belief in me never wavered even during the occasional bouts of temperament and stress that are always part of the creative process. I have a treasured souvenir of one particular episode that erupted just a few days before the opening.

It was a fairly exhausting time with daily rehearsals and nightly performances; we were all tense and tempers tended to be slightly ragged. John came to me late one afternoon with a new song, the last one to be added before the opening.

'We've gotta put this number in tonight,' he told me.

'What are you talking about?' I answered. 'I'm not putting that number in tonight – I can't . . .'

'You've bloody got to . . .' he insisted. 'You've got to learn it and put it in tonight – I'll work with you . . .'

'I can't . . .' I said.

'Of course you can,' he yelled.

'Can't,' I yelled.

'Don't call me a c____t!' he shouted.

'I didn't call you a c____t!' I yelled. 'I said, "can't".'

'I bloody well heard you!' (At the top of his lungs now.) 'Don't call me a c____t . . .'

'Oh, stuff it!' I hollered, stalking out of the hall: 'I'm not putting that in tonight . . .'

The upshot was that I learned the song and it went into the show that night.

A short time later at the *Billy* recording session, John presented me with a magnificent Piaget watch as an opening night gift and, beautifully inscribed on the back, were the words: 'C____t – Thanks for *Billy*, Love, John.' Later on he told me the delicious story of going to Asprey's in London to buy the watch. His description of the ensuing scene of purchase and the dialogue that followed is treasurable:

Scene: Asprey's, London.

Enter: John Barry, customer, dressed in slightly Mod musician's threads, explaining to a clerk he would like to buy a Piaget watch as an opening night present for Michael Crawford.

Asprey's Clerk (dressed in formal grey morning suit – terribly BBC London): 'Yes, sir, I heard the reviews were excellent. A lovely choice, indeed. And would you like to have the watch inscribed?'

John Barry   (terribly BBC Bradford): 'Yes, I would actually. It has to be done rather quickly . . .'

Clerk: 'Absolutely no problem at all, Sir. And what would Sir like us to put on it?'

John: 'C____t – Thanks for *Billy*, Love, John.'

Clerk	(one eyebrow discreetly raised): 'Aha . . . But what exactly would you like us to put on the watch?'
John:	"C____t." That's capital C . . .'
Clerk	(quickly interrupting): 'Yes sir, I know how to spell it . . . "C____T", you say? Would you like that in script, or in block capitals . . .?'
John	(tired of the whole thing): 'Look, just write it . . .'

And write it they did. I have that particular treasure to prove it. I hope I never have to take it in for repair.

The years of doing *Billy* inevitably took a physical toll. I was exhausted, no question about it, and I needed a complete rest. In addition, all the day-in, day-out dancing had caused severe varicose veins to develop in my legs – not exactly a glamorous ailment and hardly life-threatening, but a very painful, unsightly condition. In the spring of 1976 the doctors recommended an immediate operation to have my legs 'stripped' of them. It would require, they said, several months of recovery time. I checked in to hospital the night after I finished the run.

The hospital staff knew me from the show and from the times I'd been along for appointments, so there was a light-hearted atmosphere – but underneath all the joking, I was secretly terrified.

First, my legs had to be shaved and my nurse took about an hour to do it. Matron kept coming in to tell her to get a move on. 'Well, I don't want to do any damage,' the nurse replied. 'I'll be doing damage to you if you don't get a move on,' said matron. 'A pair of legs have never taken that long to shave!' But my legs, it appeared, were not the issue at all: I had to be shaved around the groin as well. The young nurse had obviously been plucking up courage to finish the job; now pressed, she proceeded to the task. Both of us were quite overcome with the embarrassment of it all.

I was a sight to behold when she finished: in its semi-bald state my body had only a few tiny tufts left here and there – the way a chicken looks just before its backside is stuffed with celery and onions.

I was taken down early for the operation, but I know I didn't really come round from the anaesthetic till very late that night – apart from one moment in recovery, that is, when some nurse slapped me, saying, 'Michael, Michael, how are you, Michael?' and I muttered something like, 'Well, uh, I, uh, uh, well, I'd feel better if you weren't slapping me round the face . . .'

I had been plagued with the thought that I might have an erection during the operation, having been told it is a common occurrence. With the exception of the surgeon, there were only women in the operating room, all very attractive too. Oh God, I thought, what happens if I'm dreaming about those good-looking women, and while the surgeon is operating he looks up and he sees . . . Well, (and you'll pardon the pun) how would I ever live it down!

I think I must have spoken about my fear to the anaesthetist, but she put my mind to rest. I wonder if she spoke about what I said to her during the operation. I remember seeing scenes in films where the surgeon and nurses chat about things like the weather or the price of bacon, anything to break the boredom, while the patient just lies there under the knife, shaved, plucked and bare-bottomed.

When I finally came round in my room, my tongue

felt the size of a lorry blocking my mouth. 'Water,' I
murmured, 'I need water . . .'

In bustled the very strict Irish night nurse. 'What's all
the noise in here!' she asked.

'Water,' I whispered again, 'some water!'

'Oh, yer awake are ya,' she said.

'Uhhh . . .' was all I managed to murmur.

She gave me some water. 'Well, now yer awake, I'm
going to give you a bed bath.'

Suddenly, I could feel the pain. 'Oh, no,' I struggled;
I didn't want to be touched. 'I don't want a bath.'

'Now don't be a durty boy! Y've got to have a bath!'

'But I haven't been anywhere . . . I haven't moved!'
What the hell does she imagine I've been doing? Do I
look as though I've worked up a sweat? I couldn't have
moved if I'd wanted to.

She made a grab for one hand which went fly-away,
an uncontrollable limb that had nothing to do with the
rest of me. If she hadn't stopped it, it would have
whipped full-circle round my head; she'd have had to
duck to get out of its way. She gave me her sternest no-
nonsense-now expression and proceeded to wash my
hands and face. Like a sad, rag doll, all I could do was lie
there.

'Right,' she said. 'Now y've got to wash yer private
parts,' she said. She rinsed the flannel and handed it to
me. 'You can do that yerself.'

'But, I haven't done anything . . .' I answered, in weak
exasperation. 'It's just been lying there.'

'Now enough of that kind of talk!' she said.

So under her stern gaze, I obediently lifted the sheets
and looked down. 'My God, Nurse, look at this!' I cried
out in shock.

'Will you stop it!' she said. 'I'll not be lookin' down yer
sheets!'

'No, no, no!' I protested. 'You've got to look at this!' She looked down too, and saw the bright red bow tied securely round my privates. The nurses had done it while I was in recovery. There was even a card attached, with a simple message: 'Get Well Soon!'

CHAPTER 18

BILLY WAS STILL running at Drury Lane when Gabrielle found a new house for herself and the girls. I bought it for her as part of our settlement agreement and they moved away from Wimbledon. How very matter-of-fact this all sounds, but there is nothing I could write which would convey the misery and sense of dislocation we all felt.

I gave up the little Russell Gardens flat and moved back to Wimbledon to act as a kind of caretaker until the house could be sold. It was for only a matter of months. I lived in what used to be the sitting room, with just a small amount of furniture and a mattress on the floor.

But the sale of the house brought some financial breathing space at last and, not long after, fate and circumstance combined to smile in the person of a good friend, Shirley Conran, who was later to write many international bestsellers, including *Superwoman* and *Lace*. Embroiled in her own bitterly unhappy divorce – is there any other kind? – she was very low and seemed desperately in need of encouragement when she finally spoke to me about it. I referred her to my own lawyer and, once she'd made arrangements to see him, I drove her along to his offices hoping to lift her spirits with a little support. I didn't see her again after I left her there, but she later wrote to thank me for my help. She ended her letter by adding, 'If ever there's anything I can do for you . . .' and on impulse I decided to take her up on the offer. I called her and explained that I needed somewhere to live. 'In your travels,' I said, 'if you should see a place with cottages in the country . . .' The timing was perfect. Shirley had just done a feature for a women's magazine on Woburn Abbey. 'They have a lot of tithed cottages,' she said. 'I'll find out from the estate people there . . .'

Bless her, she called them immediately and put me in touch with the agents for the Woburn Estate, an area as lush and beautiful as any place in England. I fell in love with the countryside at first sight, but nothing on the estate was available. I was persistent, however, and asked to be shown anything and everything in the area. The very first place I was shown was an old thatched cottage, really tiny; you had to bend way down to get through the front door. 'I'm afraid this won't do at all,' the agent commented. Undeniably the house had more than a few problems: the back wall was falling off and the grounds were almost flooded. But for some reason it held enormous charm for me. I was instantly besotted.

The agent, quite undeterred by my enthusiasm for the place, continued to drag me around to other properties but I knew what I wanted. The cottage owners were another couple in the middle of a divorce. They had to sell quickly and I knew I had to have the place. I don't think I gave a thought to whether I could afford it or not – hardly standard Crawford practice – I bought the place immediately 'warts and all', and I've lived there happily ever since.

The roof is re-thatched now, the windows replaced,

the rooms enlarged slightly and, hopefully, the visitor is enveloped in a feeling of warmth and coziness the minute they walk through the front door. There's the smell of beeswax on the wood, and the glow of polished brass; there are photos of family, friends, and loved ones. The heat from the Aga brings life to the floorboards in the upstairs bedrooms. In the winter the log fire burns brightly, with the smell of applewood drifting through the tiny rooms, and during the summer months the family arrive on Friday night and we all sit around the old pine table in the kitchen indulging in a glorious 'fondue', no television, no radio, just conversation, decent wine and lots of laughter. Then it's early to bed so that we're well rested for the barbecue the next morning.

I converted a beautiful old outbuilding next to the cottage as a new home for Nan. She was ninety-three when she came to live with me, sharp and chirpy but, alas, her eyesight was failing badly. As I write, her little house has been empty these past few years – these days it's used as a guest cottage for the family; they love the place every bit as much as I do. I built a pool there, I made ponds, I put in fences, with help from the village. That whole year of 1976 was a grand time of discovery for me. I was forced to rest for a few months on account of the operation – as much as that is possible for me. (You'd be hard-pressed to find the phrase 'Complete Rest' in the Crawford lexicon.)

I acquired a good amount of chickens and sheep, together with a few geese. I read a book on self-sufficiency and it became my second bible. I started my own garden and began to grow everything I ate – a pastime which absolutely delighted me. To be able to dig a new potato out of the soil for lunch! To have fresh eggs and home-grown vegetables! I hadn't tasted anything that good in years.

With the divorce came all the related consequences of not seeing the children as much as ideally I would have wished and, like it or not, I became the quintessential weekend father.

Of course, I insisted on dragging Emma and Lucy into my new world of self-sufficiency, even though the glories of a freshly harvested potato were never quite as apparent to my children as they were to the father who had grown it. They had lived through Daddy's various enthusiasms over the years and were understandably cautious about my return to the soil. Sunday luncheons were something of a sore point; they never knew what we were going to eat. Everything on the dinner table was strictly Crawford produce. The only thing that didn't come from my garden was the beef bought from the farm up the road.

On one particular Sunday the girls were treated to a huge and unidentifiable blob of dark green vegetable. There were suspicious sidelong glances between them, and from the corner of my eye I could see the offending leaves being poked from one side of their plates to the other in a vain attempt to make them disappear.

'Come on, girls,' I ordered, eager for them to share my new discovery. 'Eat those greens . . .'

There was a lot of kicking going on under the table. Lucy was just eight, and not quite up to questioning what was on her plate, but Emma was ten, and therefore braver: 'Daddy, what is this?'

'It's full of goodness and nourishment,' I said. 'That's all you need to know.'

But Emma had the bit between her teeth now and was not to be put off. 'I don't think that's fair, Daddy, I think we should know what we're eating . . .'

'It's nettles,' I told them, enthusiastically, adding, 'and they're full of iron!'

I think they were too stunned to say anything much. Avoiding their looks of pained reproach I managed to get them to eat half the nettles, but you can imagine the conversation when they got home:

Gabrielle:	Did you enjoy your day?
Girls:	Yes.
Gabrielle:	Yes? Well, what did you have for lunch . . . ?
Girls:	Lamb.
Gabrielle:	Lamb? Yes, and . . ?
Girls:	Potatoes.
Gabrielle:	And?
Girls:	Stinging nettles . . .

Understandably the lawyer was on the phone to me first thing Monday morning. 'Look,' I protested, 'nettles really taste good if you don't overcook them. Like spinach . . . a little salt and pepper . . .' (Where was his sense of adventure!) 'They don't sting or anything; I mean, the sting is gone! I had it myself! I'd never put anything on their plates that I hadn't eaten myself . . . and I survived!'

My protests fell on deaf ears: All children's menus must now be cleared in advance!

I've got a photo at home of the two girls standing next to an aircraft, their sleepy eyes practically closed. My friend, Jo-Anne, is there too with an early-morning look. And me? Why I'm standing there with them, wide-eyed and bushy-tailed, with a grin on my face as big as an aircraft hangar.

I met my friend Stuart Carrie in 1977. There were great celebrations of the Queen's Jubilee all over England. One nearby village invited me to make appearances at its street party, visiting people's houses and old people's homes in the area, judging the fancy dress, and generally helping to raise money for local charities. And when I'd done, the man who had asked for my help, who'd organised everything and driven me round, said, 'Look, if there's anything I can do for you in return, please let me know.' Now, knowing that the village was situated very close to an airfield I said, 'Well, there is one thing that I'd love to do. I've had the desire to fly all my life.'

Within a week he called me back. 'Sunday morning,' he said. 'I've arranged with a fellow called Stuart Carrie, he's the Senior Air Traffic Controller at Cranfield Institute — meet him at the airfield.' God, this is *wonderful*, I thought. I felt as if I were flying already.

'I've got a surprise for you tomorrow . . .' I announced to the girls. 'What is it, Daddy?' they asked suspiciously. 'It's not more nettles, is it? You're *not* going to cook nettles for lunch!' 'No, no, no,' I assured them. 'It's nothing to do with food or anything, it's just a surprise.'

I had arranged to meet Stuart at 8:30 am at the airfield. Well, 8:30 on a Sunday morning . . . no one's awake in England at that hour, apart from the vicar and the milkman. Of course, I had hardly slept at all. I bounced in to wake the girls. 'Uggghh, Daddy, what is it? What's happening?'

'It's time,' I said. 'It's time for the surprise!'

'This *early* Daddy? Can't we have a *later* surprise?' I was having none of it. This was going to be a great day. Out of bed, everybody! Rise and shine!

Accompanied by my less than happy crew, I arrived at the airport. Our pilot was there to meet us. 'Hi, I'm Stu Carrie,' he said.

'Hi, I'm Michael Crawford,' I gushed. 'I'm really excited about going on this trip.' I turned to walk to the field and walked straight into the wing of the plane. I neglected to mention that in the photo I've described, in addition to my proud grin, my forehead seems to be slightly swollen. My dignity may have been slightly damaged – but nothing could ruin that day for me. Here I am, *me*, I've finally joined the Air Force, and I'm standing alongside my first aircraft!

Stu Carrie kept looking at me sideways as I climbed into the plane, not sure what to expect next. He had received special permission for us to fly over parts of central London, and we flew at an altitude of about fifteen hundred feet. I wanted to reach out and touch the flags at Buckingham Palace and the flower-planted rooftops near Dolphin Square. Those first moments over London gave such a lift to body and soul, I could scarcely breathe. I turned round to the girls, still slightly half-asleep: 'Look, there's where you live! We'll call Mummy as soon as we get back.'

As we flew back over Essex, across and back up to Bedfordshire, Stuart said, 'Would you like to take the controls?' We were now up to three thousand feet. I could hear *The Dambusters* theme tune throbbing in my head. I nodded.

'You have control,' he said.

If only he knew!

By now even the girls were rather impressed that their father was flying the aircraft. The sweat ran down my face. With blood and heart pounding I stayed on those controls almost until we landed. After landing, our group headed straight into the club, and I bought drinks all around. I was so excited. And you can imagine how excited Mummy was, when she learned that a single-engine aircraft had flown over the house with her children in it! The lawyer was on the phone at 10.00 am the next morning. I didn't see the girls again for a month!

Even before I'd left *Billy* I'd agreed to do Bernard Slade's two-character play, *Same Time, Next Year*, the following spring, partly because it represented a complete change of pace. It was already an enormous hit in New York (it ran for years on Broadway). The play was about a couple, each married to another, but involved in a longtime affair; it was funny and touching and bittersweet, and called for the characters to change and age over a period of twenty-five years. I thought it represented an exciting acting challenge.

It would be delightful to report here that *Same Time, Next Year* was a smashing success, but it wasn't. We opened to middling reviews at the Prince of Wales in late September 1976. Eric Thompson (father of Emma and Sophie) was the director; he was a brilliant and inspiring man, but sadly my co-star Frances Cuka and I had not much in common, little rapport and even less of the stage chemistry needed to portray convincingly an adulterous couple happily spending stolen time together in bed. From day one, you know whether or not you're going to hit if off with someone. We were working together rather than living together in the show. There's a big difference: every minute is hard work, and the situation becomes more difficult with each passing day, because there isn't the natural trust in what the other is doing.

Frances left the show after four months and was replaced by Michele Dotrice. Perhaps it was foolish for the two of us to team up again: both of us had spent the past several years trying to escape our *Some Mothers* incarnations, but the roles were such a radical departure for us as a team that we thought it might spark an entirely new image, and perhaps even save the production. Box-office receipts picked up considerably for a while (well, of course, it was 'Betty and Frank Together Again!'), but still it was obvious the play was never going to be the success in London that it was in New York.

At the same time, after much hesitancy on my part, I was persuaded by BBC director Claude Whatham into doing two Václav Havel works for television, satirising the repressive Czech society responsible for the persecution of Havel, their most famous dissident playwright (and now the Czech President). I had my own doubts about doing anything quite so serious on television, believing that the audience's identification with me as Frank Spencer might detract from Havel's message, but here again was an opportunity to escape typecasting and I accepted the challenge. The critical response was wonderful, but the viewing figures only fair: Michael-Crawford-As-Serious-Actor was obviously not something TV audiences wished to see.

I'm not much given to introspection about the choices I've made in my career, but I think I based my decision to do another series of *Some Mothers* in 1978 on the theory that 'if you can't lick 'em . . .' And so, five years after those first episodes that changed my life, I accepted the offer. By this time Michael Mills had transferred from the BBC over to Thames Television, so we went with a new director, Sidney Lotterby, who had just had enormous success with *Last of the Summer Wine*. He was excellent to work with, and had great enthusiasm for physical comedy.

Michele signed on again – no one else could possibly have replaced her. She was, as always, absolutely stoic in the way she put up with my teasing and practical jokes, but it took months for her to recover from a segment in which Frank dances a Highland Fling, wearing a kilt. At rehearsals I'd always worn a pair of Union Jack shorts underneath, but on the night of the show – to Michele's surprise and horror – I wore nothing at all. It was a delight to watch as she instinctively became a real-life Betty, frantically holding her skirts wide, as she tried to cover me from the camera eye.

That little bit of naked tomfoolery, by the way, resulted in another spate of letters to the BBC from Mary Whitehouse, England's self-appointed censor and guardian of the public morality. She was quite a character, always writing letters to the Corporation about Frank Spencer. She called the show obscene, and said that I was obsessed with my private parts because I kept rubbing my arm down the outside of my leg. I don't want to imagine the kind of men Mary was obviously used to dealing with: I certainly wouldn't want to meet them on a dark night.

Once again *Some Mothers* was a hit – and this time, America called. One of the television networks had decided to create their own Frank Spencer character for New York. The temptation was lovely, but only momentary. New York wanted a five-year commitment. Five years! I'm too old to be doing this now, I thought. Besides, the idea of Frank Spencer living in New York was too depressing to contemplate: America's level of tolerance for eccentricity is notoriously limited. The poor man would be a street person – or dead – within a week of his arrival.

The doctors discovered a lump in my left breast in the summer of 1978, after I'd finished the second series of

Some Mothers, and an immediate biopsy was ordered. A simple procedure, they told me, just a day or so in hospital. Breast tumour? I was totally shocked; surely I wasn't alone among men in believing that only women have to worry about such things?

I decided to keep completely quiet about my medical problem. Indeed, I've never said a word about it to anyone and I tell it now only because of the insight it gave me on my life at the time. I suddenly felt very much alone. It was after I entered hospital – in the midst of filling out the admission forms, to be precise – when I was confronted by the line that asked for 'Name of person to be notified in case of emergency'.

How could I put down Nan, a fragile ninety-three-year-old? I remembered how once as a child of about six or seven I'd made Nan promise she'd live to be a hundred. Could the unthinkable be about to happen? Could I be about to die before Nan did?

Then again, how could I put Jo-Anne's name down on the form? We were involved, but not living together. I certainly didn't want the children to be the first to know, nor Gabrielle. It sounds totally idiotic, but the only thought that crossed my mind was I don't want anyone to know I'm dead – they'll be upset!

So I wrote in the name of my agent – Michael Linnit – trusting he'd know the best way to deal with any awful eventualities. I think if he had known about it, he might have wished my obvious confidence in his abilities wasn't quite so absolute.

A report was later sent to me from my surgeon, the kindest of men, Mr John Maynard, at Guy's Hospital, London, dated July 18, 1978. 'Dear Mr Crawford,' his letter began, 'The histological report on your left breast tissue showed only increased fibrosis . . .' Mr Maynard briefly concluded: '. . . there was no evidence of malignancy.' Wonderful words, welcome words indeed. But another such tumour was found a few months later and just before Christmas I had to return to hospital for another biopsy. Again, it was non-malignant.

It's all over now, a long time ago, and I've long since been given a clean bill of health. But I've never forgotten the experience of lying in that bed alone and frightened. It was a gift in a way. It's not as if I was struck by the lightning bolt of spiritual revelation. All I had to do was to walk through the children's wards seeing those amazingly brave, often terminally ill little souls, to gain a whole new perspective on life and death and one's own vulnerability. I realised I'd been given a chance to do something more with my life. So a year that had begun rather self-pityingly ended as a celebration. I was alive and I was healthy. I felt very fortunate.

CHAPTER 19

FOR SHEER LEWDNESS and crudeness, one would have to search long and hard to find a character lower than David Finn. If a man like Finn moved into your neighbourhood, it would be a clear signal of a precipitous drop in property values. Face covered in hair – more bird's nest than beard – he scuffed about in dirty sneakers, leg warmers and pyjama bottoms; his clothes were the grimy repository of cigarette ash, and marmalade from a late breakfast. But if he looked creepy, he behaved worse, a loudmouth slob. He was, in short, absolutely everything I wanted to be on television: the complete opposite of Frank Spencer.

It was my original *Some Mothers* director, Michael Mills, now a producer at Thames, who offered me the gift of the David Finn character in the 1979 television series *Chalk and Cheese*. Jonathan Pryce had starred in the pilot, but elected not to do the series. I thought he had made such an impressive job of creating the characterisation of David Finn, that I shamelessly borrowed some of that persona. I enjoyed playing the role enormously, even more so because I was working with Michael again.

We started off as number one in the ratings and finished, I think, at number seven with viewing figures of 18 million: it was very respectable, but by our previous standards, it wasn't a triumph.

I don't know who hated the character of David Finn more – the fans of Michael Crawford (or should I say Frank Spencer?) or my grandmother. Loyally, she always switched on the television when the time came for an episode, but she adamantly refused to watch the screen while the show was on, insisting instead on sitting with her back to the set. If that wasn't bad enough, I was also swamped with hundreds of letters complaining about me playing such a part. If Jonathan Pryce had played the role, they might have adored it. But not 'our Michael'. 'We'd much rather see him do Frank . . .' I didn't want to hear any more of it. Michael Mills was keen to do another season – certainly more than the eight shows I had agreed to do – but I declined, and suddenly something else was offered that seemed a great deal more important.

Every now and then when an actor is very lucky, he'll read a script or hear a song, and he'll know his name is written all over it – he knows it's something he must do. I'd just been sent a script and a music tape for a show called *Flowers for Algernon*. It was about a mentally retarded man who participates in a scientific experiment, becomes a genius and falls in love with his therapist, only to discover at the end that he will regress again and forever into his former state. Mental retardation is an obviously thorny subject to depict in any form, but to approach it as a musical play seemed to me incredibly brave and daring. The Daniel Keyes novel had become something of a cult classic and the film version, *Charley*, had earned its star Cliff Robertson an Oscar, so the story was already well known.

The 'Algernon' in the title, by the way, is Charley's best friend, a mouse. I trained and worked with one for months – he was brilliant, a real star. We even had a song and dance together, a little vaudeville routine where he'd run all the way up my arm and sit on my head, or else he'd scuttle up one arm, around my shoulders, then down the other side. Then I'd put him on the ground and strut off stage, while Algernon followed close behind me. Our little act used to bring the house down. I kept him (along with two of his understudies) in my dressing room. My long-suffering dresser, Kate Aarons, hated the mice, and I would drive her crazy letting them crawl over my shoulders, or when I lost one in the dressing room while I was rehearsing.

The moment I heard that wonderfully spare score by Charles Strouse, I knew it was something for me. I was enthralled; I hadn't even finished listening to the tape and I was already playing Charley in my head, and pursuing a hundred ideas of how I could further connect with the character. The music, the story, everything about the show moved me profoundly and inspired me. I don't think I have ever had such an immediate response to a project.

I knew of Charles Strouse, of course, the prolific, ebullient American with a list of Broadway and West End hit shows a mile long. *Flowers for Algernon* was very different from his *Bye Bye, Birdie* or *Annie*. Charles described it in fact as a kind of chamber musical – small in terms of size of cast and orchestra perhaps, but it was a powerhouse nonetheless.

Jo-Anne loved it as much as I did, and I knew it was a project we could work on together, something we had wanted to do ever since we had been dance partners in *Billy*. (She later danced in the show and assisted Rhoda Levine, the choreographer.)

The British director Peter Coe – a man I didn't know at all – had sent me the script. Peter was best known, I suppose, for his direction of *Oliver!* and was at that time Artistic Director of Edmonton's Citadel Theatre in Canada and had just directed *Flowers*. It was arranged that we should meet early on, before rehearsals, and it was clear from the start there might be fireworks ahead. Peter and I were theatrical chalk and cheese; we couldn't have been more different if it had been planned that way.

Peter could sometimes be aggressive and very arrogant in his approach. But he was also brilliant, sophisticated, cultured (I'm sure he'd read a hundred books for every one of mine), slightly patrician in manner, and as complicated and cool a cookie as you'll ever meet. It was touch-and-go for a while. Both of us could be verbally combative, and we proceeded to stake out our own philosophical claims early on. For example, I use the word 'we' a lot whenever I discuss a production with anyone; I love working within an ensemble unit, as part of a team. Peter however was not quite as strong on the 'we' concept as myself.

From the beginning I insisted that I wanted at least a degree of consultation regarding casting. Peter's view was that casting was his concern and none of my business. 'Fine, if that's the way you work . . .' I huffed at him, 'if you want to do it without consultation . . .' And I stormed out of the production, only returning a few days later after a conciliatory phone call from Peter who assured me that we could indeed work together and he would agree to a degree of consultation. (A degree was what he promised and a degree was exactly what I got – I felt he never exactly overwhelmed me with it.)

For a while rehearsals resembled some primitive territorial dance: my finger waving under his nose, his under mine, as both of us shouted, 'That's it! . . . that's final!' We'd stalk away in opposite directions, pause a second, then turn back to face one another and one of us would say, 'Well, of course, if you'd rather . . .' And we'd burst out laughing. Two very different people, travelling totally divergent paths, attempting to reach the same shared goal – the best production possible.

I know I am a very visceral performer, all heart and guts on the sleeve, supercharged, hyper-emotional. And easily moved to tears: I cry when I sing a sad song in class. Peter was completely the opposite; he never showed emotion at all. He'd sit and watch me impassively, squinting hard in total concentration. He was bearded and had a habit of gnawing his bottom lip with an avidity that half-convinced me the surrounding black roots must surely taste like sweet licorice. The more emotion I put into my performance, the harder he'd chew on the 'licorice', particularly at that point in the show when the character Charley realises he is regressing again into that nightmare childish state – he knows he is slipping away and he hates it.

> . . . I won't go back, not at this stage
> Into the dark, into that cage.
> I'll find a way that I can stay
> Charley, Charley, Charley . . .

I had a tremendous emotional involvement with Charley, and when I sang those words in a strange juxtaposition of character and actor, I felt as if I was standing outside of myself. I became my own audience, watching the man, rooting for him, and I wept whenever I rehearsed the song.

'What makes you cry there?' Peter asked.

'I don't know,' I said. 'It isn't self-pity . . . It's the feeling that I won't go back, I can't go back . . . it's frustration, anger.'

'Try it again,' he said, 'and this time hold back, pull the emotion back, way back, and then let it go . . .' It was like an emotional slingshot. He encouraged me to explore and examine the pivotal words and phrases of the song's lyrics, and urged me to use these lyrics as the root of a portrayal of honest emotion. Peter showed me how to strip a song to its lyrical bare bones, to build and develop the emotional content until it became an extension of the character. He made me understand that it was okay to let the emotions go to any extreme within the context of the song – to the heights, in fact – as long as I had properly constructed my character along the way and prepared the audience for it. The audience will then accept all the emotional heights you set as you sing. You can't just stand on a stage and cry and expect your audience to cry too.

In preparation for *Flowers for Algernon* I visited hospitals for the mentally handicapped, not as an entertainer as in the past, but rather as an observer. I read somewhere that we never actually act the truth, that we simply mirror it, interpret and embellish it. The single most important thing in my mind was to treat the subject of retardation with the dignity it deserved. I didn't want the innocence of Charley cheapened by caricature. Whenever I toured those facilities I remembered gentle Sam who had swept the floors in the David Grieg shop when I was a kid in Bexleyheath. He was very much like Charley, though, unlike him, Sam had his independence and a sense of his importance in life, his self-respect – something that could be easily lost within the confines of an institution. I had my own little corner backstage where I would go before a performance just to think about the man, and the naïvety and total innocence that made up his world. In that corner life somehow became slower, simpler – someone would call my name, I'd turn around and suddenly be the adult-child that was Charley.

There were two very gifted actors who played Charley's doctors: Aubrey Woods, the aggressive, no-nonsense Dr Strauss, and Ralph Nossek, the gentler Dr Nemur. Ralph had the most beautifully kind voice and when I was Charley, I loved him. Whenever Ralph spoke to me on stage, I felt as if he might be my dad or some kind uncle. We shared a wonderful little scene together where Dr Nemur puts Charley through the Rorschach Test. I always wanted to do the test to please Ralph.

I'd like to single out another of the leading ladies most special to me. There are a few to whom I am particularly devoted because of the partnership we shared: like an expert tennis partner, each of them made me work that much harder. Michele Dotrice was one, and Cheryl Kennedy, my *Flowers* co-star, was another.

Cheryl had fallen in love with the show, just as I had, after hearing only a little of the music tape. Her calm assurance saved me on more than one occasion. Just before the opening preview it was decided I should sing 'Whatever Time There Is', the love song Cheryl had originally sung alone. I didn't know the words at all and resorted to having them written out and held directly behind Cheryl's head in the wings, a patchy solution at best, and one to be avoided, as I'd learned from the mad old days with Harry Corbett in *Travelling Light*. Now I totally miscalculated: it was so dark in the wings I couldn't read a thing. But before complete panic set in

Cheryl took me in hand and simply spoke the lyrics to me, gently talking me through the song. She was a wonderfully calming influence on me and on the whole company.

Flowers for Algernon opened on June 19, 1979 at the Queen's Theatre, and divided the critics. Those who loved the show adored it, and gave me some of the best reviews of my life. Those who disliked it were mostly put off by the subject matter.

Nan came to see the show, of course, although by now her eyesight was very poor. I made sure she was seated in the front row, but even then I'm doubtful whether the show was more than a colourful blur to her. Still, her hearing was very acute. In the first act, as Charley begins his journey from imbecile to genius, his progress is dramatised as he sings about some of the books he is reading, beginning with *Robinson Crusoe*, moving to the more challenging *Dr Jekyll and Mr Hyde* ('It's good . . . but it's simplistic'), and ending with a fast-talking synopsis of *War and Peace* (all in a style wonderfully reminiscent of Danny Kaye's superbly intricate patter):

> . . . André goes off to war and Lisa dies but leaves a son.
> And Nikolai is fighting too, they fight Napoleon.
> Pierre's wife's name is Ellen, she's the daughter
> of Prince Vasily;
> Pierre will go to war, instead he sets his peasants
> free.
> Did I forget to mention André has a sister too,
> and Ellen has a brother, or is this too
> much for you?
> When André meets Natasha, he loves her heart

and soul, but she meets Ellen's brother,
he's a cad – that's Anatole . . .

I held the song's last note on and on and on, as long as I
possible could. At the end I had to turn to Cheryl's
character and say quite breathlessly, 'Did I do good?'

And before she could utter a word a voice rang out
very clearly from the first row, 'You did wonderfully,
darling.' It was Nan.

I died. Oh my God, I can't believe it!

'You did – you really did!' she insisted.

Cheryl couldn't say a word, and there were tears of
laughter in her eyes as she stared at me trying not to
collapse entirely – until I started to laugh too. Afterwards
Nan told me how much she loved the show. 'But it won't
last, you know,' she said. 'It won't last.'

'Nan!' I said, 'I've just had some of the best reviews
I've had in my career!'

'I know you have, darling, and you're wonderful. But
it won't last.'

I was secretly spooked by her remark: it was a strange
thing for her to say. How could she know? She couldn't
even *see* the show.

It lasted, with previews, just six weeks. And when it
came off, she said, 'I knew it wouldn't last. I just knew it
wouldn't last!'

'Naaaaaaannn!'

A theatre company will often pull together more solidly
in defeat than during a successful run. With
disappointment staring us right in the eye, we closed
ranks. When the closing notice was posted for *Flowers*,
the whole company got together and decided to take

salary cuts; I said I would work for nothing. Everyone made sacrifices in an attempt to keep the show going. To be honest, none of us could understand why we were being threatened with closure just two weeks after the opening; the houses had been good, the audiences receptive. Management blamed newly instituted VAT and spiralling ticket and production costs, etc etc.

Our last Saturday matinée was particularly difficult to get through and I can only recall parts of it, particularly the special feeling of warmth throughout: we were as one with the audience. Kate, my dresser, painted an accurate portrait of the gloomy scene backstage at our final performance. 'That last Saturday night we did the show, we had to absolutely drag Michael on stage because he was so distraught. On the very last change, we were waiting for him in the changing room and he didn't show up. It was a real quick change, I remember, and I thought, my God, where is he? I went up and found him in the wings, and he was sobbing, and I literally had to pull him into the quick-change room. Of course we were all crying as well . . . and we had to push him back on stage again. It was so sad, I can't tell you. The crew, all of us, everybody on the show was just crying their eyes out at the end of it.'

Well, we went down, but it's nice to know we didn't sink without a trace. The endeavour was indeed so dear to us it was decided to do a recording of the show, if only to have a lasting souvenir for the cast. Charles Strouse and I put up several thousand pounds for the project and with Cheryl Kennedy's help we were able to get space for a day in the studio near Pie Island owned by Pete Townshend of The Who.

Neither the engineers nor the musicians bothered to watch the clock or worry about their pay cheques. Charles Strouse's wife, Barbara Siman, helped to produce the record and I assisted in mixing the sound. We got it done and, as with the show, it was a labour of love from beginning to end. And now, with all the people who mention it to me, who say they saw *Flowers* or heard about it, or say they have the record and they love it, it's difficult to believe we actually closed in six weeks. We are all grateful it is remembered with such affection.

Just after the bitter disappointment of *Flowers*, an invitation arrived to present an award at the Australian Film Festival. It included two airfares and hotel accommodation. Of course I jumped at the opportunity to go. Jo-Anne had been working very hard too, and I knew this would provide a rare opportunity for both of us to have a holiday as far away from everything as possible. She was already working on another project and arranged to meet me later on, so I decided to go on ahead to Thailand and experience some of the exotic sights of the Orient before catching up with her in Sydney.

I got off the plane in Bangkok carrying a passport loaded with visas to go to all kinds of places, and a travelling medical booklet as thick as an encyclopaedia with immunisation charts. I spotted a Thai woman at the end of the gangplank half-carrying, half-waving a sign that said 'Mister Cwarfer' – and knew I was expected.

My welcoming committee of one had been sent to guide me through the intricacies of Thai immigration, which she did with admirable dispatch, and then led me inside the terminal where I was greeted by another representative, a genial, ginger-haired Irishman who was the assistant manager of my hotel.

He bustled me into a waiting car and, as we drove to the hotel, he pointed out some of the sights along the route. The heat was extraordinary that day, and the humidity only served to exaggerate the already pungent smells of spice and sweat and swamps. A strong aroma of cooking wafted from every Bangkok street corner as well as from the thousand wooden barges on the Chao Phraya River that form a kind of floating city within the city. At first glance it was hard to tell exactly what was being cooked, until the Irishman pointed out some of the Thai delicacies that included insects and small unidentified animals, and some other items the thought of which made this Western stomach bounce about like a cork in the English Channel.

My red-haired friend called later that evening with an invitation to sample some of 'Bangkok's night life' – as classic a bit of descriptive understatement as I've ever heard. We'll have a 'real look-see', he said, and mentioned a rather seedy area of the city called Pat Pong. The plan was to have a quick beer in one place and move on to the next. We made a date to meet and began making the rounds of the bars, something you have to experience to believe. There were girls of every shape, size and description – hordes of them, swarms of them, and they stuck to us like flypaper. The Irishman positively relished my astonished response; I know my blushes matched the colour of his hair.

This may all sound incredibly naïve, but I have never been able to come to terms with that particular kind of sexual frontal attack. Bangkok was like some giant sexual supermarket and for a few tourist dollars, everything imaginable was immediately and energetically available.

A girl came and sat beside me on our first stop. 'You 'Merican?' she asked.

'No, no.'

'Eeeengrish?'

'Yes,' I said, 'English.'

'Austraryian?' she asked.

'No, English,' I repeated.

'Oh,' she said, 'I like Eeeengrish!'

'Oh, well, terrific,' I said. I had been trying to give up smoking (for the hundredth time), but started again on the spot. She could see I wasn't being particularly responsive and after being subjected to a couple of my banal questions ('Tell me, what do you do during the day?') she wandered off, no doubt insulted, and mumbling what sounded like the Thai for 'jerk'. She was replaced in mini-seconds by another girl who sat as close as possible without actually perching on my lap.

'You don' rike me?' she said.

'Yes, I do rike you,' I said, 'very much. But I'm you know, uh, I'm listening to the music . . .' That was pretty stupid. With five gyrating topless Thai girls bouncing in front of me on top of the bar, this hardly constituted a meeting of the Bangkok Music Appreciation Society.

'You don' rike me . . .' she pouted. 'What you want? You want my sister?'

'No, I don't want your sister.'

'You want my brother?'

'No, no,' I said, 'certainly not, certainly not!'

'Ahhh,' she said, 'I know what you rike . . .' She left me for a few seconds, and returned again giddily arm-in-arm with an extraordinary beauty.

'Well, hellooo,' I said. 'Uh, do you want a Coke?' My Irish host and his friends were laughing at me now, delighted at my obvious interest in the girl. Face flushed scarlet with the combination of beer, heat, noise, and more beer, shakily lighting another cigarette while one still burned in the ashtray, I felt ridiculously out of place. But the girl was really charming and by the time her friend came back to check our progress, we were getting on quite well. 'Ah,' she yelled above the din, 'see,

I know what you rike! You rike George here!'

'George?' I said.

'Yes, that's my name, George,' replied the gorgeous transvestite I'd been chatting with for the past fifteen minutes. In typical 'Cwarfer' fashion I leapt to my feet, scattering beers, Cokes, and cigarette ends over my companions and made a beeline for the front door, followed by the Irishman who was totally convulsed at the turn of events. I found over the course of a few days that such knee-slapping practical jokes comprised the general tenor of his humour. Doubtless he'd been the sort of boy who likes to slice up minnows and sneak them into the vicar's sandwiches.

On my last evening in Bangkok I met up with him again, and this time he brought a friend – an Australian physician from Hong Kong whose sense of humour was at least as crazy as his. I happened to mention that I would like to have a really good oriental massage before I left Bangkok. I still felt completely wrung out from the flight and all the subsequent late-night carousing. Our host said he knew an establishment that would accommodate me. Dammit, just a straight massage, I warned him: no kidding around this time, I've got to get on a plane tomorrow morning. Right, he said, I know just the place. I must have been out of my mind to believe him.

The three of us drove to somewhere in downtown Bangkok, and eventually pulled up and parked in front of what looked like an ordinary Chinese restaurant. Inside, however, the resemblance ended. We walked down a long narrow corridor covered floor-to-ceiling in busy flocked wallpaper and reached our destination, a vast wall made of glass, behind which sat one hundred or more girls neatly laid out on shelves like a cold cut display in one of those refrigerated cabinets at Marks &

Spencer; they were of varying widths, heights, and sizes, and each one wore a number. The girls all appeared to be vastly amused about something and giggled as they looked out and pointed at the men who peered in on them.

I was told to pick a number (just like in a supermarket) and that girl would give the massage. 'You choose one for me,' I told my companions. 'I'll be quite happy. Just see who's good at doing a massage.'

They left, then reappeared, and signalled for me to meet them at the door on the side of the cage that served as a kind of human check-out counter for the girls who met us there to take us to our rooms. An absolutely beautiful girl came out first. 'Is she mine?' I asked. 'No, no, she's for the Doc,' the Irishman grinned. The next girl came out, a real stunner. 'That's my girl,' said our host. The door opened again and another girl appeared. I can't imagine how I had missed her among the others, she must have weighed 200 pounds. 'She's your girl . . .' my companions laughed. 'Well, great,' I muttered rather lamely, 'just as long as she knows how to give a good massage.'

The girl and I joined the others in the lift but we were promptly ejected. It appeared 'my date' added slightly too much bulk to the elevator's already overburdened machinery. Doc and the Irishman howled with delight as the doors closed on the two of us – Stan Laurel and his oriental Oliver Hardy – and I waited in some dismay as the lift, shaking with their hilarity, creaked its way up to the fifth floor.

The two of us got into another lift – by ourselves this time – and rode in solemn silence; she obviously spoke little or no English. The lift doors opened, revealing another dimly-lit corridor in this architectural rabbit-warren which eventually led us into a long room. It was actually two rooms; one with a sunken bath and a kind of Li-Lo sitting next to it on the floor, the other with a massage table.

'In there,' she pointed. None of that sentimental twaddle here. This lady obviously meant business.

She started to run the bath. 'Take your crows off . . .' I did as I was told (after all she constituted about two of me), but not knowing the procedure I decided to opt for modesty, keeping a towel draped around me. 'Take dat off,' she ordered.

As I dropped it, the door swung open and in walked a waiter with a Coke. 'Ohhhhhhhh, put dat away,' he said, pointing disgustedly in my direction and then hurriedly left the room. I began to pick my towel up but, 'You get in . . .' she ordered, so I dropped it yet again and put one foot into the bath.

The water felt glacier-fed. 'I can't get in that!' I complained. 'It's freezing.'

'You get in quick,' she pushed me. 'I go wash yoo back . . .'

'Oh, dear God!' I howled. 'Well, wash it quickly . . .'

That finished, she knelt by the side of the tub and pulled the Li-Lo onto the tile floor. 'You rie on Ri-Ro,' she commanded. 'Get on Ri-Ro.' I must have looked apprehensive because she proceeded to wig-wag a few hand signs to demonstrate she was about to give me a body massage. I finally did as I was told and lay down on my stomach while she stood behind me. Some slight movement of hers made me glance up at the mirror in front of me. Her towel fell to the floor and I saw the full horror of my predicament. For a second she stood behind me, her arms now extended straight out at her sides as if in some sort of ritualistic pose, two massive breasts now hanging free.

Then suddenly, and with the weight of a collapsing building, she fell straight on top of me. The Ri-Ro exploded – not one centigram of it remained intact – and I lay splattered across the tile floor, buried under a ton of flesh with one of her great breasts clogging each of my ears.

For a moment I thought she had rendered me deaf as well as impotent. It was an enormous relief to hear a sudden banging on the wall and voices shouting: 'Hey, what you do in theah!' and 'What you do to her!' What I do to HER! My nose was squashed flat to my face and my parts flat to the floor, like a bunch of well-trodden grapes in a French winery.

She rolled off my broken body, knelt beside me and whispered gently in my ear: 'Hey,' she said, 'you wan' anyfin' speshul?' We had obviously reached a ticklish crossroads in this negotiation.

'Well,' I mumbled, not giving way an inch, 'I'd like you to do my neck, I'm still pretty tense . . .'

'No, no,' she tittered through her little white teeth, the only tiny part of her anatomy, 'somethin' speshul, extra?'

The ending to this story, although anti-climactic, was touching rather than funny. I finally made her understand I was only interested in the massage and none of the extras, and thanked her.

'You velly nice man,' she said, as if I had given her a gift. She smiled a smile that was obviously kept for very special occasions – of such charm and sensitivity that for a moment she was very pretty – and I suddenly felt like a complete cad. She never said another word to me, but led me to the lift and turned away just as the doors closed in front of me. Then, one inch at a time, the lift began to creak and moan its way back to the lobby.

I said nothing about the evening to my night's companions who waited in the hall outside. (Bugger 'em, I thought.) The pair of them were tickled to death with self-congratulations at the construed success of their little enterprise. They were still laughing the next morning when they drove me to the airport and put me on the plane to Australia.

My next memory is of the flight to Sydney and the enormous gentleman (even sitting down he looked seven foot), a very affable German businessman who sat next to me, a real high-powered type. He was, he told me, 'in rubber goods'. After my experiences in Bangkok, I didn't care to touch that one. But he was very expansive and told some funny stories, and the trip passed quickly. His English was good, but his accent was quite thick and he had trouble with his 'th's so that 'everyzing was like zat'.

Just before we landed he leaned over and nudged me with his enormous elbow in a companionable way to signal he was about to give a little free man-to-man advice: 'Szoh,' he said, 'zis izzz your first visit to Auztralia?'

'Yah,' I said, laughing nervously. 'I mean, yes . . .'

'Mr Spray vill come now,' he said, 'sroo ze aircraft, and sprraaay us all . . .'

'Pardon?' I said. I hadn't the slightest idea what he was trying to tell me. After a few more friendly nudges that sent me ricocheting off the window, he managed to explain that one of the crew would be walking through the aircraft to aerosol the passengers – a practice employed on certain airline routes from Third World countries to make sure that unwelcome creatures of unspecified identity do not get off the flight along with the passengers and make themselves at home in the country of destination.

'Make shooor . . .' he nudged, 'zat you cover your mouse ven he spraaays you!' he said.

'I'm sorry?'

'Ven he spraaays you,' he commanded, 'cover your mouse!'

Well, I thought, I've heard it called lots of things over the years, but this is a new one. Still, having been nearly castrated in Bangkok, I decided not to risk losing it again in the course of an aerosol spray job. Anyway my companion seemed to be an authority on this kind of travel so I solemnly follow his advice: I covered my 'mouse' with a large newspaper and waited for the spraying to subside.

We landed in Sydney and my German friend and I said our good-byes, and I walked towards my next stop – the line through Immigration.

Some Mothers had been a great hit on Australian television for some considerable length of time, which delighted me, of course, but feeling the way I did, I donned my usual 'disguise' – an ordinary pair of reading glasses – and hoped not to attract too much attention. It soon became very clear I hadn't a thing to worry about.

'G'day!' boomed the clerk at the Immigration counter. I swear you could have heard this guy from the balcony of the Sydney Opera House.

'Hello, there,' I piped back.

'So . . .' he said, peering at my passport, 'so yer an actor, are ya, Michael?' I could hear the people on the line behind me fan out to take a look.

'Yes.'

'And what are you doing here in Australia?'

'Oh, I'm just having a little break,' I said.

'Oh yer outta work, are ya?' he bellowed.

'Well, actually, I'm just having a . . .' I suddenly panicked: I don't have a work permit. Is presenting an award on television the same as working? What if he asks to see my work papers? They won't allow me in the country! I'm not going back – there's no way I'll let them re-spray me back to Bangkok!

'Ummmm, just here for a holiday . . .' I muttered.

'Yer outta work, are ya?' he repeated. The woman directly behind me couldn't contain her curiosity a second longer, and circled right around to have a look at me. Unimpressed, she just shrugged her shoulders and went back to her place in the queue.

'Ahhh, not exactly,' I replied. 'Well, I suppose I am . . .' But then without another word he passed me through.

As I passed through the gate into the terminal, I was spotted by a woman representing the Australian Film Festival.

'Michael Crawford?' she asked, rather tentatively.

'Yes.'

'Oh dear, I don't know how to put this!' she said, clearly upset.

I froze suddenly. It must be some terrible news from England – something has happened to Nan or the girls!

'What is it?' I said.

'I don't know how to say it . . .'

'Well, just tell me!'

'There's been a strike . . .' she said, 'and the awards have been cancelled. We've brought you all this way . . . and we don't know what to say . . . I'm so sorry to have inconvenienced you.'

I breathed an audible sigh: 'Well, there have been things in my life less forgivable than being flown first-class to Australia . . .'

'Well, I don't know how to make it up to you,' she said. 'What we'd like to do is send you north to Cairns, to the Barrier Reef, and you can have a holiday there for a week on us . . .'

'Well, that's very considerate,' I said. 'That'll handle my pain very nicely.'

That may have been one of the best holidays of my life. I flew to Cairns, and Jo-Anne flew from London to meet me there. In no time we made friends with the managers of the sailing club. They were wonderful people, and not averse to a 'stubby' (the little bottles of beer found in Australia). We were out on a sailboat everyday. Everyday, somewhere. It was paradise. What a great country Australia is. This was to be the first of many visits and the start of some lasting friendships.

Before returning to London we flew on to Bali, where Jo-Anne and I had our first experience of an earthquake – an enormous shock, that lasted an eternity of twenty seconds, destroying churches and other buildings around the countryside; its strength registered six on the Richter Scale.

I remember standing in front of our hotel when it struck, under an ancient tree in the garden. The girth of its trunk must have been seven or eight feet across, but still it shook and bent like a young sapling caught in the wind. I spotted Jo-Anne standing terrified on our third floor balcony, and all I could do was yell an encouraging 'Jump!' at her. JUMP?! Thank God she ignored me completely and survived to tell the tale. What do you suppose I had in mind? I mean, up to that moment we were getting on very well indeed.

After our return to London, I went to Los Angeles to talk to David Bell, the head of London Weekend Television, about a television special. (Bruce Forsyth was also there working out his own television special with him.) Jo-Anne came with me and we saw John Barry and his wife, Laurie, who were now living in California. We were their guests at a Sunday 'Super Bowl Party' at the home of Sammy Davis Jr. Jo-Anne and I were dazzled by all the familiar faces from the Hollywood television and film establishment in his living room – David Soul and

Michael Glaser from *Starsky and Hutch*, among others – in addition to old friends like Jackie and Joan Collins.

It was the very first time I met Sammy, arguably the most dynamic talent of his time. His extraordinary face made him look as if he'd spent his life walking into closed doors – which, of course, in a sense he had. But not even the experience of being both black and Jewish in the army had made him bitter, and the warmth of the man shone through his battered exterior. He treated racial problems with a humour that perhaps made people listen and learn more than they would have done otherwise. And, despite all his success and the glamorous company he kept, he continued to be as eager and enthusiastic as any fan.

Sammy's generosity was legendary and staggering, a fact to which I can personally attest. In the course of our conversation with him, Jo-Anne and I told him we were hoping to visit Las Vegas. He was delighted: Vegas was his kind of town. When are you going? he asked. Tomorrow, I told him. Leave it all to me, he said, and without another word he left the room to make a phone call. When he returned a few minutes later, he gave strict instructions; when you get there, go to Caesar's Palace, it's all taken care of.

The next morning, Jo-Anne and I flew to Las Vegas and went, as Sammy had instructed us, to Caesar's Palace, one of the best-known hotels on that colourful neon-lit street known as The Strip. We arrived to a rather perfunctory reception at the front desk – until I said my name, whereupon everybody snapped to immediate attention: 'Oh, Mr Davis called . . .' the manager said. Mr Davis called; that was our golden key to open every door in the city.

Sammy had booked us into a suite the size of Buckingham Palace. The room, we were told, was complimentary. (I'll never forget the place; there were mirrors everywhere, on every wall, even on the ceiling. When Jo-Anne and I woke in the morning and looked up, I thought the people in the room above me were staring at us.) Sammy had also booked us in to see all the top shows in Las Vegas – Ann-Margret, *Hallelujah Hollywood*, all the programmes at the MGM Grand – and each one was complimentary. And we had only just met him the previous day.

Michael Linnit called shortly after we returned to London to say that the Walt Disney company had sent a script for me to read, a comedy-thriller called *Condor Man*, a spoof of the James Bond films. I was excited by the prospect of working with the Disney studio, and especially with Charles Jarrott, the accomplished British director of *Anne of the Thousand Days* and *Mary, Queen of Scots* and that beautiful film *The Dove*. I was called back to Los Angeles by Charles a few weeks later to test for *Condor Man*. Against all the odds he chose me for the part.

Well, our European locations were sublime – Paris, Zermatt, Monte Carlo – and the film also meant a reunion after fifteen years with Oliver Reed.

I'm convinced that playing Ollie's brother in *The Jokers* was the only thing that saved me when the two of us filmed *Condor Man*. Even when the script was a little thin, Ollie was bound to give it his all. In this one he played the enemy, a murderous Russian agent, and remembering his penchant for living roles, I feared for my life.

For the first few weeks of production he remembered the good old days when we were 'brothers' and every now and then, for old times' sake, he'd give me one of his crushing bear hugs on the set.

Ollie had a few late evenings on location with *Condor*

Man. I recall the night he threw his tuxedo into the sea from the window of his Monte Carlo hotel room. (Our cost-conscious company manager rowed out at dawn in a little boat to catch it before it floated away and disappeared entirely into the Mediterranean.) That same night Ollie wandered into my room while I slept and, without a word and for no readily apparent reason, he turned all the beds except mine upside down. Then he turned around and left. 'Thank you, Ollie,' I said, as he went out the door. He always left me alone just as long as I said thank you.

Our leading lady had a slightly rougher time of it, and Ollie clearly felt her talents were unfortunately (for her) far below Ollie's high standards. I recall they had a scene together in a helicopter where she was supposed to be terrorised by him, but in take after take, she was entirely unable to project enough fear for Ollie's taste. So while they were in flight for a final shot, Ollie actually opened the 'copter door and threatened to throw her out. She had no doubt that he meant every word, and the glance of fear that crossed her face at that moment was very real.

As time went by Ollie grew ever deeper into his character. He always spoke with a Russian accent now. One night, on location in Switzerland, I sat by myself in our local hangout and saw a grim-looking Ollie sitting alone in a corner of the bar. He looked up and saw me, 'Come here and hafffff a dreeenk!' he said.

'It's okay, Ollie,' I said, 'I'm meeting someone . . .'

Again, he growled, 'Come here and haff a dreeenk!'

'No, Ollie, really . . .'

He rose majestically from his seat and squeezed me flat as easily as if I'd been a cheap accordion. 'Cummmmm here into Russian Embassy and haff a dreeenk, you little feathered fart!'

I'm not a complete fool; without another word I went

'into Russian Embassy' and had a drink with Ollie. Of course, from that moment on and throughout the rest of film production, I was known as 'Condorman, the Feathered Fart'. Thank God it didn't make the billboards.

CHAPTER 20

JUST AFTER I had finished filming *Condor Man* in late 1980, some blessed soul (I wish I could remember who it was) told me about a very exciting, very physically challenging production in New York. It was the new Cy Coleman musical called *Barnum*, based on the life of the flamboyant American circus showman. I asked Michael Linnit to look into it for me and he soon discovered that none other than Britain's very own high-flying impresario, Harold Fielding, was going to bring the show into the London Palladium but hadn't as yet decided on the casting.

If his name is unfamiliar to you, let me explain. Harold is an English theatrical institution on the grand scale; he has produced or managed just about everything and everybody during his illustrious career. He was a child prodigy on the violin and has an encyclopaedic knowledge of and abiding appreciation for music. In his time Harold has presided over everything from the Philadelphia Orchestra's very first trip to Europe to the burning of Atlanta six days a week in the London stage production of *Gone with the Wind* at Drury Lane.

Harold has done it all, and although he's a diminutive five-foot-two, his outsized reputation casts a long shadow before him. He is the last of the great London impresarios in the grand sense of the word. But he would also be the first to tell you that his secret weapon for success was his late wife Maisie, his greatest friend and confidante and his beloved silent partner, twenty-four hours a day, for almost forty years. He never made a decision without her.

Although Harold became a dear and loving friend, whom I find rather huggable, we certainly didn't start off that way. It took Harold quite a while to warm to me and from the start he made it crystal clear that he was the boss; he certainly didn't want some actor throwing his weight around, especially in the area of casting where, as the reader is already aware, I have a few opinions of my own and am rarely shy about expressing them.

'Casting, Mr Crawford, will be done by my director,' he informed me one afternoon in his best aren't-we-grand manner, so merrily at odds with his high-pitched voice. Then, quite ignoring me, he said, 'Mr Linnit, if your client wishes to attend [auditions], he may sit at the back of the theatre providing that's agreeable to my director.' Most happily, 'my director' was Peter Coe, who by now knew me very well indeed.

It was agreed in early discussions with Harold that Michael Linnit and I would first go to the States to have a look at the Broadway production. The tale Harold tells to anyone who'll listen is that I excitedly called him at the interval, so enthused that I couldn't wait for the final curtain, and shouted long-distance, 'When do we start? When do we start?' Harold loves that story, but there's not a bit of truth in it.

Of course the real story hasn't quite the flair of Harold's version. Michael and I flew to New York and went to the matinée at the St James Theater, a lovely old Broadway house perfectly suited to musical comedy, and much favoured by such musical giants as Rogers and Hammerstein in the past – it had been home to *Oklahoma!* and *The King and I*.

The afternoon was made immediately memorable by a run-in I had with a woman who would have made a great saloon bouncer. She stopped me before I had a toe inside the theatre. 'Whaddya got in there?' she yelled at me. 'Well, it's a tape recorder . . .' I couldn't finish the sentence. 'Yer not allowed to take recorders in there!' she blasted. 'I'm with the production actually . . .' I explained. 'I don't care what yer with,' she said, 'yer not allowed to take that in there!' By that time all traffic into the theatre had halted while everyone waited around for some burly New York cop to carry me off to the slammer. Fortunately the house manager succeeded in restoring order without any bloodshed.

Of course, she was within her rights; it's strictly forbidden to bring recorders into theatres during a performance and I'm a hundred per cent behind the strict enforcement of theatre rules, having more than once been blinded by camera flashes while attempting to walk the wire. But there had to be a better way of saying it. The public is, after all, doing us a favour when they come to see a show. (By the way, that same usherette came to London and saw *Barnum* at the Palladium. She even came backstage. 'Hey, you remember me?' she bellowed. 'I used to be . . .' 'Say no more,' I said. 'Of course I remember you – you've been indelibly engraved in my memory for years!')

The amazing *Barnum* company in New York, with its stars, Jim Dale and Glenn Close, was a joy to behold. After the matinée Michael Linnit placed a call to Harold from our hotel at about ten pm London time. 'Hello,' he said, 'is Mr Fielding there?' There was a long-distance echo as someone answered, 'No, solly, not heeyuh now. Who calling?' We knew immediately there would be no conversation with Harold that night.

It's always been an open secret among people who know him well that whenever Harold doesn't want to speak to someone, he pretends to be the Chinese houseboy and takes a message. His business day was over, he was tired and this is how he dealt with it. So we got the 'Chinese manservant' and decided we would speak to him at his office the next day. Michael told him then that we liked the show enormously, although we both had some minor reservations. We saw the show again a day or so later, before returning to London to start negotiations. Agreements were finally concluded in early January 1981, and I left for New York to train for three to four months with the Big Apple Circus School.

Led by its entrepreneurial artistic director Paul Binder, the Big Apple Circus has become a wonderful New York institution: a small one-ring circus, much closer in feel and presentation to the European circus tradition than to the huge Ringling Brothers and Barnum & Bailey three-ring spectacles.

I finally got to see one of those Barnum & Bailey extravaganzas at Madison Square Garden. It was an enormously complicated affair filled with spectacular animal acts – baboons on motorbikes, chimps on stilts, one bear who walked about precariously balanced on his hind paws, and another who bounced on a trampoline. Yet another bear stood on his great front paws twirling rings on his hind feet. I saw fifteen clowns jumping out of a tiny Volkswagen, and one unforgettable clown who walked out hilariously dressed as a giant mouth with an enormous tongue hanging out. There were camels, elephants, horses, zebras, sixteen stilt walkers, one of whom could do a double back-somersault, and a giant production number at the finale with colourful cardboard serpents that coiled high overhead, holding pretty girls in their mouths. The circus was a dazzling display of sound and colour images, and I'll never forget my first sight of it. While it bore no physical resemblance to our production, it gave me the rarest of opportunities to bear witness to that amazing breed of people known as circus performers. I met with them, talked with them, for days on end, and many are still my friends to this day. The love and dedication they have for their art is what I so desperately wanted to convey to our audiences.

My training schedule was such that after the first few weeks I could have qualified as a candidate for the monastic life. Still, I couldn't resist the occasional stolen pleasure of a late evening, like that of January 25, 1981 when I went to see my friend Jane Summerhays in the musical *Sugar Babies*. (The date remains in my memory because the American hostages had just been released from Iran and paid a triumphant visit to *Sugar Babies* that night. The curtain was half an hour late going up waiting for them, and when they finally arrived every man, woman and child in the theatre stood to cheer as they trooped into the stalls. It was a spine-tingling moment.)

Jane and I had known each other since 1978, when she came to London from New York to play the role of Sheila in *A Chorus Line*. Tall, about five-foot-ten, ebullient, like a young Rosalind Russell with a Lucille Ball laugh, she was very charming and quickly became a friend to all of us. My daughters had liked her very much indeed, and I had invited her to the cottage for Christmas that year. It took us months to recover from the experience!

Jane thought it might be fun to decorate the

Christmas tree American-style, with strings of cranberries. Trying to find cranberries in 1978 in England was not an easy task, but find them we did – boxes and boxes of them – and needles for the berry-stringing as well. (I could see the girls looking sideways at each other, remembering when I'd given them stinging nettles, and I was stricken with the sudden mental image of sending them home to their mother with pricked, bloody fingers and covered with berry stains. I wouldn't see them again for a month!)

We strung cranberries for hours and far into the evening. I think we were all secretly wishing we'd opted instead for a good old-fashioned English Christmas. We even tried to delegate some of the work to Nan, but it was far too intricate for her failing eyesight. But when it was finished, the tree looked wonderful; it was draped in garlands of berries – nothing else, just covered in berries.

I was delighted when Jane came to watch me rehearse at the circus school. The 'school' was simply space rented for teaching and practice purposes in a high school gymnasium on the edge of a rather dicey neighbourhood in Manhattan known as Spanish Harlem. When I walked in, I was half expecting to see lions and elephants and performing clowns; there was none of that, but the spirit and tradition of the circus and its extraordinarily dedicated performers was everywhere. Some of those circus professionals had trained Jim Dale and the New York and touring *Barnum* companies, and later on they trained some of the Australian company. My teacher and mentor was called Sacha. He had been a circus performer since he was a child in the old Czechoslovakia; he was a brilliant teacher and a bit of a tartar, who demanded total commitment, concentration, and dedication. Even when

I practised without him, I'd often spot him sitting in a corner of the gym watching my every move.

I swear I used to see him munching raw chicken legs. As I say, he was a hard man . . .

I was the oldest 'pupil' in the school. God knows, with all the aches and pains I suffered in the training, there were times when I felt certain I was the oldest man alive in New York. It was amazing and, I confess, slightly mortifying, to come to class and see mere toddlers, the tiniest of circus-family children, tumbling and doing tricks on the trampolines and trampettes, and performing awesome acrobatic feats. The circus people who practised with me weren't actually pupils at all; they were professionals from places like Las Vegas and other American cities come to train for a new show and to improve their skills. All I could do was stagger about, doing my best, while the kids tolerated the very elderly 'Uncle Michael' in their midst. I felt intolerably foolish at times, but the key to their respect was in the effort – to take the work seriously, to keep on trying to give your all. If you did that, you were accepted and embraced as family.

My day commenced with a warm-up that had been unquestionably designed by a world-class sadist: forty-five minutes of bending, stretching and pounding, followed by forty press-ups on a cold concrete floor has never been my idea of a pleasurable way to greet the dawn. It felt like doing time in an old East European labour camp – and Sacha was the guard dog.

Once the morning kinks had been ironed out, and provided my thirty-nine-year-old body was still mobile, the actual circus training would begin. No one else was learning to walk a wire, so I worked on my own, attempting to negotiate a wire that had been stretched two feet above the ground and twenty feet across that large, spartan room. To keep myself upright, I'd imagine that my body was somehow invisibly connected to the ceiling; my eyes would find one point directly ahead of me on which to focus at the end of the wire, and then I would walk, always with total concentration. Then the heart-thumping day arrived for me to step out into space onto a wire the thickness of a pencil and pulled taut almost to snapping point and now it was at a height of seven feet from the ground! That put my head approximately the height of an average ceiling. The only thing that ran through my head was the old circus adage Paul Binder told me: 'You miss the trick, you break your neck.'

I couldn't be convinced that I'd ever be able to walk those thirty loooooong feet across the room without falling or, at the very least, splitting myself in two. I stood there, shaking and talking to myself. Come on, you've got to go, just take two steps . . . go on and fall, but go, GO! I knew that unless I learned to walk the wire, I wouldn't be able to play the part. What better motivation for an actor to go up there and try again! My instincts were quite right, of course: I got halfway across and fell, grabbing the wire with my hands – that was the rule, always grab the wire on the way down, it breaks your fall – before I landed on the padded floor. I fell constantly, sometimes scuffing the wire and grazing an arm. Over time I gradually built up calluses on my hands and feet as a dancer does. Finally, after about three weeks of tentatively creeping across that wire, I gained a degree of confidence and skill. Later on I calculated the distance I travelled during the five years I played in *Barnum*. In all that time I must have walked about a thousand miles of wire – and I'm proud to say that, in all those years, I came off it only about eight times. And even on those shows I never failed to get across on the second attempt.

After I'd learned the wire, I wanted to try everything else just on the slightest chance that some of it could be used in the show. I learned to juggle, to do spins and tricks on the ropes, and to fly on the trapeze (even though I knew the insurance people would never allow it in the performance). The experience of jumping into space off a platform from a height three times that of the average room, while holding onto a swinging bar just twice the thickness of a conductor's baton is, to put it mildly, character-building. I could hear the ever-watchful Sacha shouting, 'Pike, pike!' (Pike? What in hell's he talking about? Pike? That's my grandmother's name!) 'Bend, Michael! Bring those legs up! Pike!' (Pike, hell! all I want to do is stay alive!)

Ultimately I was able to add some extra stunts to the London production; I slid down a rope from the roof of the theatre to the stage for my last entrance, and finished the first act with a stunt called 'the web'. This involved hanging by one arm from a rope, and swinging around with such force that I was lifted horizontal to the ground, spinning so fast that, if it weren't for my size 9 shoes, my trousers would have shot straight off the end of my legs and ended up in the circle. The result of this spectacular trick was that for the first two months of our run I usually threw up during the interval at every performance. But it made a great close to Act 1.

Beyond all else my one great personal ambition was to be able to ride the unicycle. As you may remember, bikes have always been my special passion ever since Herne Hill and Sheerness. I used to watch the circus folk on their giant unicycles, balancing the children on their shoulders; it all looked so fantastic that I was determined to learn that too.

I can unequivocally attest to the fact that a giant wheel does not stay naturally or comfortably ensconced under the crotch. In order to ride it, the upper part of the body must remain rigid while the lower portion keeps moving about in the often vain effort to maintain stability. Moving, now backwards, now forwards, constantly attempting to stay steady, you try to keep the cycle under control, but the great wheel has a mind all its own and will suddenly lurch forward and completely run away with you. Then, just as suddenly, as you gain a bit of balance you're flung backwards, while the saddle pushes your private parts so far up your backside, the thought crosses your mind that you've definitely seen the last of them.

My circus skills were never outstanding, but I became reasonably proficient at several of them. Beyond that I learned to present those skills with a great sense of pride, given as a special personal gift to the audience. That's the real spirit of the circus.

Our company was a young, fresh, hard-working family of artists. The show was full of verve, a kaleidoscope of colour and music and the kind of spectacular stunt work I love to do. Yet from the very beginning of rehearsals and until we opened in our first preview in May of 1981, I was never sure that any of us was going to survive the emotional circus going on behind the scenes.

The American team that created *Barnum* on Broadway was made up of very experienced men who knew each other well. Cy Coleman, the composer, was a mainstay of Broadway and the popular music charts, writing hit songs for top stars like Frank Sinatra and Shirley MacLaine. He'd already been involved with shows like *Sweet Charity* and *I Love My Wife*. Michael Stewart, the lyricist, had won honours as librettist of such great hits as *Bye Bye, Birdie* and *Hello Dolly!* The show's co-author was Mark Bramble, who later worked again with Michael Stewart on *Forty-Second Street.* It was a very high-powered group and I was very enthusiastic about the opportunity to join the team.

But I'm not so sure the feeling was entirely mutual. While I was training at the Circus School, I worked with Cy Coleman on some of the difficult high-speed, tongue-tripping songs in the show. I know I sang at least at the same pace as Jim Dale had done on the album, but Cy was fairly critical of my performance in those early sessions and I felt a little demoralised. The Americans were always polite, but it was obvious they were generally not thrilled with what they saw as happening to their show.

A key ingredient in the New York creative team was missing entirely from our London rehearsals: Joe Layton, the multi-talented director/choreographer who had directed the original production. Joe had also worked with some of the other members of the American team in the past, and was much respected and entirely trusted by each of them. Other commitments had prevented him from accepting the London assignment, which was why Peter Coe had been appointed our director.

As so much had to be done with movement and choreographic styling (never Peter's main forte), Buddy Schwab came from New York to work on the production. Buddy is an American dancer-choreographer who had been Joe Layton's assistant on *Barnum* in New York, and over the years would work on the show in London, Manchester, Australia, and countless other countries around the world. I loved him. Buddy was the soul of encouragement and always great fun to be around. He was a dear old hoofer, a real character. A bit highly strung and forever puffing on a

Marlboro, his favourite response to absolutely everything was 'I know' (pronounced 'Eye-grnohhh'). Like Peter Lorre with a sinus condition. 'Buddy,' I'd say to him, 'I shouldn't have done thus-and-so . . .'

'I know,' he'd answer.

'What?'

'I know,' he'd say, 'I know you know you shouldn't have done thus-and-so. But you did.'

'Yes,' I said.

'Right,' he'd say, 'I know.'

It was apparent almost from the beginning that there were going to be major differences in concept between Peter and New York. Peter had strong opinions about absolutely everything and he was never one to tolerate that which he considered to be flippant. The Americans, in turn, seemed to find him intractable and condescending. Peter felt that *Barnum* in New York was just that little bit too light, too 'throwaway'.

Beyond that, I had seen some very minor things in New York that I felt we might do differently in London. For one thing I wanted more of a relationship established between Mr and Mrs Barnum than I saw in New York. I wanted a relationship that conveyed a deeper partnership between the two very disparate lead characters; the flamboyant, head-in-the-clouds Barnum and his loving, pragmatic, and no-nonsense wife. I thought that Mrs Barnum's death near the end of the show lacked sufficient emotion in the Broadway production; I wanted the audience to really miss the lady in our London production.

The Americans disagreed with virtually every idea Peter or I had, and it was extremely difficult to contest the logic of their basic argument. Why in hell should we change anything for London on the word of relatively unknown Englishmen, when the show is already a hit in

New York? (If it ain't broke, don't fix it!)

The Americans knew that Peter had directed *Oliver!* in 1961 – his peak career year, in fact, when he had three hits (*Oliver!*, *The World of Susie Wong* and *The Miracle Worker*) running simultaneously in the West End – but that was twenty years before, and they were interested in present successes, not past glories. So, very early on, we were given to understand that we were dealing with their 'Bible' and even the most minute changes would be fought tooth and nail. They were as one in not wanting us to tinker with the smallest portion of the Broadway version of *Barnum*. There were great battles back in England whenever there was any attempt to change the odd word, often involving lengthy angry transatlantic telephone calls, and equally indignant correspondence. In fact, at one point, legal action was threatened.

The acrimony was, in my view, threatening to envelop the entire company by the night of our opening preview in London. Those of us in the British production felt that because the New York management was impossibly inflexible in its attitude, our production was being needlessly and rather aggressively undermined. Adding to my own stress were the problems in my private life. Jo-Anne and I had parted not long before. She wanted marriage, and I didn't. Since my break-up with Gabrielle – no matter that I may have loved again – I hadn't reached a point when I felt confident enough to remarry. (Actually, I've done more than enough to further that institution. Almost every woman I've been involved with gets married to someone else within a matter of months of our breaking up. And Jo-Anne was no exception. She married shortly after we parted, lives happily in Australia, and remains my dear friend to this day.)

I had barely eaten or slept for some three days before the opening preview and was in a state of near-collapse.

That night, as I sat in my dressing room I suddenly found myself unable to speak; my head went down with a thud, hitting the coffee table – I must for the first time in my life have had a blackout. The doctor was called and he ordered me to the hospital. Reluctantly, I was half-carried out of the theatre with Harold holding me firmly by one arm. 'Now, Michael,' he kept whispering, 'don't wobble as you go out. We don't want to upset the company . . .' As far as I can recall, he was the one doing most of the wobbling, although I could hardly blame him since he was the one who had to call off that first preview performance.

I was taken to hospital, given something to help me sleep and awoke hours later feeling remarkably peaceful. After all the arguments and anxieties of the past weeks, it was so marvellously quiet that, for a brief moment, I actually thought I might be in heaven, until a nurse brought me some hospital soup. I wanted desperately to get back to rehearsals, but it took about two days before I felt well enough to leave – and then, as always, I did it my way. I got up, got dressed, and checked myself out by climbing through my opened ground-floor hospital window. I've often wondered who paid the bill.

Perhaps my escape had been a bit too sudden, because my head was still swimming from the sleeping pills when I got to the theatre. The dress rehearsal had started just as I arrived and I could hear my understudy saying, 'Barnum's the name . . . P. T. Barnum . . .' I even surprised myself by yelling, 'Oh, no you're not!' at the startled company, as I walked out on stage and pushed him aside: 'Barnum's *my* name . . .!' There was silence from the front of house where the stunned management people sat, rooted to their seats in disbelief. I looked as if I'd just escaped from Colditz, but we began the rehearsal all over again. Our leading lady, Deborah Grant, hung onto me throughout the rehearsal, determined to make sure I didn't decide to walk the wire. If I had, I'm sure I would have been back in hospital permanently.

The next morning Harold organised a press call, to show that I was back – up and running. The photos were surely some of the worst that I've ever seen of myself! But press calls are vital to a show.

When our delayed first preview night finally materialised, the Americans trooped in off the New York flight, jet-lagged and weary. The audience response was really good, but word filtered backstage that Michael Stewart thought the show was still too slow and had left at the interval. At the curtain, however, when two thousand eight hundred people at the Palladium rose to their feet cheering and shouting, the British producers and management turned to the Americans sitting behind them. The Americans smiled and, in a sporting gesture, they bowed in unison to their British counterparts implying, yes, maybe we were wrong after all.

We were still not altogether out of the woods, though. The show hadn't had much of an advance sale. The name *Barnum* wasn't exactly a household word in England, and when you mentioned 'circus', a lot of people were simply turned off.

But then came our opening, and a set of rave reviews. And while it didn't happen overnight, the show soon took off; new phones had to be installed in the Palladium box office to keep up with the booking.

We played to packed houses for two years, the first straight musical comedy ever to run at that huge theatre for such a length of time. Audiences came from all over, even from 10 Downing Street – Margaret Thatcher and her family were enthusiastic fans – and more than a million people saw the show in the first year alone. The lavish praise from the press was matched by that from our peers. I shall never forget Robert Morley's remark that, in fifty years in the theatre, he had never seen anything like *Barnum*. The success of the British production was especially gratifying to me in that it vindicated Peter Coe, who had fought for his ideas against substantial resistance.

I was nominated for an Olivier award for *Barnum*, one of the great thrills of my life. Robert Morley presented the award. After reading out the name of all the nominees for Best Actor, he said, in a very kindly and flattering gesture, 'Obviously, there's no contest this year, the winner is Michael Crawford.' He didn't even open the envelope.

The only thing in my mind was the memory of the night I 'won' – and lost – the British Film Academy 'Best Newcomer' Award. My God, I thought, not again!

'Michael Crawford is the winner . . .' Mr Morley repeated. Reluctantly, I walked up to the stage, feeling uncomfortable for myself and the other performers.

'I really think . . . well, to ease my mind, Mr Morley,' I said to him, 'would you open the envelope?'

'There's no need!'

'Please open it.'

Eventually I had to take it from him and open it myself.

'There,' he said, 'what did I tell you?'

The audience was laughing all the while. They must have thought it was a pre-planned routine. But when I made my way back to the table, I found I was drenched in a cold sweat.

It didn't take long for me to discover that my daily commute between the cottage and the theatre was going to be a killer. I had to find a place closer to London. I settled on a house in Islington shortly thereafter and, while it was fine as it was, I had my own ideas for renovation. I sought the advice of some designers I'd dealt with a few years earlier when they'd been working on a promotion for *TV Times* wherein various celebrities had a 'dream room' designed to their specification – a bath with jacuzzi, a new bedroom, that sort of thing – to be installed in their homes later on, if they desired.

I had thought it a great idea and designed a garage as a combination workshop and workout area at the cottage.

I asked the company officials who had organised the original promotions whether they'd ever thought of doing an entire house. No, they said, but what a good idea. How incredibly wrong we all were.

The company designer and his helpers filled my head with new idea after new idea (well, that was their job after all) until the day came when I found myself standing in the cellar with every floor above me partially removed, staring straight up through four storeys to the bright blue sky.

Months passed, and while the deadline for being photographed in my completed 'dream house' hovered, the builders had to work Saturdays and Sundays to complete the job, which prompted a court order from my neighbours who objected to the noise. The order prohibited the use of hammers and anything mechanical at the weekend. I was afraid to whisk an egg on Sunday morning lest I be carted off to prison.

The house was finished eventually. I stayed on for a couple of years in Islington, but I loathed it. It wasn't a home at all; it was far too *Homes and Gardens* for me – beautifully decorated but the atmosphere was like that of a show home. I never once used the upstairs, and I knew I would never feel comfortable there.

It was through my friend Sue Barbour (a mainstay, with her father, Peter, of the *Barnum* company) that I found the flat I had always wanted. She knew how much I hated the Islington house and, through her real-estate contacts, she heard about a place on the docks in Wapping. I had a special feeling about the place from the first; it was where I wanted to be – right on the water and the Thames of my childhood memories.

In 1986 Wapping was the site of an angry industrial war, one of the worst in history, which raged for months between the newspaper unions and Rupert Murdoch. It was a sad and often scary commute, passing by the long lines of strikers. The weekends were the most difficult. It had become traditional on Saturday nights for running pitched battles to break out between the strikers, the police, and the usual collection of anarchists who turn up at every public event with a mind to incite others to physical violence. The streets were completely blocked off at night, and most residents found getting home a circuitous and unnerving proposition.

It took me weeks to discover my own route, and I learned never to take my car after the experience of driving home one evening and having a brick hurled at me. My solution was to travel by cab along a convoluted back way that delivered me behind the scene of the demonstrations. One Saturday night I arrived home from the theatre carrying all the weekend shopping – the joint, potatoes, bread, my vegetables, everything. Laden with five Marks & Spencer bags and my sports bag slung over my shoulder, I put on my glasses and a baseball cap, hoisted the groceries, and climbed out of the cab to face the marchers. They were out by the thousands that night, and the mood was less than hospitable. 'Will you be alright, mate?' the driver asked.

'Oh yes,' I said, 'I'll be fine.'

But it was obvious I had only one option open; I had to join the march, and I did just that, loudly taking up the chant as we marched – 'Murdoch Out!' – jostled and pushed along with the thousands of other demonstrators. I really need this, I thought; eight shows a week and I have to march three-quarters of a mile around Wapping on a Saturday night just to get home. I could see my building in the distance. The marchers started to fan out, moving off in a circle. This was my chance to branch off in another direction, hopefully without being noticed. But the burly gentleman next to me saw me turn off. 'Where you going, mate?' he called after me.

'I'm setting up a field kitchen down to the right here,' I explained, 'to make some sandwiches for everyone . . .' and I showed him the weekend shopping.

'Good on ya, son,' he shouted. 'Good on ya.'

'Good on you too,' I shouted back '. . . I'll see you later.' I waved, did a right wheel and ran like hell.

The show had been running for some time when, one night in 1982, the young championship figure skaters Jayne Torvill and Christopher Dean came to see *Barnum*. They were England's idols of the moment; they had just won the World Championships and their amateur careers were now at a peak. Chris and Jayne came round to my dressing room afterwards, along with their great friend and trainer Betty Callaway, to talk about the act they hoped to put together. They were in the midst of creating a new routine for the upcoming competitions and had already decided on a circus theme. I suggested if they wanted to use music solely from *Barnum*, our music director, Mike Reed, might perhaps arrange something for them. Tell us the sequences you'd like, I told them – comedy, romance, etc – and how you would like to mix and blend them. Up to that time skaters in England had never had musical arrangements specifically produced for their needs. They usually had to use spliced taped musical material; it often sounded awkwardly amateurish and disjointed.

Our backstage chat generated a lot of ideas and enthusiastic planning. The team – Chris, Jayne, Betty Callaway and myself – first worked out the sequences for the routine, starting with a fair amount of excitement and comedy, segueing into romance, and ending with a spectacular 'big finish'. Mike Reed cleverly arranged the music to reflect this and recorded it with musicians who'd agreed to work on the project for a shoestring because Chris and Jayne were wonderful young people, competing in an amateur event and representing Great Britain to the world. It was a combination that drew the maximum effort, care and love from everyone involved.

Jayne and Chris would come to watch the company's warm-up at the Palladium, and I attended some of their training sessions, working with them on certain aspects of the circus routine such as mime and tumbling, and how to do things with hats as props and generally assisting in any way I could, artistically and choreographically.

When I finished my run at the Palladium in March 1983, I went to New York on business and then flew directly to Helsinki for the World Figure Skating Championships. Betty Callaway, myself and those talented youngsters spent happy hours there together at practice sessions. I watched Chris and Jayne rehearse the *Barnum on Ice* routine until it was as near to perfection as they could make it. I'll never forget the euphoria of that glorious night of the championship when they went on to win the competition again with straight sixes – perfect marks.

In the course of our time together we discussed their plans for the future. Once they decided to turn professional they were going to need an agent, accountants and lawyers. I offered advice where I could, and I suggested that instead of going to a large sports agency, I would instead introduce them to Michael Linnit, where maybe they'd get more attention. I planned to take a year off to work with the team on their next routine and, at about the same time, Buddy Schwab and I had an offer to do *Barnum* in Italy. Buddy would stage the show and, for the first time in my career, I would direct. The timing of that project seemed to be heaven-sent, so well did it synchronise with Chris and Jayne's practice schedules.

I was about to embark on an exciting new adventure – or so I thought. But as my mother used to say, 'What is to be, might well not be.'

Or something like that.

CHAPTER 21

WHEN BUDDY SCHWAB and I flew to Rome in September 1983, my image of Italian theatre was based solely on the success of their tailoring. I had been lulled into a false sense of security by the certainty that an Italian design guaranteed an admirable fit on a pair of trousers, and for some reason I felt equally certain that casting and directing an Italian stage production would be an unqualified joy. But within half an hour of our arrival at a padlocked theatre and the vain attempt to pick our way through eight and a half tons of scaffolding to get inside, we began to have some niggling doubts about the venture. However, after a few hours more, when I was beginning to feel like a minor comic character in some mad Italian opera, I seriously started to contemplate a renewed attempt at enlistment in the RAF.

Auditions were scheduled to begin at ten o'clock one sunny Monday morning. There was an immediate minor hitch in the proceedings when we discovered that the set from the previous show was still standing. Management insisted that before auditions could begin, the set had to be dismantled there and then. 'But I thought that was being done overnight,' I said.

'No, prrroblem,' was the answer. 'Eeess no prrroblem at all . . . We do theees now, you cuma back at lunch time. Why don't you go forra walk. You cuma back, and we be rrready for audition!'

I looked at Buddy and said, 'Well, if they seriously think they can strike that set in less than two hours, then this is going to be absolutely the place to work!'

'I know,' said Buddy, lighting his fourteenth Marlboro since breakfast. I was very impressed and, ever the optimist, we strolled out of the theatre and down the road to have a look at some ancient Roman ruin or other.

We returned two hours later expecting to see a bare stage and a dazzling display of Italian technical efficiency, and found instead one lonely Italian stagehand armed with a hammer, gazing at exactly what we had looked at two hours since. 'Ai, yeesss . . .' he mumbled to himself, 'there is theees . . . and there is theees . . .'

Out of nowhere our very amiable producer appeared on the scene. 'We are not quite ready for you yet!' he cheerfully explained. 'Why don't we go and have a beeyouteeful lunch . . . I take you to lunch my fren . . . Then we come back, it will be gone, and thena we start the audition!'

'But where are the artists wanting to audition?' I asked, thoroughly bewildered by now. 'We'll be glad to see them in the lobby, we need to be doing *something* . . . we're only here for two or three days.'

'Ah, my frens,' he said, 'you cast in no time! Two, three days be enough for casting.'

And so we went off and had a wonderful meal and our producer proved himself a most convivial host, and after our 'beeyouteeful lunch' we returned and found there were now three men pondering the still unstruck set, trying to decide what should be done.

'Well,' I said, 'it looks as if we've lost the day, doesn't it . . .'

We left the theatre that evening certain that everything would be better tomorrow, and dined again with management. (I'll say this for the experience: we were always kept well fed.) But when we arrived at the theatre the next morning, we found the set only half down and layers of dust everywhere.

It took another two and half days for the stage to be cleared and in that time I hadn't seen one artist who would do for any kind of role in the production; either an actor had a great voice for the role of the ring master, but had only one leg (I swear it!), decidedly one fewer than is needed to walk a wire with any real alacrity; or he had a good speaking voice, but couldn't sing a note; or he (or she) could dance and do all sorts of tricks, but could barely speak (or sing) a line. We hadn't even met our star yet, a well-known Italian pop singer.

Our producer, meanwhile, tried to put the best face on things and held a gala reception to introduce me to the press. It was less than successful because none of them spoke English and my Italian is strictly confined to the translation of restaurant menus. I remember nodding a great deal and lapsing into an occasional gracious 'gracias', dipping into my limited Spanish on the principle that if I couldn't be Italian, I'd try to be as Mediterranean as possible and hope that would do. It was then that I was finally introduced to our star, a Cliff Richard lookalike, young, very handsome-looking, and with a good voice. I felt it might be necessary to develop the humility of the Barnum character which I thought essential to make him endearing but, with work, I thought he would do very well.

I returned to England, then back to Rome again; the

producer even dragged us to Milan for a few days in an attempt to pull a cast together. Circus people arrived from every corner of the European continent to audition for this production. Most of them would only work if their entire family was cast, but usually half the family couldn't sing, or they were too young, or too old, or too large, or too grotesque. They were all fabulous characters, mind you, but far better suited to a Fellini film than a Broadway musical.

One of the most difficult roles to cast was that of Joyce Heth, a black woman who was supposed to have been one hundred and sixty years old and George Washington's nurse – one of the great Barnum 'cons'. We were desperate to find a black woman with a great voice somewhere in the city of Milan. By this time our producer was reduced to dragging people in off the street to sing for me. Then suddenly, the day was saved. They found about forty black singers, men and women, who spoke both Italian and English as well. They did part of their routine singing spirituals for me. Everyone was so delighted, so moved, so thrilled – so relieved – to think we'd finally found someone in Milan who could actually sing. Up to that moment I'd begun to suspect that every singer in the city had been locked away for safe keeping at La Scala.

When the group finished, our applause was thunderous – even the crew backstage put down their hammers long enough to clap. In the end I chose four out of the forty to finish our circus cast. Our producer was thrilled: 'Ah, Meester Crawforttt, you are soooo thorrrough! We knew you are soooo correct!' and he stood by my side as we started to negotiate terms with the group.

I said to the troupe leader, 'I'd like to cast this lady and that lady there, and you, and if it's possible we'll have one other as well.'

'Well, that's not possible,' he said. 'The group cannot go on without me.'

'Well, if there's a problem,' I said, 'I mean, if we have to lose you, we can take this other man . . .'

'No,' he said, 'you can't have him, he's essential to our singing group . . .'

'Ah, I understand,' I said. 'Fine, then we'll take the two ladies . . .'

'No, no,' he said, 'because this lady is married to one of our members and she cannot leave . . .'

'Well, what about this lady here, I mean, for the role of Joyce Heth . . .'

'No, you see, it impossible,' he said. 'We're only in Italy for two days.'

'You're WHAT . . . ?'

'Well, you see,' he said, 'this gentleman [he indicated our producer] asked us to come in and sing for you.' And they had done just that, apparently having not the slightest knowledge of why they were auditioning or for what. They were only in Italy for two days as part of a round-the-world goodwill concert tour from the island of St Lucia, in the West Indies.

'You mean, we've spent the entire afternoon . . .' I said to the producer, 'are you telling me we've wasted four weeks of our lives going backwards and forwards . . .' Words failed me. I was beginning to froth at the mouth.

'I know,' echoed Buddy, who was now smoking two Marlboros at once.

'No, no, no, everytheeeng will be fine,' he said. 'You wait!'

We travelled back to Rome for a last attempt at casting our Jenny Lind, and were sent two possible candidates to audition for the role. One was the producer's girlfriend. By no stretch of the imagination was there the remotest possibility of that lady being cast either as Mrs Barnum (her first choice) or Jenny Lind. I gave her an hour's audition in order to give her every opportunity, mostly to keep our producer happy. Still he was a good sport about it: he thought it was a great idea right up to the end when he gracefully conceded defeat. ('Eye duhn't waaant to interveeer . . .')

One of the last to audition was a quite beautiful woman who couldn't reach most of the notes and as far as I could see didn't have much to offer in the acting side, but had the finest pair of breasts I'd seen since the chicken cacciatore platter at Luigi's buffet display in the lunch hour. When I said no to this lady, I turned to hear a voice from the back of the theatre: 'Wait a mineeet,' it said, 'I duhn't agrreee . . .' This time, it was our leading man, who had suddenly decided to contribute a lira's worth of his opinion to the production, and in his opinion she was 'magnifico'. When next I caught sight of our young hero, he was up in the circle with the lady. I can't actually swear to what they were doing up there, but there was definitely a little movement in the third and fourth rows of seats. It was at precisely that moment that I knew without a doubt I was in the wrong production, at the wrong theatre, in the wrong country, at the wrong time of my life – and in no way did I have the patience to be a director. I went back to the hotel, had a long, long discussion with Buddy, who was now up to two packets of cigarettes a day. 'I can't do it Buddy, I honestly cannot do it.' 'I know,' he said, sympathetically. I then packed my bags, went straight to the airport and got on a plane. Buddy stayed on, directing as well as staging the show. They ended up with a terrific cast and the production was an enormous success. My Italian experience taught me that over there they may make it look as if confusion reigns, but that's just a question of style. In reality they have everything under control.

I related my Italian adventures to Michael Linnit when I returned to London, only to be told that Torvill and Dean had decided to create another kind of routine, and that they would be working alone. It was disappointing because I'd arranged my whole year around Italy and directing *Barnum* in order to enable me to work with Chris and Jayne. Slowly, the twice-a-day phone call relationship with Michael Linnit began to disengage; our phone calls became less and less frequent, and Michael became more and more involved with the skaters' careers. In the end, he wrote me a letter suggesting a parting of the ways.

So I lost my agent as well as a year of my professional life. I was particularly sad because Michael and I had enjoyed a fine ten-year relationship.

Chris and Jayne remained dear friends and I cherish those wonderful months we spent working together, watching their amateur career climb to its magnificent climax. I'm pleased to note that they were there in the theatre along with Michael Linnit, sharing a rather glorious night of my own, the Broadway opening of *The Phantom of the Opera*.

I spent the last months of 1983 winding down at the cottage, mainly with Nan, who had become increasingly frail, although she remained determinedly feisty to the end of her days. You wouldn't want to tangle with her over Margaret Thatcher. Oh boy. Margaret Thatcher couldn't do anything right, not even if she'd visited the cottage in person to tell Nan she'd won the pools.

But beyond caring for her, I could barely rouse myself from the persistent malaise that was dogging my career. I felt paralysed, seemingly incapable of taking any kind of action. It's little understood outside our profession that setting up work projects often requires six months or more. It all takes time – whether someone is writing a series or producing a play – and the actor is forced to live through endless periods of time waiting for the phone to ring. I had no work, nothing was happening, and I was beset by the actor's usual niggling doubts about his self-worth and self-imposed paranoia. I seriously began to question whether I would ever work again. My God, I thought, this is really the end. I'm even too old for an Air Force desk job.

Then suddenly (and quite improbably) I was offered the opportunity to compere a new game show imported from America called *The Price is Right*. I had anxieties about doing something so far removed from anything I'd ever done before, but I honestly felt I was on the brink, and that I needed to stand up and perform again, no matter in what. Negotiations went on for weeks and the deal was finally just about set. I had the video tapes sent to me from America and I ran them constantly, practically memorising what they called their 'Bible', a weighty tome that listed all the rules and information one must attend to on that show. It was down to the wire, four days before Christmas – I'll never forget the day, or the lady I was with, a dear old friend from Liverpool called Wendy.

I told her what I was going to do. She listened to me gravely and then said, 'You can't do it, luv. You can't do it.' I suppose I was waiting for someone to say that to me.

'You know, you're right,' I told her, 'I can't. It's not what I want at all,' and even at that late date, I knew I had to turn it down.

Life seems to turn on just such tiny moments.

It's odd remembering that I was within a few days of completely changing the direction of my life and career. If I had taken the job, I doubt I would have continued to work as an actor – and to think what I would have missed!

Then I had the idea of doing *Barnum* again – but this time, I thought, do it for television.

I suppose it might have been perceived as a backward step returning to *Barnum* – but I believe in the old adage ' a working actor is better than a starving one'. By putting *Barnum* on television, we would be producing a permanent record of a performance, something people on the stage rarely have the opportunity to do. I put the idea to Harold Fielding and he unhesitatingly agreed to it. I am forever indebted to him for taking the risk and unknowingly helping me to restore my belief in myself.

An Australian company already owned the video rights to *Barnum* and it was Harold's thought to take the new production away from London while he did what he could to acquire broadcast rights. We would meanwhile reopen the old Manchester Opera House, which had been shut in 1978 after serving for a while as a bingo hall. I think I only agreed to his plan because I knew it meant that at the end of the run we could produce the television show. I never dreamed what a grand time that city had in store for us all.

While I was in Italy my mind would often wander back to the cottage, which had become a haven of family happiness. There had been a gradual healing in my relationship with Gabrielle over the years. We were now friends, and she would often come down and stay at the cottage with me and the girls, and also bring along Sam and Harry, her two lovely boys from her new relationship. They were now part of a wider and very happy family that also included an Irish setter called Starsky. On summer Sundays there was always a barbecue. The calm centre of the fun, as ever, was Nan. I can picture her now, sitting with her legs dangling in the pool, or lying on a swing-bed in the garden, gently swaying, her voice meandering out from under her wide-brimmed sun hat, as she contentedly sang the odd line from 'Sweet Rose of Tralee' or 'Galway Bay'. Every evening she'd have to be inside at six-thirty on the dot in order to watch *Crossroads*, and every two weeks the priest would come round to give her communion.

My favourite new toy was a bright red ride-on lawn mower. Nan desperately wanted to have a go on it, and I treasure some photos I took of her chugging along, her white stick balanced across the handlebars and Starsky running in circles around her, making sure she didn't drive into the pool.

On arriving back from Italy, I found that Nan had taken to her bed. Phyllis, who looked after her so caringly, hadn't wanted to worry me while I was away, but there definitely seemed to be something wrong with Nan. I could see she was very tired now. There was no fight left in her at all. All the frustrations of rheumatism and the wheelchair and her blindness had quite exhausted this amazing and resilient ninety-nine-year-old lady.

The doctor had recommended she go into hospital for tests, so I arranged to take her. When she was registering, they asked her when she was last in hospital. We worked out it had been in 1898!

She was put in a little room off the main ward, and there we stayed for the next three weeks. I'd drive down at seven in the morning and leave at eight at night. In between I'd tell her some of the stories I remembered that she'd told me as a child, tales of her beloved Ireland, of poets and princesses. Then she'd say to me, 'You must sing, Michael, you must sing,' and very,

very, quietly I'd sing some of the old Irish folk songs.

We had taken a last grand trip together down to Sheerness the year before. I had hired a Winnebago van to accommodate her wheelchair and I brought along a few close friends, Stu and Sue Carrie, who had been so kind through the years, and lovely Jane Watts from *Barnum*. Like a queen travelling in her own private coach with all her courtiers about her, Nan set out to visit that special part of England we called home. She said she wanted to have 'a look round' Sheppey; it had been years since she'd been back there. Her sight was quite gone by now – or only very misty – so I talked the sights to her and described the passing scenery and all the changes that had been made since she'd seen it last.

'Do you remember the Black Prince,' I asked her, 'and the road through the hills and across the top of Dartford?' Of course; she knew it all. I tried to explain that we didn't use the old route anymore; there was now a six-lane motorway bypassing it all. She listened intently and tried to imagine the changes, but it was clear that she wanted to go home the old way. So I changed direction and got stuck, of course, in interminable traffic, but it was worth all the wait. Her face lit up; she could actually feel the difference. 'We're going past the railway lines now,' I told her, and she knew it. Then over the bridge, and we were on the Island. She held her head tipped backwards, as the blind sometimes do, as if she could 'see' it all by sniffing the air. Her home, and all her life. It hurt my heart to watch her.

We stopped in at the home of my old boyhood friend Tony Clayton and his charming wife, Margaret. He and I had lost touch over the years, during which time he had become a teacher. We took lots of photos and waxed lyrical about haystacking and hills and long-ago adventures, and for just a moment we were kids all over again.

After the visit to Tony we drove to the site of Nan's old home in the Crescent. Sydney House sat there still, but the welcoming look of those two big front bay windows was gone now, quite hidden behind hedges grown four feet higher than when I saw them last. And the house was painted grey and white, no longer the pale green and cream that I remember and which seemed just right to me: the perfect colours for that seaside island.

I got out of the van and walked past the place. I could see a woman inside watching us from behind one finger-lifted curtain. She finally opened the door and stepped outside: we were obviously there for a reason. 'Is there something you wanted?' she asked.

I introduced myself and Nan and told her we used to live there. 'This was my Nan's place,' I told her, 'but it's always been my favourite house.'

'We've made some changes,' she told me, a little apologetically, and very kindly invited us in.

'I don't think so, no,' I said. 'It's very kind of you, but no.' I told her we didn't want to intrude. (Only half the truth, I didn't want to see the changes.) We simply wanted to visit the place again and feel the atmosphere, I told her, and we looked for a little brick wall I'd built for Nan; it was almost a relief to see that that small relic of the past hadn't vanished along with everything else. (I went back to see it again only recently; my brick wall is still standing there.)

After three weeks in Bedford Hospital they let me take Nan home. When she returned I remember her saying, as I got her out of the car, 'I didn't think I'd be coming back here.' It sounded so mournful. 'I thought I was ready to go,' she said, almost as though she was disappointed to see the cottage again. I was selfishly so saddened to hear that; I suppose that in my heart I knew she was simply echoing my fears.

I can still recall the sharp feel of Nan's thin shoulders when I carried her, lifting her off the bed to take her to the bathroom. She was like a baby, helpless in my arms, and it occurred to me then that I was doing for her what she had done for me when I was a baby.

In the end I believe she simply willed herself back into hospital. She'd only been home a few weeks when I took her back again for the very last time.

Nan died on the morning of August 20, 1984. Ninety-nine years old. My best friend. She was clear and in control almost to the end.

I don't know why I was still with her when she died. With rehearsals starting the next day I would normally have left early in the evening. Visitors and family had stood vigil most of the afternoon, but after everyone left in the evening, I lingered on. I sat in the armchair next to her bed, holding her hand, watching her and praying, as she lay there unconscious. I was just dropping off to sleep when she suddenly squeezed my hand; I opened my eyes, and she died. It was just as peaceful as that, the kind of death we all pray for—with serenity, and a hand to hold.

All these years later I still can't bear to think about those last moments. I keep on hoping that I did enough for her.

I took the ring she always wore off her finger: she called it her wedding ring, a little silver band decorated with a blue enamelled Maltese cross. (Was it Charlie's or Mont's? I'd forgotten to ask her.) I remember I had to sign a form to take it with me. 'Sorry, Mr Crawford, hospital regulations, y'know.' I gave Nan's rosaries to Emma and Lucy: Nan was a loving friend to both of them and they had delighted in having long, secret, female chats together. I think the girls enjoyed sharing their confidences with her and hearing all the stories she used to tell about what their father did 'when he was your age . . .' Children love that sort of thing. I was never allowed to know what the conversations were about; I suspect some of them were of the never-trust-a-man variety.

Later on, when I went through her things, I found two hundred pounds she'd squirrelled away in all the purses she loved to save. I put the money into 'The Edith Pike Trust Fund'. I want her name kept alive. One day, when there's enough, there will be a plaque in a hospital room or ward identifying it as having been given 'In loving memory of Edith Pike'. Even better, it might just simply say 'Nan's Room'.

Chapter 22

It's a real hardship for performers, especially those with families, to have to travel out of town on a production for any great length of time. Deborah Grant, the original Mrs Barnum, Sarah Payne, our Jenny Lind, and Ginny McGustie, our exuberant Joyce Heth, were all unavailable, and we had to reassemble an entirely new cast for Manchester. I have to say that the second company of *Barnum*, as a whole, came closer to being a real family to me than any I've ever been a part of. They were special beyond belief and the memory of them all is still dear to me. They were young, generous, eager kids willing to try anything, working constantly to improve tricks for the show.

Peter Coe was again our director, but this time there was never a question of my being excluded from the casting process. In fact, Peter didn't show up at all until we were a couple of weeks into rehearsals. I used to joke about it with the company: you'll see Peter on the first day of rehearsals, I told them, and on the last day, but you won't see too much of him in between. To tell the truth, the main work at this point was the circus training and staging. The fine tuning of performance was much further down the line. So, Buddy 'I know' Schwab would supervise daily rehearsals of who did what and where.

Peter had another little foible. He sometimes left halfway through an opening night and before the opening night curtain he would gather us together: 'Don't worry if the reviews are terrible tomorrow . . .' he'd say. I remember he gave that kind of pep talk, if you can call it that, to our *Flowers for Algernon* company, and he did it again before the opening night curtain of *Barnum* at the Palladium. 'Just don't expect the critics to like the show,' he said, 'then you won't be disappointed.' We all looked at each other nonplussed, and went on in a completely paranoid state, each of us worrying, 'What in hell does he know that we don't?'

Danuta and Terry Parsons were our resident circus trainers. Danuta, an aerialist, was a beautiful, diminutive four-foot-six Polish powerhouse of an individual. Her husband, Terry, was an ex-clown who had been with the Barnum, Bailey & Ringling Brothers circus. I had first met them when I was training at the Big Apple Circus School and I was delighted when they could join us for the second production of *Barnum*. Danuta and Terry were always there for the company, and as a result the production never lost its original feel, its spirit, or its sharpness. All this helped us remain a very tight unit.

Buddy, Terry, Danuta and I auditioned hundreds of circus specialists between us – jugglers, stilt-walkers, and aerialists. And if they felt inhibited by the fact that outside their own specialities they weren't as adept at singing and dancing as some of the rest of the company, they could always take comfort in the knowledge that I was handicapped in absolutely every area of performing. That show was a great leveller for all of us.

I had originally asked Cheryl Kennedy to come to

Manchester as Mrs Barnum but she had to decline. Having only just returned from a ten-month tour of America she quite rightly felt that her teenage daughter needed her mother about the house. So Eileen Battye became our Mrs Barnum; she had auditioned for the first company and had been turned down. When she auditioned the second time, two years later, her warmth as the character radiated like a shining star against the competition. I wondered why we hadn't seen this at the first audition. 'I just gave a bad audition,' she said. How fortunate for us she returned. She became surrogate mother to the entire company, myself very definitely included.

Michael Heath was the ring master and my understudy. He's a wonderful-looking character, and I loved to watch him do his stuff at our daily workouts before the show. Michael would charge into the hall, head and body bent at an odd angle as if pushing against a gale-force wind, while his arms swung at twice the speed of his gait. Michael wasn't terribly athletic, although he was convinced otherwise and was willing to try anything. A flesh-coloured gap always showed just above his ankles, because he pulled his trousers up to a point just below his rib cage. Nevertheless, sporting a handsome handlebar moustache, he was the embodiment of a 1920s beach lifeguard, alert and ready to take on any challenge.

When we finally arrived in Manchester for rehearsals, the city was experiencing a period of expansion and renewed vigour. It had endured years of decline after the War, with factories closing and industry moving away from the area, but the city had managed to hang on, and in time attracted new businesses and opened up new cultural opportunities.

There was a small group of entrepreneurs, led by

Forbes Cameron, the rock-and-roll promoter, dedicated to saving some of the splendid Manchester theatres, including the beautiful old Opera House, from demolition. I think the reopening of the Opera House was viewed as one more positive sign of the city's new lease of life, and we were welcomed accordingly. The advance bookings totalled over a million pounds and people queued around the block for weeks for tickets. And they kept on coming. From Manchester, of course, but also from surrounding counties and cities – from Sheffield, Birmingham and all over the north of England. Coach parties made the journey from as far away as Scotland, and everybody had a whale of a time. We played to sell-out business throughout the entire six-month run, and it was like having a party every night of the week.

One of the most exhilarating things about our stay was the way the city made us feel a part of the community. The company responded by doing a bit to entertain the children in all the Manchester hospitals, and our mail at the theatre was heartwarming and, just as often, heartbreaking.

It began with Vanessa. Her teacher wrote to me at the theatre telling me about this little girl who was suffering from leukaemia. Vanessa had been a great fan of Frank Spencer and hoped to see a performance of *Barnum*. I visited her at the hospital, and later on we had the two front rows removed from the circle so that we were able to bring her to see a performance from her hospital bed. She was a very dear and brave child, and an inspiration to the entire company.

Vanessa was being treated at the Manchester Children's Hospital which, at the time, was trying to raise desperately needed funds for its bone-marrow transplant unit. The hospital was running a Christmas card campaign, using a card design which had been drawn by another child-leukaemia sufferer. After Vanessa's sad death, I felt I should do everything I could to help the campaign carry on in her memory. With the help of disc jockey Susie Mathis, Piccadilly Radio got behind the project as well, and eventually the Christmas cards were sold all around the city, in shops and restaurants, even in the health spa next door to the theatre.

As part of the campaign the whole cast of *Barnum* was asked to sing carols in the Manchester Free Trade Hall, the home of the great Hallé Orchestra. It was broadcast on television and radio, and the press was also there. The idea was for the company to sing one carol together, then I would do a solo of the verse of 'The First Noel', and the company would join me for the chorus. I was nervous even during rehearsals. I kept forgetting the lines and stringing the wrong lines together. ('In fields where they lay, in fields, where they lay . . .') That old devil, stage fright, really took hold. I knew I wouldn't have the words in front of me and I was, as usual, absolutely terrified I would dry up.

The company marched up the High Street on Christmas morning, everyone dressed in *Barnum* jackets, and me hiding behind my glasses. We entered the hall, my glasses came off, we were greeted by all the dignitaries, and the service began. The whole company sang a carol together and, with a mouth full of cotton and my heart doing the tango, I walked to centre stage, just in time to hear someone say, 'Well, thank you so much *Barnum* company . . . and now on to our next guest . . .'

I was left standing there with my mouth open, all ready to go, and completely forgotten by the compere. (What a wonderful Christmas present!) The cast, of course, knew how nervous I had been (and how pleased I was that I didn't have to sing). I could see some of them standing at the back of the choir; they began to giggle and tried to signal the compere that he'd passed me by, and one of them put up a sign, 'What about "The First Noel"?' The cast never let me forget about 'The First Noel' that never was.

During the run I was asked to present an award at a ceremony honouring the recipients of the *Manchester Evening News* Theatre Awards. It was then that I was introduced to the paper's editor, Michael Unger, a very modest, easygoing man, and we hit if off immediately. After our company left Manchester, it was through Mike Unger and the huge campaign mounted by the *Manchester Evening News* that the new bone-marrow transplant wing was finally completed. It was only then that I discovered Mike's own lovely teenage daughter, Sarah, suffered from leukaemia and that he had kept it a secret from everyone. I used to call her from the theatre in London when she went into hospital. She subsequently died there, a brave and beautiful girl. Her friends still come to see me even now, long after her death.

The new bone-marrow unit of the Royal Manchester Children's Hospital in Pendlebury, Salford, was eventually dedicated in December 1988, three years after our Manchester run. I was asked to officiate at the unit's opening ceremonies. That honour, that feeling of community, those wonderful people in Manchester, gave us all the feeling of totally belonging, a gift not easily repaid.

When we began our run in Manchester, my sole objective was the eventual videotaping of the show.

There had never been a thought of another run in London, but our Manchester success paid off with an invitation for the *Barnum* team to return to the West End. We all thought it would be great to bring it back briefly. I thought twelve weeks would be perfect, and that would be the end of it; then we would finally get to do the oft-promised video. But by opening night we had taken another million pounds in advance bookings, and it appeared that the video might be put off indefinitely.

Still the company stayed together, because none of us wanted anyone else to make the video, and we had grown into such a family that none of us wanted to leave the nest. Besides, the video represented a fair amount of money for the company, so the Victoria Palace became our home for the next eighteen months.

That we all spent so much time together, as much off-stage as on, was the reason for the cast's closeness. It was the warm-up that really did it. The daily ninety-minute warm-up began at five in the afternoon and twelve noon on matinée days. The skills we performed on stage had to be continually practised. And the risk of injury if we didn't warm-up sufficiently was never far away. Everyone was valuable to the show; it worked liked a complex jigsaw puzzle, and anyone in the wrong place at the wrong time could cause the most ghastly accident. Thanks to everyone's diligence, that never happened. We all got to know each other very well, and everybody had a sense of humour. Amid all the grunts and groans, there was always the intermittent sound of laughter generated by the company's collective insanity. It was the only way to survive. We were all in there suffering together.

Suffer is precisely the right word. This was no ordinary musical show – the physicality of it was exhausting; the days were long and gruelling. Just getting through it made us all stars in our own right, because each of us accomplished things we never thought ourselves capable of doing before. Some of us even discovered we were destined for it. Jane Watts, my girl at the time, had never been on a trapeze in her life but found she was a natural. She had trained as a dancer, but was born for the circus. Jane later met and married a real circus aerial artist and spent her days happily whirling dangerously in mid-air, suspended from a strap held fast (I pray) in her husband's teeth: now *there's* a man who's really had to learn when to keep his mouth shut.

Some of the world's most complicated practical jokes were hatched during those sessions; the gags would run on for days, sometimes weeks, and I was invariably the favourite target. Absolutely nothing was sacred.

Take for example my trip to Greece. I confided in Michael Heath that I was going on holiday there. Don't let anyone know where I'm going, I told him. A major mistake. Michael saw the brochure on my dressing room table with the name of the hotel on it and promptly went out and had it photocopied, and when I walked in to warm-up the next day, I found everyone reading a copy of my 'secret' hotel brochure. But it didn't end there.

Michael Heath's sister was employed by a travel agency at the time, and he had her pinch some of their headed note paper on which he typed a letter thanking me for booking the entire company on my holiday to Greece. 'Dear Mr Crawford,' it read in part, 'Thank you for your booking for 40 people on the island. If you will please forward £4000 in advance payment . . .' This was accompanied by a pamphlet detailing the glories of the island:

> . . . *this island nestles like a mole hill in the cool and shark-infested waters of the northern Aegean.*

*It is one of the more peaceful islands which
explains the presence there of the large American
'Peace for Greece' camp . . . The island boasts a
wide range of traditional Greek restaurants,
ranging from the poor tavernas of the east to the
poorer tavernas of the west . . . Water sports
abound and include shark-baiting, shark-sailing,
shark-fighting, and shark-riding. Local craft-
work of interest includes shark-tooth necklaces,
stuffed sharks, shark's heads and sharkskin
suits . . .*

The letters would arrive almost daily for weeks, each a
little more elaborate than the last: 'Dear Mr Crawford,
We have agreed to a discount on your holiday price
providing you agree to do the cabaret at the hotel. Where
would you like us to erect the wire – over the swimming
pool . . . ?'

Then, ever so gradually the letters took on a more
serious tone, and eventually threatened legal action if I
didn't come up with a four-thousand-pound advance
payment. One day Michael Heath's sister, dressed in her
travel agent's outfit, arrived at the theatre and marched
through the front of house with a 'policeman' who
'arrested' me on the spot. He clamped some handcuffs
on me and they left me there cuffed to the wire for half
an hour while the rest of the company simply ignored me
and went on with the warm-up.

And then there was the blackmail caper. We had a
running joke at warm-ups based on the traditional public
school brand of humour where everyone is called by their
surname and given a nickname. I was the 'Headmaster';
Heath was the 'Deputy Head' because he was my
understudy. I had the use of two dressing rooms at the

theatre: one downstairs where I actually dressed, the other upstairs, which I used for taking a nap or as a kind of receiving room for guests. Michael waited until I went upstairs to sleep one day and, accompanied by two girls from wardrobe outfitted in schoolgirl uniforms, he went into the downstairs room wearing boxer shorts, a headmaster's cape and mortar board, and carrying a cane. He got another member of the company to take photos of the girls being spanked over his knee and in some other provocative poses that I will leave to your imagination. They even got into my jacuzzi together. Michael had the photos developed, cut his face out of the shots, superimposed my face from the programme photograph, and photocopied them.

Then, one by one, he sent them to me through the post, along with blackmail notes threatening that if I didn't come up with thousands of pounds, the photos were going to be published. I showed them to Heath. 'I can't believe it,' I said to him. 'That's in my dressing room!' The letters arrived every few days, the threats growing more awful each time. I became more than usually paranoid and watched everyone at warm-ups, muttering to myself, 'It's got to be him . . . maybe it's her . . .' It wasn't until our Christmas party that I was let in on the joke. Heath videoed the whole thing – you should see my face!

But if humour was the company hallmark, generosity was its heart's blood. I awoke one morning to the performer's nightmare: I couldn't sing a note and my speaking voice was only just there. When I arrived at the theatre, I spoke to Michael Heath: Either I miss the show, I told him, or I could do one other thing – I'll do the dialogue and have you stand in the wings and sing the songs while I mime to them. Without a moment's hesitation Michael said, 'If you think we can pull it off, let's do it.' That night, I walked on stage before the performance began to make the announcement. 'Ladies and Gentlemen, before we start this evening, I have to tell you, I have very little voice. My voice is virtually gone, which gives us two alternatives: either I don't do the show at all – or someone else will sing the show for me and I can do the dialogue.'

The applause for the latter suggestion made it clear I would be performing that night. I introduced Michael to the audience and told them, 'He's going to be singing the songs tonight and hopefully – like his hair – you'll hardly notice the join. I hope you'll bear with us. Off we go!' Michael has a splendid voice and after the initial awkwardness the audience completely forgot about what was happening and settled back to enjoy the evening. We did it that way every night for a week. Michael had every right to say no, but his unfailing generosity was characteristic of that special group of players.

Maisie Fielding was the generous matriarch of the company (and indeed, of Harold's organisation), always there when you needed her. She was primarily in charge of supplying costumes for the production, along with her super-efficient assistant of forty-two years, Jeanette Peters. Harold was notorious for running a tight ship when it came to salaries; Maisie, on the other hand, spared no expense on lavish costumes.

She died tragically and unexpectedly during our run at the Victoria Palace. She had been in the theatre as usual all that week and died the following Sunday morning. The Water Rats – a theatrical institution that raises money for retired actors – were holding their ball that night, and many of the company were going to be there. I kept the news from everyone so as not to let the charity down, but it was a very difficult evening to get through.

Maisie's death left Harold completely bereft and, if

anything, closer to our company. There was a beautiful and moving memorial service for her in a lovely little church off Hanover Square. Four of our company sang Bach's 'Jesu, Joy of Man's Desiring'. I sang Cy Coleman's beautiful 'The Colours of My Life' for her with the whole company singing harmonies:

'. . . And if from my side, my love should roam,
The colours of my life will shine a quiet light to lead her home . . .

When I saw Harold at his office later, he showed me a shawl of Maisie's that he kept there.

'I just can't throw it away,' he said. 'It's not silly, is it?'

'If you're silly, then we both are,' I said. I told him that for as long as I could remember I didn't want the pillow slip changed on my mother's bed after she died because I could still smell her head on it. Not until that smell had faded could I have it washed. And I can still smell my Nan on the pink bed jacket she wore in hospital. I keep it in with my clothes, and when I go in to take out my clean clothes, I grab hold of it and give it a kiss. I've kept Nan's old fur coat and my mother's old overcoat. It might be foolish, but I saw them in those clothes so often that they always remind me of special moments. 'You keep the shawl, Harold,' I told him. 'Sit it there next to your desk and hug it whenever you need it.' It's still there. He'll never remove it – that's Maisie. Maisie's still there.

We were still sold out at the closing, but it was absolutely time for me to leave. I was totally exhausted. I had already cut out a matinée performance and, typical of Harold, rather than have the audience see someone else perform for me midweek, he let us drop the performance entirely, while still paying the company its full eight-show-per-week salary. Harold believes implicitly in his audience's right to see what they've paid for.

I've had greater personal success in other roles, but I had the time of my life in *Barnum*. For me, nothing will surpass those years. My memories of that time are all joyous, only marred today by the knowledge of Peter Coe's tragic death in 1987 in a car accident. And I would be extremely remiss if I didn't confess here that there isn't a doubt in my mind that, with the exception of Tyrone Guthrie, Peter Coe got more out of me than any director I've ever worked with. It was Peter who knew how to focus my energies and concentration.

Barnum (and its company) had all the qualities I treasure most about this business. It had the colour, the music, the glamour and the excitement. It had the very demanding circus skills, the adventure, the danger and the thrills. It offered, too, the camaraderie that one dreams about finding in a company. Only when a whole company gives what we used to give do you have the sense of togetherness, rather like a great sports team in action. When I think how far I've travelled from the day that I cheated with the relay team at school! We really won this race, fair and square, and what a great feeling that was.

CHAPTER 23

IN THE SPRING of 1984 I went to see the last preview of *Starlight Express*, the new Andrew Lloyd Webber show at the New Victoria Theatre. I bumped into Andrew (whom I'd met socially once or twice) at the interval and in the course of casual conversation he mentioned, almost in passing, the possibility of my doing a role in his new work in progress, *The Phantom of the Opera*, based on the Gaston Leroux tale of a hideously deformed man's doomed love for a beautiful singer.

Apparently Andrew had first become intrigued with the idea of *Phantom* following Ken Hill's short-lived play in east London that year, for which Sarah Brightman had originally been approached to play Christine. Later on, Andrew broached the idea of a musical *Phantom* to Cameron Mackintosh, who had presented *Cats* and *Song and Dance*.

The project had been through several changes, all of which had been well publicised. I told Andrew I'd be very interested, of course, but after that evening, I never heard another word about it.

The following year I heard a recording of the title song

by the rock singer Steve Harley, and saw the accompanying music video with Harley and Sarah Brightman, and just assumed Andrew had decided to go in the direction of a rock opera (and Steve) and had simply forgotten about me. (I believe Andrew's earliest thought was to do something along the lines of *The Rocky Horror Picture Show*. Indeed, *Phantom*'s title song with its heavy rock beat, a survivor of early versions of the show, sounds almost an anomaly; it has a totally different feel to the other songs in the show.) I was disappointed, certainly, but that, as far as I could see, was that.

I've since learned that as Andrew continued to compose the score, and after he read Leroux's gothic thriller and recognised its romantic potential, the direction of the music began to change dramatically. Gradually his score assumed a more classical style, something that didn't particularly suit Steve Harley's voice.

In the months that followed, I read reports that half the world was auditioning for the part of the Phantom, and then, for whatever reason, Andrew thought of me.

The stories abound about how and why I was cast for the part, and I honestly have no idea what to believe: Sarah Brightman was sitting downstairs during one of my singing lessons, heard me and mentioned my name to Andrew; my singing coach Ian Adam had recommended me to Andrew; Andrew had seen me in *Flowers for Algernon* and remembered me. However it happened, it represented another miracle in my professional life for which I thank that Great Casting Director in the Sky.

In April 1986 when the announcement was made that *Barnum* was closing, Cameron Mackintosh called my new agent, Duncan Heath, to ask if I'd still be interested in doing *Phantom*. Still? I hadn't thought anyone remembered me. No matter.

Andrew and Sarah came to see *Barnum* just before we

closed. (The adrenaline was really pumping that night; everyone in the company was hoping that Andrew had come to make him or her a star.) Afterwards, I suggested we eat in a restaurant that wouldn't draw attention to us. It was usually empty. Andrew completely agreed, until we got there and he tasted the food. 'Did it not occur to you to wonder why there was never anybody here?' he said. I think the main purpose of the meeting was to see if there was any chemistry between Sarah and myself, and it went very well as far as I could tell. Sarah was charming and obviously very excited about this great opportunity. And Andrew, pushing his plate to the side, enthusiastically discussed his plans for the show. At his request I gladly went a few days later to meet David Caddick, his musical director at the Really Useful Company. The three of us sat and talked in the music room of Andrew's beautiful house. 'Listen to this,' he said, and he put on the recording of the overture, the flip side of the Sarah Brightman–Steve Harley hit record.

The music made my hair stand on end. In fact it seemed to arrive in my body and take me over – I wanted to prowl like a cat. I know I started to work at that instant even though I hadn't been accepted for the role. I looked up at Andrew. I said, 'It's bloody marvellous! I've got to do it, Andrew.'

Within a few weeks it was arranged for me to meet the show's American director, the Tony Award-winning champion of Broadway, Hal Prince, who had worked with Andrew on *Evita*. There was a lot riding on that meeting: it had been some fifteen years since I'd auditioned for a role. There were the usual preliminary introductions all around and finally I just said to Hal, well, shall I sing it for you and see what you think? (Hal would later finish this story at a party on my last night of *Phantom* in New York: 'I didn't quite know how to ask him to get up and sing something,' he said, 'but before I had to think of anything, he offered to sing for me . . . and the moment he started, I knew we had the guy.')

Andrew was very enthusiastic. When I finished, he was bouncing up and down on the couch. 'Bravo, Michael, bravo! It's so much better now than the last time you sang for me,' he said, 'and knowing you, I'm sure you're going to make it sound even better.'

Dear God, I thought, how much more does he want? I thought I'd been brilliant! 'Oh, good . . .' I grinned, instantly overwhelmed by the usual Crawford paranoia. I've busted my braces working for two weeks to get that song right – and he wants more! There is no way I'm going to be any better than I was tonight!

But Andrew and Hal obviously thought otherwise, and on May 19, 1986, the announcement was made to the press that I had been cast as the Phantom.

Some things never change. The excitement of getting the call – you've got the job! – never diminishes. This was as big and as exciting a moment for me as when I was cast in *Hello Dolly!* twenty years before.

There were some understandable industry comments about the 'strange casting' – this dramatic role was undoubtedly far removed from anything I'd done in the recent past – but Andrew and Hal gave me the chance, and I am indebted to both of them. I knew it might be a daunting task to put this Phantom on his feet, but from the beginning I felt a real strength about it. Deep down I knew I could do it. Thus began a new regimen of singing lessons, practising five and six hours a day, and two-hour sessions with Ian every single day of the week for the next two months.

The search for the look of the Phantom took up an

enormous amount of time from the very beginning. In the earliest stages of the production, even before contract negotiations began, I spent weeks consulting with Maria Björnson, our genius of costume and production design, and Christopher Tucker, famed for his work on the film of *The Elephant Man*, who had been commissioned to design the Phantom's hideous face.

Over the months, Chris experimented with every conceivable kind of make-up to overcome the physical restrictions imposed on us by the live production. My ears and nose had to be kept clear so I could hear the music and breathe freely, and my mouth had to be kept clear so that I could be completely understood when I sang. The idea of wearing a half-mask was Maria's and it solved all our problems, save one: the Phantom was a romantic figure and the exposed side of my face had to be appealing to the audience (no small feat). So, in addition to the foam latex pieces needed for the Phantom's skull, lips, cheekbones and deformities, Chris designed some additional prostheses to straighten my nose, giving the exposed side a Valentino look.

There were some concerns about the amount of time it took to apply all the make-up: it originally took two hours to prepare my skin and glue the prosthesis into place. (We quickly learned that the prosthetic pieces had to fit like a second skin because, in the early days, the glue didn't hold well, and the bottom lip was often loose. I dreaded Sarah walking away after our big kiss wearing my lip!) Then my face had to be painted and highlighted, and the make-up blow-dried and powdered to prevent the foundation from cracking. An application of lubricating jelly to give the face a translucent glow and to keep the make-up from looking too powdery completed the process. I added contact lenses as a final touch of my own; one blue lens for the exposed side, and an opaque

lens for under the mask which rendered me alm[e]
on that side.

August 18, 1986 marked our first day of rehearsals at 'Awful House', where I'd rehearsed *Billy* and *Flowers* years before. The place was much improved, but everyone was tense, and I was full of trepidation, as I always am on the first day of anything. At least this time I felt prepared. I couldn't practise everything beforehand because Andrew hadn't completed the score yet, but I had already worked for months on the Phantom's two big songs in the show, 'The Music of the Night' and 'The Phantom of the Opera'.

Hal Prince asked everyone assembled to say their name and what they did in the show, but for some unaccountable reason, I couldn't bear to say my name aloud. When my turn came, I croaked something unintelligible which prompted a few turned heads and a raised eyebrow or two. I felt certain that the suspicions of some of the operatically trained cast members that I was totally wrong for the role were reinforced on the spot. (Sing? Why the man can't even speak!)

Then Hal took the floor and, using Maria Björnson's model sets, he 'talked' the company through the entire show. A break followed, and those of us who knew each other, however slightly, huddled together by the coffee machines to make nervous small talk until Hal reappeared – then rehearsals began. I didn't know it then, but this was already a long day for Hal. He likes to work half-days, something I understand because I'm exactly the same, a piece of news that may shock those who wag an accusing 'workaholic' finger at me. I prefer to work from very early morning until, say, two o'clock. Then I try to pack it in; my thought processes diminish markedly at the first sign of the afternoon sun.

We began the rehearsal with the auction, the very first

scene in the show. Everyone else, said Hal, could go. He sent the dancers to another room to work with our choreographer, Gillian Lynne, and told the music people to go downstairs; so he had everybody out and occupied, except for me, who continued to linger in a remote corner. Hal appeared to be very nervous that day – as we all were – and I thought I'd stick around and wish him 'lots and lots of luck, it's great working with you' at that last moment before he started rehearsing his first scene. I skulked about in the corner wiggling my fingers at him trying to attract his attention, hurriedly turning the gesture into a just-brushing-the-hair-behind-the-ear movement when he looked right through me. He acted like he had no idea who I was when he finally fixed his eyes on me. All he knew was that I was there and I wasn't supposed to be in that scene.

'What are all these people doing in here?' he shouted. 'I don't want anybody in here but the people in the scene . . .' All these people definitely meant me. I couldn't have moved faster if I'd been hit by hot fat.

Rehearsals for *The Phantom of the Opera* were a very different experience for me. I was isolated from the rest of the company much of the time, spending most of my day in a small room downstairs next to the boiler room, working with an accompanist on voice and movement for five or six weeks. Later on, whenever there was a scene or a run-through, I was called in to join the others, adding my character to the scene. It was almost as if I was outside the show, not of it, but that worked rather well, simply because of the nature of the role I was playing; although the Phantom is only on-stage for about thirty-five minutes, his invisible presence must suffuse the entire theatre while the show is going on.

Hal gave me great leeway in the development of the character. He provided a loose framework to follow for a scene and I'd pursue it. He envisioned the show as a romance on a grand scale rather than as simply the horror tale it had become over the decades through film versions, and he saw the Phantom himself as a mysterious ideal – sophisticated, sensual and seductive. I felt there had to be an inherent nobility about the man, along with an exquisite vulnerability and the passionate pride that is his ultimate undoing. He is, in sum, an extraordinary man, with all the qualities that word suggests; unique, gifted, monstrous, remarkable. Hal and I threw ideas back and forth, and he'd say either yea or nay to certain things I was doing; it's the way I love to work. I don't like being held too strictly to a particular line, and the kind of freedom Hal provides nurtures creativity and helps the artist bring more to the script than the writer may have actually written.

Some of the staging can happen almost by accident. During early rehearsals, at a point at the very end of the show when Christine leaves the Phantom for the last time, Sarah Brightman's veil fell off. I went over to pick it up, and I buried my face in it – I could smell Christine. The perfume seemed to remain, one tiny thing that still gave physical comfort. It was just like Harold Fielding with Maisie's shawl, or me with Nan's bedjacket.

I cried, 'Christine!' – my head buried deep into the veil. Then, barely audibly, I said, 'I love you . . .' It was kept in the show because it was a moment to which people completely related. In fact so much of that role came out of little truths. I'm sure the audience always sees through a phony gesture.

Maria Björnson was Hal's collaborative equal from day one of the production. From the very beginning she was interested in my input on costuming the Phantom, and we had countless productive consultations between us with Hal and Philip Linke, who had made all my costumes since the days of *Come Blow Your Horn* and had always brought me good luck.

Because the Phantom is masked and thereby limited to the use of his hands and body movements to communicate his unspoken love to the girl (and to the audience), the costuming provided an essential aid to his expression. The cut of his waistcoat influenced the way he stood and sat, and the stiffness of the upper body emphasised his air of pride and nobility. I recalled my grandfather Monty's high lace-up work-boots – I always thought there was a slightly pathetic look about them – and I had a pair made up for me to wear. They were the perfect thing, I thought, to accentuate the Phantom's inner vulnerability.

I was particularly thrilled with my appearance. I looked wonderfully, theatrically grotesque, and I was absolutely convinced that even my friends wouldn't recognise me. I was quickly disabused of that theory while rushing down the stairs in the full horror of my make-up to a dress rehearsal. Joss Ackland passed me in the stairwell, walking in the opposite direction on his way to the street. 'Hullo, Michael,' he said casually, 'how are you?' I stopped for a second. 'I'm sorry . . . ?' I murmured, in a hurry. 'Joss Ackland,' he reminded me. 'Joss! I'm sorry,' I said, 'I didn't recognise you . . .' and we both burst into roars of laughter at the irony of the situation.

By the time we reached our run-throughs I think we all knew we were on to something very special, given the scope of Hal's staging, Maria's sets and costuming and Andrew's sumptuous score.

When we began our previews, we were still experiencing more than the usual technical snags – hardly surprising in view of the complex network of machinery and computers we were using to produce the breathtaking special effects that are a hallmark of the production.

My own particular cross was the ornate gondola that ferries the Phantom round his subterranean haunt. It was navigated from the wings by a remote control device, not unlike the way a model car is operated. I think it safe to say that it was none too reliable.

Our stage manager, however, insisted that the system had great potential and we should stick with it. So for the first time in my life I decided to keep my mouth shut. It was the dumbest decision I ever made.

I recall the evening of our first public preview when everything seemed to be going as intended, as the Phantom manoeuvred his boat through the misty canals. The gondola halted right on the mark. I got out and walked around it, plucking Sarah's hand in mid-air, pulling her out of the boat and past me into position for our next scene.

Her eyes suddenly widened in a warning glance, and she looked past me to a point directly behind. As she moved into place, I let my eyes wander and was horrified to see the gondola was following me around like some kind of giant pet. Whenever I stopped, it butted me on the backside. I tried to be very cool. I grabbed the bow to lift the boat back into position, hopefully before the audience became aware of what was happening and started to laugh; the last thing we wanted to do was break the mood of the moment. Finally, I managed to heave it into place, but it was so heavy that I found myself completely out of breath just as I started to sing 'The Music of the Night'. In the five minutes it took to finish, I thought I was going to have a heart attack.

After the show I heard all sort of comments from well-wishers about the number. 'Ah the feeling . . .' said one friend, 'the emotion you put into that song . . . !'

Every one of the previews was a nightmare; I would step on the boat and wonder what was in store. Would the boat stop on the mark tonight? Or would we end up across the road at the Haymarket Theatre in the middle of a Peter O'Toole soliloquy?

There were other technical problems as well, the kind that made us wish for the good old days when props and scenery were moved around by human muscle. At one memorable preview, Sarah and I had just embarked on the final confrontation scene in the Phantom's lair. On-stage, the organ was programmed to slide alongside me from stage left and the Phantom's throne was cued to appear from stage right. The computer-driven candles had risen through the stage and the trap doors – all 136 of them – had closed tight. That was my cue to fling Sarah into the middle of the stage – but just as I did, all the trap doors opened up again.

We had to weave our way around the open trap doors, not an easy task when the stage is covered in a fog of dry ice; one wrong move, and . . . Of course, I knew I wouldn't fall through the hundred smaller trap-openings that housed all the candles, but there were thirty-six other buggers out there that worried me greatly.

In a state of total confusion, we continued to sing. 'This fate which condemns me to wallow in blood, has also denied me the joys of the flesh . . .'

To add to the chaos, the massive 'Don Juan' bed – a prop from the previous scene – rumbled back onto the stage again, and the organ, which had suddenly developed a mind of its own, rolled off.

'This face, the infection, which poisoned our love . . .'

Sarah was rooted to the floor – I couldn't tell if she was acting or panicking – I walked towards her slowly, more cat-like than usual, lifting each foot carefully before gingerly setting it down again, insinuating my way through the sea of candles that kept popping up and down in a kind of mad phallic display. Midway across the stage, unfortunately, I chose exactly the wrong place to stop and felt one of those eight-inch candles thrust its way up my trouser leg. For the moment, I was trapped.

'This face that earned a mother's fear and loathing. A mask, my first, unfeeling scrap of clothing . . .'

I think I hopped around a bit in the effort to free myself. The bulb at the end of the candle was lit and it was burning my calf. Clear at last, I continued to 'pussyfoot' my way across to Sarah on stage right.

'Pity comes too late, turn around and face your fate, an eternity of this before your eyes . . .'

At precisely that moment, some unseen anarchistic hand took control of our computer system and everything on stage went completely mad.

The throne slid into the wings, then came back on again, and the bed popped in and out like a cuckoo clock. The portcullis was due to descend as well and if any of us was standing in the wrong place, he or she would most certainly have been pierced straight through the head. At last, one of the crew had the presence of mind to pull the bed off the stage with his bare hands; all the trap doors closed again, and a degree of order was restored.

I had some friends out front that night who came to my dressing room afterwards and we indulged in a brief post-mortem. How did it look? I asked them. They all swore solemnly that they hadn't noticed a thing. (But that always seems to be the case: whenever anything goes wrong at that point in the show, the audience is usually so engrossed in the story they never seem to notice a thing.)

Most of the kinks were ironed out by the time we opened at Her Majesty's Theatre on October 9, 1986 to an audience that seemed genuinely thirsty for the romantic spectacle they were witnessing. If we had any questions about what we'd done that evening, they were quickly answered by the cheering, stamping, standing ovation that lasted nearly ten minutes.

Still, none of us could have predicted the events of the next months – the worldwide press coverage, the unprecedented public interest and demand for tickets, the extraordinary audience response, and all the honours and awards that followed.

The Olivier Award nominations were announced just weeks after we opened and *Phantom of the Opera* was included. The date for the ceremony was set for a month later, in December. I have always found the waiting pure hell. Have we won or haven't we? (There is always the chance that in the eyes of the industry you have somehow failed if you don't win and, of course, there is the fear that your career will grind to a complete standstill as a result.) I pinched a stack of the 'Nominated for . . .' signs that management were given, and papered my dressing room walls and the bathroom with them. 'Nominated for Best Actor in a Musical' was glued over the toilet – it helped to break the tension.

Emma and I attended the ceremony in December. Emma, my daughter, who I had known since three hours after she was born, had grown into a beautiful and caring young woman I felt very proud to have by my side. Lucy was still at college in France, but had sent a treasured crystal for me to hold and bring me luck. I was now feeling like one of the early Christians waiting for a thumbs-up or thumbs-down sign from the Emperor. I found it almost impossible to enjoy the evening.

When they read out the award for 'Best Actor in a

George Sewell (Santa) none too happy with his Christmas elf.

Beware the low flying angel of the lord.

Three sleepy people: Jo-Anne, Emma and Lucy. Captain Crawford's first flight (with bruised forehead after walking into wing).

Lucy, Gabrielle, Emma.

MC with Algernon.

As Condorman – halfway up the Eiffel Tower – this caps the humiliation of the satin pageboy suit.

Barnum, London
Palladium 1982.

MC helping Michael
Heath to walk the
wire, *Barnum* 1984.

Nan in her favourite hat
with newly hatched chick.

Right: Nan in her favourite
hat, training for the British
Grand Prix, aged 98.

Save the Children,
Uganda.

Phantom, London, my team – Sarah, Kate and Tiffany – a sad farewell.

Below: Bob Hope Show – Los Angeles 1989.

Above: Santa, *Phantom*, LA Christmas 1989.

Michael Jackson: Would you like to come to the Never Never Ranch? MC: I don't think so, Michael.

Andrew, Sarah and MC. Tony Party, New York.

HRH the Queen Mother inspects the damage.

Mort Viner, Pat Kelly, ★ ★ ★ Gene Kelly ★ ★ ★ and me.

MC 1999.

Musical', I listened carefully, as always, making very sure it was my name I had just heard before I made a move. It was. I kissed Emma, and went on stage to make a speech. 'I now understand the frustrations of Michael Gambon's character in *The Singing Detective*,' I said, 'waiting for Joanne Whalley's nurse to distribute the cream over his body; this month has been pure hell . . .'

When I left the stage I started to hyperventilate. I was dizzy and unsteady with relief and pride. Up to that moment I had steadfastly refused to admit to myself how badly I wanted that award. I had to make a mad dash to find the bathroom. I locked myself inside and wept uncontrollably, thinking about Nan and my mother and the girls, hoping they were proud of me. I finally managed to pull myself into a suitable state to appear in the press room, but by the time we finished being photographed and interviewed by the television stations, the awards were already over. It took me an age to find Emma afterwards, but then the two of us went to the ball. *Phantom* brought home a fine lot of awards that night; it was a triumphant evening for Andrew, Sarah, Hal Prince, Maria Björnson, Gillian Lynne, Andrew Bridge, the lighting designer, and the entire company, crew and orchestra.

I began to experience a burning sensation in my chest at a very early point in the run, a kind of intense heartburn which, despite my attempts to ignore and/or cure it, remained obstinately constant; nothing stopped the pain. I was ultimately diagnosed as having developed a hiatal hernia, a not-uncommon condition in singers, and one I'd gladly define in layman's language if only I knew how. All I can do is quote the dictionary (and rely on the reader): 'A condition that arises when a portion of the stomach protrudes through the opening in the diaphragm through which the oesophagus passes as it attaches to the stomach.'

The condition eventually became so acute that, on doctors' advice, I arrived at Cromwell Hospital in April 1987, for extensive tests. I thought I'd be finished by the afternoon, but whatever the doctors saw in my X-ray was sufficient for them to insist that I stay in hospital for treatment – no arguments, thank you – a piece of news guaranteed to make me crazy. At my insistence I was allowed to make a tortured call to Duncan Heath from a call box, asking him to let the theatre know I could not make the performance.

To avoid any fuss I was placed in the most discreet part of the hospital and put to bed with a strong dose of intravenous Valium to keep me quiet – not only because stress aggravates the medical problems, but because I had already made it clear to the staff that they were going to have their hands full coping with me. Completely stoned on tranquillisers, I moaned and thrashed about the bed: 'I shouldn't be here . . . I should be getting my make-up on . . . Where is my make-up . . .' The nurses must have thought they were dealing with an over-zealous transvestite.

For the first twenty-four hours, I was in a twilight zone. I was peered at, poked, prodded and examined by an unending succession of medical personnel. I have a vague memory of being marched about to various examining rooms wearing my short hospital nightshirt – wide open at the back, of course.

Later that afternoon as I napped in my room, I heard a periodic rhythmic thumping on my wall, coming from the room next door. After listening to that knock-knock-knocking for about the eighth time, I did what anybody would have done; I knocked back. It stopped. Then, nothing at all – until about a half-hour later, when it started all over again. When a nurse came by, I told her what I'd heard. 'Somebody keeps knocking next door . . .' I said. 'Can you tell me . . . ?' 'Oh, no, no,' she interrupted, 'don't worry about that . . .' 'Well, what is it?' I asked. 'I mean, I thought maybe somebody was trying to get out!' It required a little polite digging to discover that I had been placed in a room directly adjacent to the hospital's sperm bank. All that banging (pardon the expression) I'd heard was just some guy getting if off during his bank appointment and, describing the scene in purely theatrical terms, you might say I'd ruined his performance. Of course, once I'd discovered what was going on, I knocked back regularly. Later on, one of the nurses told me that the hospital's sperm deposits had dropped almost sixty per cent during my stay there. (I'm sure she exaggerated the number, but the rest of the story is absolutely true.)

The next morning, the company doctor, Dr McKee, came in to see me. I was propped up in bed, thoroughly dopey from the combination of pain killers and Valium.

'Hello,' he said, patting me on the shoulder. 'And how are things?'

Uh-oh, I thought, this is suspicious, something's going on. 'Well, I'm not very well,' I told him.

'Yes,' he said, solemnly agreeing, 'I've spoken to the consultant . . . You've got this, uh, you know, hernia business.'

'Oh?' I said, trying to muster a look of surprise.

'And how are we feeling today?'

We? 'Well, one day on from yesterday,' I mumbled. 'A bit better.'

'Uh, I've just come from the theatre,' he continued.

I was afraid to ask how things were but that was, of course, my next question. 'How's it going?'

'Ah, well,' he sighed. 'Uh, slight problem . . . slight problem. Last night, Steve, your understudy . . .' he began. (He was speaking of Steve Barton, the young American who was cast as Christine's lover, Raul, as well as my understudy.) 'Well, the first time he went down the trap door [at the opening of the second act], he forgot to bend his legs before he landed and he twisted his kneecap and . . .'

I could just imagine what had happened. When you're not used to taking that fall, the basement floor comes up to hit you before you know where you are.

'Is he alright?' I asked. 'How is he?' And I could suddenly feel the adrenaline start to pound.

'Well,' he said, 'he carried on with a walking stick last night. Since we have no other understudy ready, we're hoping he's going to get through today's matinée . . . Then we'll try to get the understudy ready for tomorrow. I gave him a lot of pain killers . . .'

So there it was – two Phantoms out in twenty-four hours.

I pictured Steve hobbling about the stage on a cane. He is as crazy as I am. We are out of the same mould, the same school of theatre that says the show must go on, no matter what. He is a fine singer, but for most of his career, he'd been primarily a dancer – he had been recruited through Gillian Lynne, for whom he worked in *Cats* in Vienna – and I knew that if he went on with that leg, well, there was the possibility he could completely ruin the rest of his career.

'Would you leave me alone,' I said, 'so I can have a minute to think.' (Of course I knew precisely what I was going to do.) He left the room and I phoned Duncan. I told him I was going back to work; I would do the Wednesday shows to give them time to get the other understudy ready for the Thursday performance and he was to alert the theatre to my plan. Still feeling dizzy, I said, 'Just have plenty of coffee waiting . . .'

After that, everything happened very quickly. I asked my visitor to get my personal doctor's approval for my plan and by the time I finished dressing, he'd returned to say, yes, I could go on, but it could be a very painful and foolhardy thing to do. 'Fine,' I said, 'that's all I need to know.' And off I staggered.

Dr McKee drove me to Her Majesty's Theatre – fortunately I remember nothing of the ride – and stopped two blocks away to park at a meter somewhere. With me firmly gripping the doctor's arm, we walked slowly in the direction of the theatre. Even with the morning's excitement and several cups of coffee, I still hadn't 'come to' yet. 'That's Michael Crawford,' I heard a passer-by say to her companion. 'Why, he's drunk!' she added, in a tone of absolute disgust.

Theatre management must have sent runners with the news, because when we arrived, the press was already hovering at the stage door. I walked unrecognised past them all, and went straight upstairs to sit in the make-up chair. My eyes were rolling in three different directions at once, and I started to down coffee again while my make-up artist, Tiffany Hicks, prepared me in a record hour-and-five minutes – fifty-five minutes faster than it normally takes. I was ready at the five-minute call, but without a proper warm-up.

The news that I'd been placed in hospital had been in the papers the previous day, so the matinée audience expected Steve Barton to perform. When the entirely unexpected announcement was made – 'At this afternoon's performance, the part of the Phantom will be played by Michael Crawford' – a roar went up from the audience; I will never forget it. It completely cleared my head. Adrenaline started to buzz. Dr Footlights was in the house. All the excitement (and possibly the residue of Valium) made me quite breathless. I must try this every month, I thought, and then I went out and did the show.

When I collapsed in between shows, the doctor came backstage to lecture me. 'You're absolutely not going to do another one!' 'Oh, yes, I am,' I argued. 'I mean, I've got the make-up on, I may as well stay here now . . .' And I took another pain killer, and slept for a while, woke up, and did the next show. The company was unbelievably supportive throughout, and the audience went crazy at the end of each performance. But at that last curtain call I knew there would be no more performing for a while. Even before I had the make-up removed, I'd already started to cough up blood.

There were reporters out in the street afterwards, pushing and hustling, their Mini-Cams running and flash bulbs popping. I think there was more of a press crush outside the stage door that night than there had been at the opening. In a mad dash, my personal physician and friend, Martin Scurr, hustled me into his car. (Bugger this, I thought, all I need is to have the press find me in a bed adjoining the sperm bank. I could imagine the *Sun* headlines: 'Was it a deposit or a withdrawal?') To avoid the reporters following close on our heels, we proceeded on one of the wildest car rides imaginable through the narrow streets of London's West End.

Dr Scurr, normally the most judicious of men, drove fast enough to provide solid competition at Le Mans. He was having the time of his life zooming in and out of the London side streets, his brakes screeching, the car turning on two wheels half the time, while a little yellow beacon flashed on the roof of his BMW. We were Crawford and Scurr, the Starsky and Hutch of medical escapees! He was flushed pink with exhilaration by the time we arrived at the hospital, positively panting with the triumph of losing the press somewhere in Hyde Park.

Sandwiches awaited us in my hospital room, along with notes from the nurses saying well done. We had made the nine o'clock news and the next day the *Daily Mirror*, which had managed to get a photographer into the theatre, had a picture of me taking a curtain call under the headline reading 'What a Trouper!' Later in the year I received an award for courage from the *Today* newspaper which Martin Scurr accepted for me. The awards were wonderful, but courage had nothing to do with it, of course. Besides, Steve Barton is just harebrained enough (or 'foolhardy' as the doctor would say) to have done exactly the same thing for me.

A letter from Downing Street followed on the heels of this excitement, informing me that my name had been added to Her Majesty's List to receive an OBE. It was the greatest honour of my life.

June 13, 1987, marked the day of investiture at Buckingham Palace. We were scheduled to be there at nine am as I recall (Emma and Lucy were coming with me), and we decided to meet at Her Majesty's Theatre and get dressed there, so as not to be all creased before we went to Buckingham Palace. I hired my friend Tony Fairhurst for the day; I knew he had a subtle brown Mercedes for all such important occasions. I couldn't believe my eyes when he turned up at the flat driving a bright yellow Rolls-Royce.

'I am trying to be inconspicuous!' I told him.

'Well, I had no choice,' he explained. 'The other car wasn't back in time, and I had to get a car to pick you up. The only one available was this Rolls.' He looked hurt. 'I thought you'd be pleased!' he said. 'You're only getting charged for a Mercedes and you're getting a Rolls-Royce!'

'Money doesn't come into it!' I said.

'D'ya know I've never heard you say that before!' he dead-panned.

'This is no time to be humorous, Tony, this is not the kind of entrance I want to make!' Covered in embarrassment, I insisted on sitting on the floor of the car on the drive to Her Majesty's Theatre, but it was such a glorious day for me that I found it difficult to stay cross with him. Besides, he was obviously so proud of the car. It was very beautiful, and so theatrical.

The four of us drove up the Mall that morning. I sat up front with Tony, and the girls sat in the back, grandly acknowledging the crowds that had gathered to watch. A group of people started waving and cheering as we drew near to the palace gates, and I recognised a lot of the fans from the stage door at *Phantom*. They had come to wish us well and we were touched beyond belief by their presence. I looked around at my girls just as the car moved inside the gates, and discovered that the three of us were dissolved in tears. We couldn't believe we were actually inside the gates of Buckingham Palace. I spent the next few seconds hastily blowing my nose, while the girls did their best to fix their streaked make-up.

Slowly the car moved round to a back entrance. We got out and were shown into a beautiful hallway, filled with paintings, that led to a graceful staircase. I left my rented Moss Brothers topper (which I hadn't worn in the first place) on a shelf alongside the hundreds of other grey Moss Brothers top hats already lined up there, their hire numbers showing on the inside bands. The staff appeared to know everyone. They were very cordial and very aware we were glowing with pride just to be inside those lovely doors. 'Ah, good morning, Mr Crawford. Good luck . . . hope all goes well.' The girls and I were separated after that. They were shown to their seats in the audience with the family members of other honorees. The rest of us were sent in another direction and herded into two different sections, OBEs and CBEs at one end of the very long corridor; the MBEs at the other end.

One of the Queen's aides came along to instruct us on Court etiquette – what we should do and how we should address Her Majesty – and another official began to call out groups of ten or twelve of us who were ushered to a place in a queue leading to the magnificent room that held the Queen and the audience. We were all keenly aware, of course, that we would shortly be in the presence of the Queen, but in the mad effort to keep up the appearance of being calm, everyone made an attempt at polite conversation, while none of us was actually paying the slightest bit of attention to a word being said.

Indeed, beads of perspiration were beginning to form on many a noble brow. The palace staff are obviously used to handing out tissues.

The queue moved slowly along until I was suddenly in sight of some of the audience. I was told to come forward and stand on a mark, then I was called upon to stand on yet another mark – trying to reach the Queen became the equivalent of a Chinese Water Torture. You have to remember to walk with the left foot forward, and the right arm goes out to shake her hand while you bow and say 'Your Majesty . . .' and wait for her to speak first.

She is a superb lady. There were hundreds of us at the ceremony that day, and the poor woman had to stand there for hours and say something personal to every one of us. The Queen has an equerry who stands behind her and whispers information about the honoree in her ear.

When my turn came I remember her saying (I heard the aide mention 'Phantom of the Opera'), 'You obviously didn't get this just for *Phantom*, you've done so many wonderful things . . .' I'm sure I was glowing. 'Thank you, Your Majesty . . .' 'And you haven't been well?' she continued. 'Are you better now?' And then we discussed my hiatal hernia and all the various solutions to that problem! This happened in the space of about twenty-five or thirty seconds, but I was worried that I was taking up some other person's time. In point of fact, when the Queen is finished she will put out her hand again, and when you take it she actually pushes you backwards to your proper position.

So then I was guided backwards – I'd been told I mustn't turn my back on her when I walked away – and I prayed that I wouldn't fall over. There were many before me who had walked up and back on crutches and one leg, and I didn't want to let the able-bodied down by tripping! I was led out of the room and greeted by the staff who seemed very pleased for me. It was a wonderful moment, like winning the Olivier, the Tony and the Oscar all in one.

The morning after *The Phantom of the Opera* opened in London, a news item appeared in both the *New York Times* and the *Boston Globe* detailing some of the critical and first-night audience response to the show. (In bygone days it was a rare London musical show that could generate such interest abroad – that is, until Andrew Lloyd Webber's billion-dollar resurgence of musical theatre on both sides of the Atlantic.) Those small items were the first tiny trickle in what was soon to become a tidal wave of worldwide press hype.

The international press quickly became caught up in the first flow of *Phantom* news and reviews, and the favourable word of mouth from Americans who had seen the London production created a media avalanche of anticipation and speculation of the casting for the Broadway production.

We all knew the success of *Phantom* in London automatically guaranteed a Broadway production, and I wanted very much to be a part of it, but I tried not to pin all my hopes on it or dwell on it too much. I knew from experience just how much can go wrong in the course of a negotiation, whether it be because of unions or finance. Still, it was difficult to ignore what was happening. The newspapers seemed filled with nothing else.

The story made for some initially positive copy in London and in the States – another smash hit for Andrew, an infusion of cash for a 'dying' Broadway, the romance and spectacle of the production itself – and then, in a kind of inverted somersault, the story turned in upon itself. Soon the amount of coverage *Phantom* was getting became the hot story on both sides of the Atlantic, and there was a good deal of media muttering about 'all the hype', which, of course, the press had managed to create all by itself. All we did was stand by and watch.

Sarah Brightman left the show in March of 1987, six months after we opened. I thought she had done a wonderful job playing Christine. It must have been very difficult for her at times, being married to the boss and also being a member of the company. I know it was tricky for us at times. But, when we started out together on that long journey of discovery and creativity, we worked very closely together and the pluses far outweighed the minuses. I sincerely enjoyed our time on stage together. It was very sad that both she and Andrew had to go through the difficult struggle for her to appear on Broadway. The union had already agreed to allow me to re-create the role of the Phantom because of my previous experience on Broadway, but in June it was announced that Actor's Equity in New York had turned down Andrew's application for Sarah to play Christine.

The decision infuriated Andrew, who resolved to cancel the Broadway production unless she was accepted. He had, after all, written the part for his wife. The world press went to town with the story, until Actor's Equity finally relented and reversed its decision in July. And from then on, the American media concentrated – with a decidedly show-me attitude – on the show's astonishing eighteen million dollars advance sale in New York.

I tried to stay out of the line of fire by keeping a very low profile indeed, refusing all interviews about the Broadway production, and concentrating my energies instead on the completion of my run in London in the months that lay ahead.

The first year of the show flew by with such speed that I'm left with only blurred impressions – a feeling of dazzled euphoria, first and foremost. A smash-hit of such proportions comes along once in a lifetime. Any actor would count himself lucky to be part of such a production. We were blessed with such supercharged audiences that the feeling of exhilaration in Her Majesty's Theatre was an almost tangible thing.

By the evening of my last London performance, I had almost become accustomed to the hoopla surrounding the show, the swarms of scalpers offering seats at a thousand pounds and the good-natured fans who camped for days in front of the theatre, hoping for the extra ticket.

From there, I went straight to New York to begin rehearsal. This time I was ready (I hoped) to take on Broadway.

CHAPTER 24

HAL PRINCE WAS the first person to tell me what a marvellous time I had ahead of me in New York – 'Kid, they're gonna be crazy about you!' But nothing quite prepared me for what was to come.

It had been a lifetime since *Black Comedy*. I hadn't adapted well to the city that first time, nor left myself open to appreciating the cultural differences of life in the States, but I had grown up a little in the intervening years. This time I resolved to return with a completely different attitude. New York had changed as well: twenty years before there had been a good deal of animosity about British actors taking acting jobs from the Americans. Frankly, we weren't wanted at all, and *Black Comedy* and its mostly British cast had been picketed for months by protesters carrying placards reading 'Hams Across The Sea'. This time, however, the welcome mat was rolled out.

Returning to New York felt a little like going to a favourite rich uncle's house for a very long stay – it's congenial and comfortable, but you still know you're going to be homesick for friends and family. (All that did happen, of course, and my phone bill looked like the National Debt during my first few weeks in the city.) I was also feeling increasingly nervous about the newspaper and television coverage of the show, which was giving new meaning to the words 'media blitz'. I had enormous concerns about living up to the incredible expectations of the press, and of the theatregoers who had plonked down eighteen million dollars in advance bookings.

I had a fine time roaming round the city in those first few weeks, enjoying an anonymity and complete freedom of movement that has eluded me in London ever since the early days of *Some Mothers Do 'Ave 'Em*. I wandered through all the streets and stores. I tried to buy a new calendar in Bloomingdale's, but the staff were all so laid back that by the time someone got around to serving me, it was already out of date. Totally unrecognised, I could walk everywhere quite freely, able to study all the wonderful characters around me, and absorbing snippets of conversation and the myriad accents on the street.

Our rehearsals began a week or two before Christmas, downtown on 19th Street in a building owned by Michael Bennett (the creator of *Chorus Line*). Hal kindly drove me to our first rehearsal. I was obviously nervous but his wife, Judy, sitting in the back, said, 'Don't worry. He's equally as terrified as you.' So Hal and I spent the rest of the trip trying to reassure each other: 'Don't worry, Hal,' I'd tell him, 'it's going to be fine.' 'Hey kiddo,' he'd say to me, 'there's not a thing to worry about.'

Our first read-through was just as it had been in London, but Hal was prepared for me this time. He said I could be excused from introducing myself to the company. He would do it instead (I still have no idea why I found it so difficult to say my name and what I was playing), and he told the company not to be discouraged, that I would come through and be good in the end.

The company didn't know anything about me or what I was like, yet they were all very kind. A few days later, the holidays were upon us and Hal hosted a Christmas tree-trimming party (a tradition unknown to me). If a bomb had dropped on his house that night, half of Broadway's creative talent would have been wiped out. Most of the people in the company knew I was alone and several of them generously invited me to celebrate Christmas at home with their families, but with typical English reserve I felt I would have been intruding, and chose to spend the day by myself.

I sat at my window late on Christmas Eve staring into the clear evening sky, watching the planes in the distance lining up for their approach into LaGuardia Airport. I felt completely at home and at one with the city. I had prepared for my own Christmas dinner in advance. I'd bought a chicken and vegetables and a really good bottle of red wine, and put out little dishes of nuts and sweets around the apartment as if company were expected. Very late in the evening I allowed myself the additional pleasure of opening one or two of the Christmas presents sent by my girls.

Early the next morning I called the family in London. They had just finished Christmas lunch by that time. 'Are you all right Daddy?' the girls asked. 'Sure, sure, I'm fine,' I told them, and meant it, but I don't think they believed me. Then it was time to make my own Christmas feast. I remember putting the oven to pre-heat. 'Right,' I said to myself, 'now I'll do the vegetables.' (No bones about it: I talk to myself constantly, a hard-to-break habit from living alone. Plus which, we hardly ever argue.) That done, I opened the oven door expecting to feel that first blast of heat that hits you in the face. Nothing. The day went downhill from there.

Over the next hours I was so preoccupied with taking the oven apart with the only tools available – a screwdriver and a hammer – that I missed Mass at St Patrick's. (I'd met a priest from the Cardinal's office who said to me, 'If I can ever do anything for you . . .' 'Can you book seats for Christmas?' I asked him. 'I hear it's difficult getting in . . .' He looked at me as if I had gone mad and patiently explained that the church was always open – first come, first served – no reservations required.)

By four o'clock I had reduced the wine level to a bare quarter bottle and was till trying to cook the Christmas chicken. In desperation, I squeezed it into a microwave oven that I discovered hidden away in a cupboard. At the sound of a *ping!* the little oven door opened and the chicken emerged, shrunk to the size of a fighting pigeon, its legs firmly trussed and in punching position. When I cut the string that held its legs together, it shot out a second, unsuspected bag of giblets at me in a final defiant fling. I gave up the fight. As far as I was concerned, the chicken had won.

By five, the wine was gone. I curled up to watch *It's a Wonderful Life* and the only sorrier sight was the frizzled Christmas fowl I had left sitting in the kitchen sink. At eight, I crawled into bed, quite thoroughly depressed, but thankful that it was far too late to ring England to complain.

The work at rehearsals intensified as we moved into January and closer to the opening. There were some differences between the London and New York companies, but I think they were mostly cultural. Gillian Lynne's naughty words used to astonish her dancers in

New York. 'All right darlings,' she'd tell them, 'I want you to bend forward and if you find that you fart when you do, don't worry . . .'

'Okaaaaaaaaaay!'

The New York crew took to wearing 'We Don't Care How They Did It In London' T-shirts, an idea I loved. I was the worst offender on that score. I was always saying, 'No, no, we didn't do it like that . . .' You don't realise you've said it until you've said it, and there's a sudden silence. *Fool, that's not the thing to say*, I'd remind myself. *You're in someone else's home.*

The press ballyhoo was accelerating as well. For a while I managed to remain relatively aloof from it all; nobody knew me and I continued to avoid interviews. I thought, I want New York to let me know what it thinks; I didn't want to tell New York anything. But it wasn't *just* New York. There were interview requests from Boston, Chicago, Miami, Los Angeles and Toronto, from *Time*, *Life*, *Newsweek* and *Esquire*, and from all the television networks. And the clamour for seats continued unabated. The scalpers were quoting astronomical prices (what in the name of heaven can any performer or show *do* to justify a thousand-dollar ticket?) and every American charitable organisation from the National Society of Colonial Dames to the Gay and Lesbian Service Center scrambled to set up benefit performances. By the middle of January the advance sale had jumped past twenty-one million dollars and every television news programme, every radio station, and every newspaper was filled with speculation about *The Phantom of the Opera*.

By the night of our first preview performance, I was in a state of panic. In England we are always being told that New York audiences don't know how to react until they've read the reviews, so we didn't know what to expect. There wasn't a sound from the audience until the Phantom entered through the mirror. From that point began a round of applause that continued unchecked through most of the evening. It was all very buoying but – as (Sir Laurence) Olivier once wrote – 'I never knew cheering to be indicative of success', and we were all very aware that there were still a few mountains to climb.

The Duchess of York came to New York to attend one of the early previews, a wonderful boost for the company. She'd loved the show in London, as did the Princess of Wales. They were both frequent visitors. There were demonstrations on Broadway during Sarah's visit, with people chanting '*England Get Out Of Ireland!*' and hordes of American Secret Servicemen lurking about the theatre, but she seemed not to notice any of it. Even later on, when she was rushed by a demonstrator outside the Waldorf-Astoria, she took it beautifully in her stride. There was a gala in her honour that evening. I arrived late after the performance and was seated next to the Duchess and her mother, Mrs Hector Barrantes. I confess to shamelessly whispering my John Noakes impersonation in their ears during the whole of the interminable speechmaking ('*Down, down, Shep; get down!*') and succeeded in breaking them up completely.

That was the night before the formal announcement that the Duchess was expecting her first child. She hinted the news to me, and I felt immensely flattered that I'd been given a twenty-four-hour head start on a royal secret. I sent the Duke and Duchess a telegram about five weeks after the birth: 'Wishing you many congratulations on the birth of the young Princess . . .' it said. 'Can't wait to show her my John Noakes impersonation.' I loved their response: 'Beatrice is overwhelmed with the prospect of your John Noakes impersonation. Her blue eyes lit up and her red hair stood up. She is a cracker. Thank you for your kindness. Love Andrew, Sarah and Beatrice.'

The countdown to our opening was launch-minus-three-nights now; the show was set. Hal came backstage to give his usual pep talk. 'Everything is going beautifully,' he told us. 'I'm really happy with it, and I want tonight's show to be like any other night. I don't want any differences, and . . .' he said, as if in an afterthought, 'we have in three major critics tonight.' I think I had a breakdown on the spot.

The critics! He meant Frank Rich, of course, the drama critic of the *New York Times* who, it was said, could single-handedly close a show in one night with just a few taps on his personal computer. I asked someone in the company where he was sitting. Eighth row, I was told, fourth seat in, off the right aisle.

My imagination was running riot. I could imagine myself near the end of Act 1, sitting high overhead hidden from the audience behind the ornate angel that sits at the top of the proscenium arch, peering down at the seats below:

Five, six, seven, eight . . . There's my cue . . .
'I gave you my music, made your song take wing . . .'
Two, three, four seats . . .
'And now, how you've repaid me . . .'
There's FRANK RICH! God, he's so young! (I'd pictured some wizened, silver-haired nabob; he wasn't even forty at the time.)
'Denied me and betrayed me . . .'
My God, he's looking right at me! (Difficult not to; I was perched high over the audience with my arms and cape extended – like Dracula about to take off for his evening meal.) *What's he doing? Is he making notes?*

'You will curse the day you did not do, all that the
      Phantom . . .' *Crikey, if I slip, I could* land *on him*
      '. . . asks of you!'

I suddenly imagined myself plummeting straight into his
lap, looking up at him and saying, 'I do apologise Mr
Rich, we don't normally do this . . . this is just an extra
bit we're putting in tonight. I do hope you'll understand
and bear with us. And you come back again now, y'hear!'

Phantom opened in New York on January 26, 1988. The
preview audiences had been extraordinary in their
generosity and by opening night, unlike any other in my
experience, all the tension had evaporated. There was a
tremendous feeling of warmth at the Majestic Theater.
Emma and Lucy had come over from London with
Gabrielle, especially for the evening, together with my
old friend Patric Walker, and the families and friends of
other cast members filled the place; they laughed and
cried and cheered at everything. (At the interval I called
Joe Allen's restaurant in London where some of the
London *Phantom* company were gathered. Whoever
answered, screamed out: 'It's Michael! It's Michael!' and
Claire Moore, who was Sarah's replacement, came to the
phone. 'It's going great,' I told her. 'They really like us
. . .' and I could hear the London crew hollering and
cheering in the background.)

At the curtain, the applause was thunderous. It was a
magical moment.

Afterwards, Emma and Lucy and I sat alone in the
dressing room and talked awhile. The big wait for the
first review had begun. The theatre was very quiet now.
Everyone else had gone to the party Cameron
Mackintosh was throwing uptown at the Beacon

Theater, redone in a Victorian theme for the evening. 'I don't want any of us to ever forget tonight,' I told them. The girls knew what the evening meant to me and how much I wanted them with me to share it. There was still quite a crowd waiting outside the stage door when we left. I signed a few autographs, then we got into the waiting limousine. We stopped at the apartment to drop off some flowers. Then off to the Beacon and the sea of faces and cameras and flashing lights that waited for us.

We had to push our way through the crowds to get inside the place, and found a hundred more photographers waiting inside as well. They were lined up in four rows, with each row having just two minutes to take a picture before they scrambled off into the night to meet some unspecified deadline. Then I was bustled into an ante-room for interviews with the network television people.

Everyone at the party stood and applauded when I was finally able to break free to join them: there were hundreds of smiling faces milling about me, some familiar, most of them not, and a multitude of glad hands thrust out from all directions for a handshake or a pat on the shoulder. I only stayed for an hour – the last to arrive and the first to leave – all I could think about was my voice and the fact that I had a show to do the next day – and I left the girls behind to enjoy themselves.

Outside on Broadway, the cold night air felt fresh and very welcome. The security people couldn't find my limo anywhere among the dozens and more lined up on the street, so I hailed a cab for the short ride home. It occurred to me on the way that I hadn't even seen a review. All the razzle-dazzle of the last few hours had put it completely out of my mind. I had the cab stop at a news-stand to pick up the *New York Times* and had only just read the first paragraph when we reached 57th Street.

I was still reading on my way up in the lift and finished just as I put my key in the front door. Mr Rich's verdict was in: we would live.

It was past midnight when I finally climbed into bed. I lay there as I had done at Christmas, alone in New York – but now, a hundred times more content.

The next day dawned positively spring-like. I didn't even wear an overcoat when I left my apartment for my checkup with Dr Wilber Gould, the throat specialist. Everyone on Broadway knew him. I saw him virtually every day of the preview and, indeed, without his help, I certainly wouldn't have been there for the opening night. The mounting pressure, along with certain sound problems we encountered throughout our previews, had added to my throat problems. Sarah went to him too – I think the chairs in his office had plaques with our names on them, we were there so often – and both of us became firm friends of the doctor and his family.

I walked down 57th Street with Hal Prince's words from the night before ringing in my ears: 'Mask or not, Mike, everybody in New York is gonna know you!' He was right. I was never recognised in those first six weeks in the city and now, suddenly, on this morning, every passer-by looked at me and smiled. I felt joyful and grinned back at every opportunity. Then I found a cab and was whisked off to Dr Gould's office on East 77th Street. I ran upstairs into reception, and was shown straight through to the consulting room. Still feeling elated, I sat down in the chair and discovered my fly was undone. No wonder everyone had been staring at me. So much for fame and glory. I rejoined the ranks of New York's anonymous faces the minute I re-emerged onto the street re-zipped!

But I became a *very* familiar face to the New York City medical establishment.

A few weeks later I felt feverish during the day, which set off the usual mental alarms. I told our stage manager about it when I walked into the theatre that evening. I don't feel well at all, I said; still, I *think* I'll be alright. No argument, he replied, we've got to get a doctor in.

I had a very strict routine throughout the *Phantom* run. I never saw anyone apart from members of the company after the half-hour call, and would either sit quietly waiting to go on, or talk to one of the staff about problems or questions pertaining to the production. But this night promised to be different.

A doctor was brought in, a woman. Now, she asked, what seems to be the problem? I think I'm a bit feverish, I told her, my neck glands are slightly swollen. Right, she said, strip off completely. No, you don't understand, I argued, my glands are *here*, round my neck. Yes, she said, but I'll have to do a thorough examination.

I was not pleased. In less than half an hour I had to go on stage to sing, Slowly, gently, night unfurls its splendour . . .' and this woman was insisting that I do a little personal unfurling right now.

I took off my robe and track suit bottoms and stood clad only in my Nike low-tops, a dance belt attached to a none too attractive elastic strip going up my backside – from the rear view I looked like a skinny Sumo wrestler. Keeping my hand modestly positioned in front of my dance belt, I bounced – it was chilly in the dressing room – from one Nike to the other. Those sneakers really do have air in them: I gurgled with every bounce.

Undeterred by this calamitous sight, the doctor proceeded to remove the stethoscope from her little black bag: 'What's all that gurgling?' she asked. 'It's my Nikes,' I told her. 'I've got a leak.'

She placed a thermometer in my mouth and took my pulse and my temperature, writing copious notes all the while. Then she began her 'tap routine': she tapped my chest, tapped my lungs and tapped my back; she tapped me all over – she tapped so loud, I heard Tiffany call 'come in' from the next room.

OK, she said, lie down on the sofa. I lay down and shot a brief glance into the mirror. I saw myself naked, except for dance belt, sneakers and full, grotesque make-up, and the lady hunched over a side table pulling on rubber gloves. It was a scene straight out of a Stephen King horror film.

'Please drop your dance belt,' she ordered. 'I have to check the prostate.' This was getting worse than the RAF physical; if I'd known what she had in mind, I would never have considered seeing her. 'And while you're doing that,' she continued, 'I need to put this cotton bud inside your penis and take a swab.'

'In the name of God, madam,' I howled, 'it's my neck! I have *swollen glands*!'

'I have to examine everything,' she told me, completely ignoring my outburst.

It seemed inconceivable that I was about to be skewered at both ends – a cotton bud in my penis and a woman doctor's rubber finger in my back passage – and I was due to go on stage in less than fifteen minutes.

'Relax,' she said.

'*RELAX, MADAM?* How can I possibly relax?' I looked at her in the mirror. 'This is not a very pleasant experience.'

'It's not exactly a bowl of cherries for me either,' she said.

She finished her examination on the five-minute call and I dressed and went on for the performance, feeling slightly uncomfortable. But I still had to go along to her office the next morning. She didn't recognise me of course, until I dropped my pants. The diagnosis: swollen glands. I'll never forget her last words: 'Will you be paying by Visa or American Express?'

$350 for swollen glands! I'm thinking of become a doctor.

The medical profession aside, I confess to having had the time of my life in New York. The celebrities turned out en masse backstage, and I have wonderful memories of conversations with people I had often read about but never dreamed I would meet.

Two First Ladies visited – Mrs Nancy Reagan and Mrs Rosalyn Carter – and Kitty Dukakis came too (an almost-First Lady). Michael Jackson was there, and Katherine Hepburn came twice. (I want you to be an official Phantom 'groupie', I told her. 'Oh, I am, I am,' she replied in her steely-edged New England voice.)

Barbra Streisand stopped by my dressing room too, with her friend Don Johnson (who insisted on using 'Richard Head' as an alias when he reserved his tickets). She was charmingly enthusiastic about how much my voice had changed since the days of *Dolly*. That was thrilling. (It was her idea to team up in a studio to sing 'All I Ask of You' as a surprise duo for her new album. It didn't work – I was far too nervous and insecure about my voice – still it's wonderful to think what might have been.)

Chita Rivera sent a memorable note backstage (*you sure know how to work a cloak, honey*), and Tommy Tune, whom I hadn't seen since our *Dolly* days, called me 'the toast of Broadway', an extraordinary compliment from a gentleman who has done rather well himself over the years.

When Burt Lancaster walked in – my hero, 'The Crimson Pirate' – I nearly fell out of the chair. 'I can't say anything,' he said, 'I'm in awe.' 'Don't say a thing,' I smiled. 'You rest your voice – *I'll* do all the talking.' I'd thought of him a lot when I'd been doing *Barnum* – he had started his career as a circus performer – he had such guts and strength. I asked him what he was doing in New York. 'I'm only here a few days,' he told me. 'I've got two movies to do.' 'You're going to be a great success one of these days,' I said. And he roared with laughter, thank God.

It was after a visit by Lucille Ball that I stopped wearing contact lenses under my make-up. She was very cross with me when I told her they'd been irritating my eyes. 'Why do you wear them,' she asked, 'when your audience can't even see them?' 'Well it's the feeling that they're *there*,' I tried to explain. 'What you're doing is a waste of time,' she scolded. 'You're doing yourself harm! I don't want to see them in your eyes again!' 'Well,' I said, 'uh, I'll take them . . .' She wouldn't let me finish. 'And don't let me hear that you put them back the minute I went out the door . . . !' Bless her heart, she was a very concerned and caring lady.

The nominations for the Tony Awards were announced in May. The agony of waiting was exactly the same as it was for the Oliviers – in fact worse, because so much is made of the Tony Awards in New York.

There is more of a concentrated theatre community there than in London. The twenty-two-square-mile area of Emerald City architecture that makes up Manhattan houses a live-in audience, and they are very, very keen. When you are a part of a successful show, every cabbie, every shopkeeper, and almost every waiter (the New

York actor's daytime job) will have read reviews and know your name – if not your face – and all about you, because if you're a hit you're bringing in *business*.

London is far more spread out; people will come into the capital from great distances to spend a day shopping or in the museums, and then, perhaps, go on to the theatre – but then they leave it. In Manhattan, which is much more compact, people more regularly go to restaurants after a show. Similarly, in New York everyone who works in the theatre lives in close proximity to the square mile of theatres, and there are dozens of 'theatre' restaurants nearby, full of writers, directors, and stars (except on weekends, when you can get a table anywhere because everyone has gone off to their country homes), many of whom live close enough to walk to work.

It's not surprising then that the Tony nominations assume a greater degree of importance in the eyes of the general public than do the Oliviers in London. There are Tony polls in the newspapers and Tony office polls throughout the city; there are Tony parties thrown by the Tony Committee for the nominees, and Tony television programmes that include predictions of the probable winners.

As the night approached I slept less and less and felt more and more under pressure, until finally we got there. The forty-second annual Tony Awards. The show was broadcast live on network television across the whole United States. Sarah and I performed the 'Music of the Night' sequence as our excerpt from *Phantom*. When we finished, I rushed backstage, got out of my make-up and costume, and set off through the labyrinth of corridors that led back to my theatre seat next to Duncan Heath, who had come from London to act as my official escort for the evening. (He actually arrived on time.)

I sat with a fixed smile on my face while Joel Grey (a

Tony-winner himself, for *Cabaret*) read the nominations from the stage. Mentally, I said four versions of the Lord's Prayer and three Hail Marys, and I could feel Nan and Mum saying the rosary with me. Then my name was read out as 'Best Actor in a Musical'. I refrained – but only just – from kissing Duncan and shook both his hands instead while he bounced up and down in his seat. It was a thrilling and unforgettable moment for me. That award said to me, you've been accepted on Broadway – now you are one of us. It was a longtime dream come true.

Poor Joel Grey was hit by the tidal wave of my pent-up emotion. When I ran up on stage I picked him up and swung him around, and then I kissed Bernadette Peters. 'So many wonderful things have happened to me here in New York,' I said, 'that by the law of averages I should be knocked down by a truck any day now,' and proceeded to thank everyone I had to thank. The only person I forgot to mention was Sarah, my co-star – something I wish I'd done – but I was too busy thinking of Andrew and Hal who had put me there in the first place and helped me do what I had done. Then I was rushed over to Sardi's restaurant to be interviewed for the newspaper and television cameras. Andrew arrived shortly afterwards. He was clearly euphoric at having received the award for best musical. I think he was still upset that Sarah hadn't been nominated, but he was obviously savouring all the honours *Phantom* had won that evening: Hal had been voted best director; Maria had won for her designs, and our 'prima donna', Judy Kaye, received a Tony for best supporting actress.

Afterwards, we headed downtown to share the awards with the company, who were holding a private celebration of their own. It was a joyous night for everybody, but I had to be careful not to get too excited, because there was a show the next day. I finally departed around one-thirty in the morning – late for me, but I heard the party went on till five.

Originally I had only been contracted to work for six months in New York, through to June of 1989, but it didn't require much arm-twisting to get me to agree to extend my stay there until October. Lucy came to stay the summer with me, the longest period of time we had spent alone together since her mother and I were divorced. Having just finished college in France and acquired a fistful of O- and A-Levels, Lucy had no idea as yet what particular career she would pursue. Her interests and experience were wide and varied, from art to acting to singing to video-editing to production management, and she also had strong qualifications in chemistry, botany and biology. Could I be this child's father? She had a summer intern job at Broadway Video, a company that did post-production work for *Saturday Night Live*. The two of us were like flat-mates for those three months, and in the course of getting to know each other again as father-and-daughter, we grew to be loving friends.

My daughter had to put up with the usual paternal fears and lectures, of course, about life in the big city and getting home in the wee hours. I was very strict about that. She hated it, and would leave an occasional caustic note for me whenever I broke the rules of the house: 'Hi there,' she wrote one night. 'Curfew was 1 am. You're late. Don't forget to lock the door and go straight to sleep because we have an early start in the morning. Black. No sugar. Thanks, sleep well. Love. L.'

I need not have worried about her. Lucy was a green belt in judo, very street-wise and, as she constantly reminded me, the allowance I gave her guaranteed that she dressed like a street urchin, so any self-respecting mugger would have automatically dismissed her as having nothing worth taking.

I'm so proud of both my girls – and of Gabrielle. It's very hard for children to come out of a divorce unscathed, so once the inevitable unpleasantness was behind us, we very consciously considered the best way to bring up the children. Lucy was more academic than Emma, who had a battle with concentration and application. She was her father's daughter. In the end, though, she put in a concerted effort, and there was much punching the air when her O-level results came through. Emma has Gabrielle's expensive tastes, but when it comes to fashion, Lucy and I stand alone – slightly lost. Lucy is the more flamboyant of the two, and also has my auburn hair and freckles. They both now work in TV production, and I'm glad to say that, over the years, they've put sibling rivalry aside and have grown closer and closer. As a child I'd been given so much by my mother and by Nan. They taught me how to love and to be happy, which are both, I believe, habits like any other, and I can only hope I that have passed, and will continue to pass, that on to Emma and Lucy.

My mind always seems to know when my body is about to have a breakdown. A week before my last Broadway performance, I caught a virus; not a sound could emerge out of my throat. It couldn't have come at a worse time.

A huge farewell party had been organised for me at the Hard Rock Café the next evening, which caught me literally between a rock and a hard place: I couldn't cancel it. But if I attended, I would offend the theatre management and the company would think, well, there's nothing wrong with him, he was at a party last night. I explained my predicament to our stage manager. I've got to do this, I told him; I feel like death warmed up, but I've got to go. I'll be alright, it's only a block from my apartment. He agreed, and I attended as planned, for an hour or so – I looked as if I was dying on my feet in some of the television interviews – and then I ran home in the pouring rain. I climbed into bed, and there I stayed for the next five days.

The last week people queued for days outside the Majestic in the quest for a ticket; some came from as far away as London and Australia. Rain or shine, they were always there: it looked like a convention of street people had hit West 44th Street. Some brought folding chairs and radios for entertainment; the truly intrepid brought sleeping bags. They slept and read, or were interviewed for the evening news, and they passed the time by singing songs, like participants in one of those hail-and-hallelujah meetings.

As the week progressed and I was nowhere to be seen, many returned tickets went begging; most of the fans stayed put and turned down tickets to go in, hoping I'd be back for the next performance and they'd be at the front of the queue.

I'd awake each morning and think, this is the day, I'm all better. But by noon I would collapse again – literally, because the virus had affected my equilibrium. I finally returned at the end of the week on the very last night.

The last performance in a show is like an opening night. Even worse, for me. The pressure is greater because I feel the audience expects more; many of them have already seen you perform and now they want to see something they've never seen before. All you can do is go out there and do a straight show; the audience's excitement will carry it away – it lifts everything.

At the curtain, the stage was strewn with dozens of roses thrown by the cast and from the audience. Then Steve Barton said some wonderful things to the audience and tears were shed. Later on, fans threw roses outside the stage door as I left for my farewell party at the Tavern on the Green. The driver had to remove a blanket of flowers from our limousine to clear the view, and as we sped away I heard people shouting from their cars, 'Who is he? What is it?' One excited Hispanic cabbie pulled alongside our limousine. 'Hey, que pasa, buddy?' he shouted at me. 'Who are you?' That last New York party was the best ever, filled with sentimental speeches and gifts and tears: a superb climax to the most exciting year.

CHAPTER 25

SHORTLY BEFORE I was scheduled to leave New York I was approached by Robert Mackintosh, Cameron's brother, about an idea he had for a London Christmas television special to benefit the Save the Children organisation. The show involved the use of the New York and London casts of *Les Misérables*, *Phantom of the Opera*, *Me and My Girl* and *Starlight Express* singing Christmas carols, and he queried me about singing a song especially written for the show by Alain Boublil and Claude-Michel Schönberg, the composers of *Les Misérables*. I loved the idea, but wanted to visit with a TV crew some of the countries where Save the Children was doing its good work, to show viewers what their donations were paying for.

All the next weeks were spent packing for a trip to Africa, getting the mandatory inoculations and reading up on Uganda, Zimbabwe and Zanzibar, some of the places we were scheduled to visit.

Sue Knight, my assistant, and I boarded a plane in London, with a stopover in Brussels to pick up passengers, before heading on to Entebbe in Uganda.

The cast of characters in the VIP lounge looked like a group of displaced persons on the last flight from *Casablanca*.

A white-haired, whisky-swilling German 'Sydney Greenstreet' – a massive three-hundred-pounder – sat impatiently nearby. There were two nuns as well as a little pop-eyed Frenchman, who might have passed for Peter Lorre. And a man sat facing me who looked like a 1940s European drug baron, complete with a nervous facial tic. Smoking constantly, a pregnant woman sat nearby with a husband in sandals and brown socks, and another child in a pushchair. An American couple completed our *Casablanca* road company: a large woman with a faraway look in her eyes and a loud, sinister laugh, with a tall, skinny husband who sat next to her, his ill-fitting trousers cut far too short. They didn't look as if they belonged together.

We boarded silently. Sue and I were seated in what was euphemistically termed 'club class' – a very small club indeed, judging by the seating standards. The enormous German sat in front of me and insisted on resting with his hands grasping the back of his head. When he pushed his seat back, his fingers went into my soup.

Instructions had been faxed to me at Brussels Airport. The television people wanted me to speak to the cameras as I walked down the steps from the aeroplane. A few off-the-cuff 'here we are, we've just arrived' words would do. So I used the flight time to write and memorise a short speech. It was impossible to sleep. Our German friend's seat was now set so far back, I could see the whites of his eyes.

When day broke we were flying across the northern tier of East Africa's rocky terrain. It looked like the surface of the moon, but gradually the barren landscape gave way to lush stretches of emerald-green jungle, and the indistinct forms of life below took shape as we descended for the approach into Entebbe. We could see mud huts now, and the sudden flashes of beautiful, exotic birds in winged retreat from the scream of our jet.

The German shot out of his seat the second we landed; he pushed everyone aside to get his bags and bolted quickly down the aisle to be the first to disembark. When the aircraft door opened, before anyone could move, some anonymous pair of hands pushed in a sheaf of papers to the steward to be given to me. 'This is what we want Mr Crawford to say as he comes down the steps . . .' 'What!' I exclaimed. 'I've just learned the whole . . .'

'No, no,' I was told, 'this is what they want you to say as you come out the door . . .'

The flight steward came to escort me off the plane first, and Sue and I experienced a brief thrill of victory as we threaded our way around the German who was waiting anxiously to get out of the door. 'Peter Lorre' was also clearly irritated by our preferential treatment, and his lizard eyes flicked a suspicious sidelong glance my way. The pregnant woman ignored us completely. She was badly in need of a cigarette and a brandy, and was intent on fighting her way off the aircraft if need be.

My one-upmanship was short-lived, however. I left the plane rumpled and jet-lagged, and clutching the new script firmly in my hand. I had to shout above the airport din to be heard by the television crews assembled on the tarmac below. 'Take the shot waist-high so I can look down and read this thing . . .' I called. 'Well,' I began, 'here we are at Entebbe,' and I stepped out of the aircraft. Then I missed the next three steps and slid down the rest, landing on my bottom right in front of the camera. 'Hello, I'm from Save the Children.'

My comeuppance was complete as I was held there

until the cast of *Casablanca* had left the aircraft. Then I was sent back up the stairs to redo the shot completely, with only the airline crew left to walk behind me as if we had all just casually arrived.

A representative from Save the Children escorted us through the terminal building and helped us through the massive stack of paperwork which seems to be a requirement wherever one goes in Africa.

The charity's Land Rovers waited outside the terminal to drive us into Entebbe, a ride of some twenty-five miles. We passed groups of uniformed teenage boys as we left the airport, young ragtag soldiers armed with rifles and machine-guns and stationed at various check points. Although they were very friendly and just waved us on when we approached, it was an unnerving sight, which served to remind us of the not-so-distant repressive past of Idi Amin and his successor, Obote.

The more one travels, the smaller the world becomes, and I have lost patience with those who maintain that charity begins entirely at home. The sights, smells and sounds of abject poverty are impossible to describe to anyone outside a Third World nation. Nothing can prepare you for the shock of the moment when the word privation assumes a human face, that of a child. The mountain of statistics is reduced to that one tiny face in front of you. Paradoxically, nothing is more uplifting than to witness the triumph of the human spirit over such hardship. We experienced it all from the moment we arrived in Africa, and it's an experience never to be forgotten.

We averaged ten-hour days of filming and travel after that, initially tracing the distribution of the badly needed cargo of vaccines (that had arrived on our flight) along 'The Cold Chain', a route set up by the government with the help and expertise of Save the Children's organisation. The trail leads from a central cold-storage facility and then, by truck, jeep or motorbike, to remote outposts like the tiny vaccination clinic I visited at Kasubi. I felt privileged to be allowed to deliver and administer a portion of the vaccine to a tiny, smiling baby girl.

The inoculation programme alone has cut the death rate of children there from such things as whooping cough and measles by as much as ninety per cent. Like UNICEF, Save the Children uses its resources on education, so that each village will ultimately be able to fend for itself. Money is spent on teaching the basics of nutritional cooking, as well as techniques for finding water, digging wells, and practising crop rotation. Education is the tool by which the hard-pressed populations of so many African nations will finally be able to gain control of their lives and future.

From Uganda we flew on to Zanzibar, via Nairobi. The flight took us over Lake Victoria, stretching two hundred and fifty miles across in some places, on towards Mount Elgon on the Uganda–Kenya border. We were lucky because the thin cloud cover permitted us a clear sighting of Mount Kilimanjaro's majestic peaks rising nineteen thousand feet from the landscape. Only at aircraft height can one appreciate the vastness of Africa and begin to realise how much the wildlife, once roaming so freely, has been pushed into small enclaves. Our pilot pointed out the vast green lawns of tea fields in the distance, planted at heights of seven thousand feet, and the Mara (meaning plain), the largest game reserve in Kenya. Mara is about thirty miles across and makes up an area of some five thousand square miles, an extension of the vast Serengeti Plain.

We landed in Zanzibar, a different kettle of fish entirely from Uganda. As was always the case, there was the bureaucracy and the endless paperwork. We found the local people very helpful and courteous, albeit slightly more aggressive than those we had encountered in Uganda. Francis, our driver, was a delightful exception; he was a charming and well-educated young man, and there was very little he didn't know about the history of each site we visited. It was our hotel in Zanzibar that brought us quickly down to earth.

Built on the site of a swamp, we promptly dubbed it the 'Mosquito Marriott'. Constructed in the 1800s – it must have looked fantastic in the time of the Sultans – it had obviously seen better days, and after the turmoil of years of war, it was very battered.

Damp heat pervaded the hotel, and I'd venture to say the air-conditioning hadn't worked properly since the day it was installed. The carpets were a hodgepodge of green and purple patterns, joined and rejoined every ten yards or so, like a threadbare patchwork quilt.

We were assigned rooms described as 'superior' – then a North Korean delegation arrived and we were relegated to 'inferior' quarters. There was no noticeable difference. All the rooms were dark and damp and devoid of mosquito netting. While I waited in my room to go to dinner – the food? chips with everything, breakfast, lunch and dinner – three members of the hotel pest-control brigade walked in, closed all the windows, and sprayed my room and all the cupboards against mosquitoes. The effect was absolutely suffocating – for me, not the mosquitoes (I think they thrived on the spray) – and it succeeded only in driving me outside into the corridor to wait until they had finished.

The bathrooms were an adventure in themselves. All the tubs had a coat of rust on the bottom, and there was no cement insulation around the piping from one room to another. If you peered through the bathroom wall (need you ask? Of course, I did) you could actually see the person in the room next door. You could, in fact, see three bathrooms beyond the bathroom next door. It made it easier for the roaches to get a clear run along the pipes, I suppose, and for the mosquitoes to fly nonstop on their bombing raids round the hotel.

The prospect of actually getting into bed held no great attraction for me and, Zanzibar being a Muslim country, there was no chance of getting a drink to help me sleep. The humidity was such that once you lay down, the sheets – indeed, the whole bed – were soaked within fifteen minutes. (They did at least change the linen every day.) I slept in a long-sleeve turtle-neck sweatshirt to avoid being bitten, which, of course, left my face totally exposed. The only remedy for that was to sleep with the laundry bag over my head – but if I had, it's doubtful I would have awoken the next morning.

My agent, Duncan Heath, was due to arrive in Zanzibar the following day. He was coming, ostensibly, to check on our progress, but I think he really wanted to visit the country because it had such a beautifully exotic name. I couldn't wait to see his face when he arrived!

I haven't said much about Duncan until now. I've saved him for last like the savoury at the end of a good meal. Harold Fielding had recommended Duncan to me when I was looking for a new agent. We hit it off immediately, despite the fact that in terms of background we are worlds apart. Duncan is the product of public school, a blond and handsome charmer who hob-nobs with the occupants of the finest drawing rooms in England.

Duncan became a good friend. He has a great sense of humour, and he is a fine agent besides – justly celebrated for his gifts as a deal-maker. Other than that, he drives me out of my mind. I am constantly lecturing him about his unorthodox dress code: it's sneakers with *everything*. 'How can you expect people to take you seriously as a businessman,' I say, 'when you wear sneakers with an Armani suit!' He walks around on the bounce – I think Duncan uses a bicycle pump to fill his Nikes – as if he is expecting an audition call from the Harlem Globetrotters.

Many of his clients complain that it is impossible to get him on the phone; he never calls you back, and he has an absurd propensity for missing appointments – a practice for which he has managed to frame every lame excuse known to man. I know, I've heard them all: 'I couldn't get in today, mate, they blew my briefcase up at the airport,' or 'Somebody banged into the back of my old Merc, damn fools!' or 'The trains were on strike,' or 'My flat was broken into,' or 'My flat caught fire . . .' or 'I had to go to my brother-in-law's . . .' or 'My dog [or was it his cat?] was hit by a car . . .' But in spite of – or perhaps because of – his idiosyncrasies, he is a joy to be around – when he turns up.

Of course he missed his flight to Zanzibar. He was called back by the customs people; he had put down his occupation as 'Agent' and they held him on a charge of criminal misrepresentation. (Just kidding, mate!) We were told he would arrive on a chartered flight – he'd managed to hitch a lift on one – due four hours later. Sure enough, Duncan travelled over in a little four-seater with, so help me, an occupied coffin for company. When he stepped off the plane, followed by the coffin, he was wearing a T-shirt with 'Jambo' written across the front of it and a turban wrapped around his head; he looked like an Aryan Arafat. It was very embarrassing.

We filmed for two days in Zanzibar. The hospital we visited had reached a dilapidated state of disrepair. Still, the Save the Children field workers had done a remarkable job in helping to modernise the paediatric ward (the equivalent of our baby special-care units). They had one incubator which, owing to the unreliability of the country's electrical system, was run by hot water bottles – one placed in each corner – which kept it warm. There are many unsung heroes among those field workers.

Nairobi was the last leg of our trip. Compared to what we had left behind, it was like a return to London. Here, at least, the children had trousers to wear; there were cars in the streets and fewer holes in the roads.

As a reward for our long, dusty labours we decided to treat ourselves to a one-night visit to a safari park which, we were told, had special provisions for the visitor to watch wild animals night-feeding at the local watering hole.

We arrived just in time to see . . . nothing. Night was falling. Well, to be fair, on the way in we did see a couple of elephants and the backsides of some monkeys disappearing into the bushes. All the rest was mud.

Duncan, Sue and I were settled in separate but adjoining rooms in the great wooden lodge-hotel. We were all absolutely famished and, after changing, we sat in the bar to await the first call for dinner. At the sound of the bell there was a mad dash to the dining room, where we ate a hearty meal and put away a bottle or two of Kenyan wine. By far the greatest number of tourists in the room were German. (I hope this doesn't sound as though I'm picking on them. As it happens, there *were* German tourists everywhere.) You could tell we were the newcomers: everyone else had rings around their eyes from pressing binoculars to their faces all day.

We finished dinner at nine o'clock and then walked outside to the lounge, just in time to catch the beginning of the evening's entertainment – a slide presentation that featured 'Animals-That-Can-Be-Or-Have-Been-

Spotted-At-The-Water-Hole-Day-And-Night-In-This-Game-Park'. We settled down on the couch to watch. Our slide-guides were a middle-aged Irishman with a thick Irish accent and an amiable young native with a broad smile and thick Kenyan accent.

The Irishman coughed once to get everyone's attention, and began: 'Hullo dere. Dis is de elephant.' And up popped a slide of an elephant.

I tried to stifle a laugh. This sweet man was doing his best, but after weeks of witnessing utter deprivation, hysteria was beginning to seep in.

'Dis,' he continued, 'is de cockatoo,' and up popped (as I was sure it would) a cockatoo slide. 'Dere's not a lotta cockatoo about dese parks,' he said.

I could feel the couch start to shake around me. Duncan, I discovered, was an even worse giggler than I was. The three of us sat with our fists stuffed in our mouths. I suddenly felt as if I was back in a classroom and expected to feel Mr Steele slap me round the back of the head with his metal arm.

Completely unperturbed, our guide continued. 'Now, *dis*,' he said (supplying his own emphasis), 'is de watah buffalo . . .' The slide went up of a large animal knee-deep in a pond.

At this point his young Kenyan assistant interrupted. 'No,' he insisted, 'dis is not de watah buffalo. Dis is de warthog.'

We kept bursting into fits of coughing to hide the laughter, but thankfully our narrators didn't seem to notice. The Germans, on the other hand, kept looking round at us, as though we'd devalued the Deutschmark. That only made it ever worse.

'And now, de hyena!'

At that point, Duncan had to excuse himself and went out onto the balcony to pull himself together. Our bad behaviour served to clear the room and when the slide show concluded at ten, we were alone. We were each handed a questionnaire, asking which animals we would most like to see at the water hole that night. We were told that if they appeared, we would be called – no matter the time – to observation platforms high above the watering hole to watch the fun. (I kept imagining a gentle knock at my door, and someone whispering, 'Wake up, wake up! De cockatoo is at de hole.')

We decided to explore a little before retiring. The high observatory platforms were full of German tourists staring out into the night, so we chose to have a look at one of the empty underground observation bunkers built into the side of the watering hole.

None of us wore jackets, and it was freezing down in the dimly lit bunkers. Every now and then we would giddily recall something silly from the slide show and burst into uncontrollable laughter again, the sound echoing along the concrete corridors. We could hear the Germans above us fulminating about all the noise – the word 'Engländer' interspersed their complaints. I'm sure they thought we were scaring off the animals.

We crept up to the window (really just a slit in the side of the bunker) and stood for a few moments in total silence locking out into the dimly lit night, waiting for something to happen. Suddenly, an enormous pair of hoofs walked over the top of the bunker and we found ourselves staring into the backside of an immense water buffalo, which promptly let loose a great squirt that splashed in all directions. To cap the performance, it finished by depositing a gigantic pile of boulder-like excretions barely twelve inches from our disbelieving eyes.

*

We were still laughing when we finally said our goodnights. I went to my room, and into the bathroom for the usual ablutions. I had brushed my teeth, when turning round to have a pee and while unzipping my fly, I heard the unmistakable sound of peeing. I hadn't wet myself and all my equipment was still in storage . . . I jumped back from the toilet in alarm. It was unreal. (*How can I possibly be doing this?*) Then I heard the sound of rustling paper: it was Sue Knight next door.

'Sue?' I called. There must have been eighteen inches between us, and the walls were as thin as tissue paper.

'Yes?' she answered, obviously startled.

'I just thought I was having a pee – and it was you!'

'*What?!*' She hadn't a clue what I was talking about.

'I was just standing here,' I called, 'and I unzipped my fly, and *you* had a pee and I thought it was *me!*'

'I can't believe this,' she shrieked, '. . . where *are* you?'

'Where *am* I? I'm in my room!'

With that I heard Duncan start to laugh. His room was on the other side of mine. He began to laugh, and he couldn't stop. Then I started too, and then Sue. In a state of enormous release, we lay in our separate rooms – although it sounded as if we were all in the same bed – and laughed for the next hour and a half. I don't think I've ever laughed so much for so long. Every time one of us managed to stop, one of the others would be off again, and then we'd all start. If there had been Germans in the rooms on either side of us, they would have heard everything. God help us if any one of them had shouted, 'Go to sleep!' – we would have gone on laughing for *another* hour.

We never did receive a night-time call to the observation platform, but by the time we left I had long joined the ranks of those who say that once you've visited Africa, you'll want to return there again and again.

Beyond the extraordinary beauty of the land, there are incalculable lessons to be learned from its people and their indomitable courage, resilience, and enduring patience in the face of war and indescribable hardship. It had been a gruelling few weeks and sometimes harrowing, but it was an often heartwarming and always humbling experience to meet the dedicated people who are striving to save this next generation of African children.

CHAPTER 26

EVEN BEFORE I left New York there was talk of my starring in the Los Angeles production of *Phantom*. My friends were full of advice about living in Los Angeles. 'Don't expect too much. It isn't New York, you know. It's a movie town ...' I heard *that* night and day – 'Theatre is just a minor attraction out there ... They don't care about stage work.'

Well, we would be doing our very best to *make* them care.

Certainly, I knew that if anyone in Hollywood cared to remember me at all, which was doubtful, it was as the skinny Cornelius Hackl of twenty years before. As far as the film industry was concerned, I had simply disappeared back into the dark recesses of theatre work. I might just as well have vanished off the face of the earth.

So I set off to rehearsals in New York in April 1989 with a store of secret hopes but few, and decidedly lowered, expectations.

Rehearsals began with a brand-new company headed by Dale Kristien, who was to become another of my favourite leading ladies. She was beautiful, wonderfully generous to work with, and we had an immediate and total rapport on stage. On the last day of four gritty weeks of work, someone made the announcement: 'Ladies and gentlemen, our next rehearsals will be in Los Angeles ...' I had forgotten that so many of the company, including Dale, were West Coast natives. A roar went up from the company; the adrenaline was really pumping, the excitement was absolutely palpable – they were finally going home. It didn't take me long to discover what the cheering was all about.

Our opening night gala at the Music Center was as glittering as any movie premiere from Hollywood's Golden Age. President and Mrs Reagan were our honoured guests. Indeed, I think most of the audience had, like Nancy Reagan, already seen the show in New York. But they came again (and kept on returning). Gene Kelly was my special guest for the evening. He gave me one of the great thrills of my life when he said how far I had come and that he was so proud of me.

Sammy Davis Jr was also there and sent me a three-foot-tall bottle of champagne. He would come again and again to *Phantom* – in London and New York as well as Los Angeles – and was one of our biggest fans. He loved to sing 'Music of the Night' and never failed to pay tribute to both Andrew's music and my performance.

It's no overstatement to say that the production immediately took Los Angeles by storm and completely captured the public imagination. Overnight, the press developed a galloping case of 'Phantom Fever' (*I* didn't say that: blame the *Los Angeles Times*). The show and our company were probed, publicised and feted. A ticket to *Phantom* became the next best thing to a season pass to the Los Angeles Dodgers baseball team – and even the *Dodgers* paid us tribute. I was invited to sing the pregame National Anthem, in front of forty-odd thousand cheering baseball fans – terrifying! So I invited Dale Kristien and about twenty-five other members of the cast and crew to join me as my choir. I was so afraid I'd forget the words that I wrote them on a piece of paper and pinned it to the back of Dale Kristien's Dodger jacket. I stood just behind her. Everyone remarked how exceedingly modest and generous it was for me to push my leading lady out in front!

It was in this slightly fevered atmosphere that I began a year of living in Southern California. I insisted on finding an apartment within walking distance of the Music Center. As in New York, I was secretly convinced that if I lived too far from the theatre, I was certain to be stuck in traffic and would miss a performance.

Now, finding such a place sounds simple enough, but it's a fairly tall order in Los Angeles. Indeed, in that city designed around the use of the automobile, there are places one can't even *walk* to. I finally rented a flat just a few blocks from the Music Center, on a street filled with the muted cacophony of sounds that will identify Los Angeles to the foreign visitor – the chorus of a million birds warbling at first light of dawn, the trilling of cicadas in the afternoon heat, the occasional whine of a passing siren, and the distant bawling of a car radio blaring music with a Latin beat.

My new digs overlooked a parking lot for the Music Center, but the view suited me down to the ground. I could watch the world go by in that parking lot. It was a microcosm of all human experience.

For instance, one afternoon I watched from my terrace as a woman parked her car and walked away towards the Music Center. A young man leaning on the gate near the entrance watched her too. When she disappeared from view, he went to work. Armed with a coat hanger, he started to break into her car. I grabbed the phone and dialled 999 for emergency. (This is very effective – but only if you're in the UK!) I kept my head low, bobbing up and down, trying to keep the man in sight while keeping myself hidden, with only the occasional glimpse of nose visible above the parapet. (You never know, I thought, he may have a gun. He may even come back after *me* now that he knows where I live!)

After a considerable scramble for information, I finally dialled 911 and got a female police dispatcher. 'There's a man breaking into a car,' I breathlessly reported.

'Where are you, sir?' she asked.

'I'm facing the Music Center,' I said.

'Are you north or south?'

'My dear woman, I haven't the foggiest idea which way I'm facing – I'm *English*.'

'You must know if you're north or south.'

'I'm facing the Music Center . . . *facing it!*' I repeated, frustratedly.

'Well, that's *fine*,' she said, 'and I'm *here*, but I still don't know where *you* are . . .'

'Well, where Superman worked is on my left . . .'

'I'm sorry, sir . . . ?'

'You know, City Hall . . . Superman . . . Isn't that where he worked?'

'I'll get someone there as soon as possible,' she said. Her tone implied deep resignation.

Ten minutes later, a police car cruised in and identified what was left of the car in question.

As the months went by, it began to appear that in Los Angeles at least I could do no wrong. Socially, I had been upgraded by the industry into that rarefied group of performers who are invited to all the most exclusive parties (and power lunches) on the Hollywood scene. But I never became part of it. Just doing eight shows a week took all the energy out of me. There was no way I could do the party circuit and hope to have a voice for very long. When I did make an appearance, I would only stay for a short time, speak very quietly, if at all, and then leave. Some of the film people couldn't comprehend it. What a terrible existence, commiserated one film actor, and shook his head sympathetically.

But I could never see the problem. I mean, would I swap the party scene for my *not* having done the Phantom?

Still, there is a price one pays for doing a long run, and I had set myself the goal of doing at least a thousand performances.

It was 'Boo' Laye – the late Evelyn Laye was 'Boo' to everyone in the theatre – who told me, 'never turn your back on success'. Her advice was golden for me. I acknowledged my debt when I wrote to her on the occasion of her ninetieth birthday. 'I did two years at Drury Lane in *Billy*,' I wrote, 'and five years straining every muscle in my body in *Barnum*. Now I've been doing *Phantom* for four years. At the moment, I'm in Transylvania at the home for aging Phantoms and I really should be alongside you, helping you blow those candles out . . .'

Nowadays, actors will join a show only for a limited period of time. The prevailing thought seems to be that staying on too long in a show can interfere with a performer's career. Maybe I didn't think I was going anywhere, so I just stayed on for the steady work.

There is always, of course, the challenge of trying to keep the character fresh through countless performances. Each day you have to dig deep into your emotions, and your powers of concentration have got to be such that the idea and images you used to create the part come alive inside you time and time again.

I would think of a little boy I once saw in a London hospital that the *Barnum* company visited several times. It was supposed to be a children's hospital, but the wards were shabby and terribly sad; the older I get the more it hurts and offends me to see that such conditions are tolerated. A stairway ran through one part of this boy's room, and his bed was under the stairwell. I'll never forget his deformed face. It was terribly distended. He sat alone, but the nurse told me his mother visited him every day. I tried to imagine his mother sitting on that bed next to him. How had she grown up? I imagined her marrying, becoming pregnant and how – through an act of love – her life had changed completely. She was destined to spend the rest of her life sitting on a bed in a cupboard under the stairs with her deformed child. Every night when the Phantom sends his love away – *Go now, go now and leave me!* – the music would swell. I'd move my hand and whisper 'Mama', and I'd think of that boy and wonder what his life would be like when his mother couldn't be with him anymore. And I would weep.

Monday was our day off and I enjoyed driving to Venice Beach – 'muscle beach' they call it – and Santa Monica. What is so wonderful about California is the climate and, of course, the lovely beaches, the tall pines, the gorgeous flowers, the ocean breezes. You may have heard all about the haze, the earthquakes, the fires and the Santa Ana winds – but once you get there, you forget about them. And the prevailing feeling is one of good health.

I spent a lot of time walking or roller-blading on the boardwalks there. They're not like the familiar slatted wooden boardwalks we're used to in Britain, but long stretches of concrete walks the width of a country lane.

They run for miles and miles along the ocean.

Sailing was another of my favourite pastimes, often with my old friend, Charles Jarrott, who had directed me in *Condor Man*. Imagine Charles as James Robertson Justice in naval gear: white socks up to his knees, baggy white bermuda shorts down to his knees – and lots of knee in between. Charles and I were sailing parallel to the coast and north from the port of Marina del Rey, towards the Santa Monica pier. A canvas canopy surrounded the back of the boat, but if we sat tall, we had a clear view around us. The wind was brisk, and we waved royally to the people sunbathing or fishing on the pier. We saw a large coast guard vessel sitting alongside the pier – they waved to us too. We sailed on for a while, until Charles decided it was time to tack (in layman's terms, he decided it was time to turn left) and we headed out to sea. Suddenly, the boat shuddered.

'What the f—— was that?!' Charles exclaimed.

'I have no idea . . . Could we have hit something?' I asked. We both stood up, looked out the back, and saw the coast guard boat closing in fast, as if in full pursuit of a drug smuggler. Our boat rocked in their wake. 'Are you two alright?' boomed a voice aimed at us through a megaphone.

'Yes, of course. Why?' replied Charles in his best damn-the-torpedoes tone.

'You know what you've just done?' the coast guard blared. 'You've just run over the old Santa Monica Pier!' It transpired that the old concrete pier had been sunk many years before, and the site was clearly marked with buoys and flags. Obviously, we hadn't been paying attention, as we were engrossed in conversation when we crossed the site, but if the water hadn't been as deep as it was, the boat's keel would have been torn off. 'Your boat would have gone down,' the coast guard explained. 'We had already radiod for help. That's why we were waving at you!'

'Oh, good Lord.' Charles sounded shocked. 'We thought you were just being friendly.' Then out of the side of his mouth, he whispered, 'Check the bilge . . . Check the bilge.' I checked: no water coming in. The coast guard escorted us a little way further, making sure that all was well, and left us with, 'You two are very lucky . . .'

'Charles!' I asked, in disbelief. 'For heaven's sake, haven't you got charts?'

'Charts!' he was aghast. 'CHARTS! For crying out loud, Michael, we're going to Santa Monica, not f——g FIJI!!' I had no reply.

Emma and Lucy came to keep me company over the months, and on one occasion while Emma was visiting, we went to Cubby Broccoli's New Year's party together. (He was the producer of all the James Bond films. I'd never met the man, but that hardly mattered: I was now on the Hollywood A-list of invitees.) We arrived late as usual, after the performance. Mrs Broccoli seated me next to Frank Sinatra. Emma and I hadn't planned on staying long, and when Sinatra told me his driver had taken the night off, I offered him a lift.

He sat in front with me, and Emma – her jaw dropping to her knees in awe – sat in the back between Barbara Sinatra and Barbara's mother. When we arrived, they kindly asked us in, and we ended up staying till three in the morning. I had a wonderful chat with him, all about breath control and the importance of lyrics – a lesson from the master. He told me that he practised swimming under water for as long as he could to increase his lung capacity so that he could hold a long lyrical line.

He called Sammy Davis Jr while I was there, because Sammy was now very seriously ill and about to lose his battle with cancer. Frank was very upset and openly weeping when he came off the phone. He was losing a very dear friend. It was the end of a show business era.

I had a new agent in Los Angeles – Mort Viner – who knew Sammy and Frank very well, and he told me wonderful stories about them. Mort had been Dean Martin's agent and great friend. He was instrumental in putting the so-called 'Rat Pack' together (Sinatra, Martin, Sammy, Joey Bishop and Peter Lawford), and many times he travelled with them when they did concerts together.

When we finally left Frank's house, he saw us to our car. He pointed to an area of the driveway. 'Back up there,' he said. I did as he asked, and I felt a little bump. Emma turned to me aghast. 'Daddy,' she cried, 'I think you've hit him.' Actually, I think we rolled over his shoe. Still, he continued to wave. Maybe he was just pleased to see us go. All the way home I had visions of the headlines: 'Frank Sinatra Run Over by New Year's Guest! Phantom Flees!'

One night Mort and I had dinner with Frank and Barbara at Chasen's. Sinatra could be a man of few words, depending on his mood, and he hated it when his few words were interrupted. The waiter came over in the middle of a conversation and said, 'Here's the menu, Sir. Can I get you a drink? What would you like to start? And what's your main course?' Frank looked at him and said, 'Listen kid, I hate interviews. Just bring me some food.'

Another night we were at La Famiglia with Frank and Dean Martin. It was always good to hear them discussing old times. These, of course, were the latter years of both their lives – Dean would die only twelve months later – so their memories were maybe not as clear as they had been. Halfway through the evening Dean announced that he had given up smoking. Frank was impressed: 'When did you give up?'

'Two days ago.'

'How did you do it?'

'I just forgot to light up.'

Frankly, after all that I'd heard about Los Angeles, I had expected the interest in the show and the clamour for tickets to quickly die down, but it was actually quite the reverse. Certainly, the mail should have given me a clue to the building interest. I shall never cease to be astonished by the power of the unsolicited letters I received from ordinary people, movingly describing their passionate feelings of identification with the on-stage creature who, in the face of certain rejection, 'Yearns for beauty, secretly, secretly . . .' The letters (often as long as essays) contained some extraordinary stuff. Some of them were quite emotionally staggering, such as one from the woman who wrote about her friend, suffering from AIDS, who came to a performance in New York and again in Los Angeles, and who died just ten days short of seeing the LA show again. She came in his place: 'We watched you through a lot of tears that night,' she wrote. And a mother wrote that I helped her recapture some of the essence of her long-dead eight-year-old son. She said she saw the show in London with her older son. 'He was completely captivated,' she recalled. 'We had a marvellous champagne supper afterwards and toasted the Phantom and each other. This was,' she continued, 'to be our very last evening together . . .' Her son was killed a few days later on Pan Am flight 103 that crashed in Lockerbie.

One of the more remarkable things about these letters

was that so many were from people who had only heard the recording and hadn't a hope of ever seeing the show.

Of course, I knew there were fans out there. There was always a queue of them outside the stage door. The queue grew noticeably larger over the months, and it soon became almost commonplace to hear of people coming twenty or even fifty times to see the show.

My 'Phantom' experience has me convinced that the main reason theatre doesn't exist in Los Angeles as it does in London or New York is only the result of logistics. LA is a vast city – almost ninety miles (about one hundred and forty-four kilometres) from one end to the other – the distance from London to Coventry – and it's made up of several smaller cities and municipalities (like Beverly Hills). It's often referred to as 'seventy suburbs in search of a city'. But with no real public transport system in place, commuting to a downtown Los Angeles theatre from some of the outlying regions can take many hours and pose a real hardship to the theatregoer.

Nonetheless, record crowds came to see us perform, and their reasons for being there and their personal stories were as varied and as extraordinary as their numbers. There was the retired Government worker who drove a two-hundred-and-fifty-mile round trip for each of the more than fifty times she came; and the accident victim who credited the show with bringing her out of the painful emotional shell into which she had escaped in the years since she was injured.

Things like these make me very proud to be a part of the acting profession. Many consider it self-congratulatory and precious, but I meet so many actors who are totally dedicated and diamond-hard in their self-discipline. I don't know anyone who says 'luvvie'. Maybe I've led a sheltered life? In my experience it's always been 'Oi you!'

When you decide to become an actor, you've chosen part-time employment for the whole of your life and all the anxiety that goes with that. No one would stick by the decision to work in the profession unless they have a vocation.

I also don't know of anyone in the profession who doesn't give their own time to freely help others. Acting is above all a healing profession.

When I got my first part-time job outside this profession, at Lyon's Corner House, I was fifteen. I had to be at work at six am. There was a bus conductor who used to watch out for all my comings and goings. Even though I could have caught a bus that ran half an hour later every day, I got up early because of this man. In manner he was a bit like an old-time music hall comedian, Arthur English perhaps, and his patter would have the whole bus laughing and smiling, and soon everyone would be talking energetically to each other and communicating. He was on his stage, and if fifty people travelled on each of the ten runs his bus was making everyday, then he was entertaining as many people per day as in a small London auditorium. The bus was his theatre of dreams.

That man affected my life. At some subconscious level I think I took in how the breaking down of unnecessary barriers and the giving and exchanging of energy could transform people. I remember, too, how when Nan came back from visiting old Mrs White down the road, making sure she had someone to talk to and that she was eating properly, she would return with more energy and more love in her than when she had left. Within a theatre a massive energy exchange takes place, the same as happens in a church or a synagogue or a temple, and, similarly, that tremendous power can be used to generate positive emotions.

When the energy comes back from the audience to the actors on stage, particularly in the form of laughter, that is often known in the profession as Doctor Footlights. In *Barnum*, which was perhaps the most exhausting show I've ever done, certainly from the physical point of view, it was the energy the audience gave me that enabled me to continue night after night.

To be a performer of any kind at any level is to belong to a special profession. I'm very, very proud to be part of it.

My year in Los Angeles rushed by, filled with promotional appearances, or a day off spent at the beach with friends. By spring, however, I finally had to face up to the fact that it was time to call it a day. I was tired; my voice and throat were raw, and I felt as if I had stretched my technique to the limit.

The announcement of my departure generated some kind of excitement. It was difficult to come to terms with the hysteria that followed – the *Los Angeles Times* dubbed it 'Michaelmania' – and more difficult still to believe they were actually talking about *me*.

Within days of the announcement, the newspapers showed adverts for tickets to 'Crawford's last performance' at a thousand dollars and up. The clamour grew steadily, along with the prices asked for tickets, and threatened to grow completely out of hand. Some of the lengths people went to to get tickets were actually quite funny. One man drove the box office crazy for weeks by pretending to be Ronald Reagan. Another enterprising punter appeared at the stage door with a note: 'Mr Crawford. My name is Eric Trump. I am Donald Trump's son. I had two tickets for this afternoon's performance, and I lost them. I've tried all over LA to find tickets to no avail. As you know my parents, I thought you could do something.' It was printed in a childish scrawl on the back of a torn envelope. When he presented himself at the stage door, he was carrying a telephone into which he spoke constantly. There was cord attached to it, but it wasn't connected to anything.

I was appalled when I read about the thousands of dollars being forked out for the odd last ticket, and I was determined to find a way for some of that money to be channelled to a local charity. I spoke to the people at the morning TV chat show, *AM, Los Angeles*, and agreed to donate my own six house seats for auction, hoping to raise a few thousand dollars that way. By the time the bidding ended, the top-selling pair of seats went for twenty-seven-and-a-half thousand – and the six tickets eventually brought in a total of seventy-four-and-a-half thousand! Not in our wildest dreams had any of us envisioned such an outcome. The proceeds went to Para Los Niños, a charity for children in poverty, and to the Equity Fights AIDS organisation.

My last performance in *The Phantom of the Opera* was on April 29, 1990, a Sunday matinée. At the curtain, Dale made a lovely farewell speech and the cast sang 'Happy Trails'. When I left the theatre I was given police protection to get through the several hundred good-natured fans laughing and milling about outside the stage door. Oddly enough, when I appeared, the scene suddenly went very quiet as if everyone thought I was going to speak to them. I walked through the crowd and shook some hands. It was all so quiet, it felt unreal. Then, as I passed through, the crowd noise slowly started up again.

Surrounded by security men, I reached the pavement expecting to find the car waiting, but there was nothing in sight. The police had ordered the car to move on or risk a summons. We suddenly found ourselves closed in from behind.

'The car's gone,' I yelled at the security guy, who hadn't seemed to have noticed. Where the hell did he think he was escorting me to? I heard Sally, my dresser, call me from a distance. 'It's over here!' she signalled – about a block away. *Over there?* I started to run, and several hundred people – mostly female – followed behind me. Lucy laughed about it afterwards. 'I never thought I'd live to see my forty-eight-year-old father being chased down the street by a horde of women!' I managed to jump into the car just before it was completely surrounded, but the fans kept banging on the windows. 'Don't look frightened, Michael! We're not going to hurt you!' I'm sure I looked exactly how I felt – absolutely terrified.

EPILOGUE

YOU'LL OFTEN HEAR members of a company in a long-running TV series or stage production refer to themselves as a 'family'. It may sound overdone to the outsider, but the comparison is apt: you are pushed together with a divergent group of people who, in a sense, you haven't chosen and with whom you may (or may not) develop a certain rapport. You live in each other's pockets within the close confines and highly charged atmosphere of the theatre or studio for a short, intense period of time. It is a microcosm of life. In very short order you begin to experience – albeit often from the sidelines – the everyday trials and tribulations and events that make up their daily lives. There are weddings, births, christenings, illnesses, even deaths – we lost three of our company of thirty-three to AIDS during *Phantom* in LA. There are friendships, relationships, sometimes even love affairs that people at home know nothing about, and which are held sacrosanct within the protective arms of the company. At the end of the day, of course, these same people go home to their actual families and lead an entirely different kind of life.

Depending upon the depth and endurance of your shared experiences, it can be a terrible wrench to have to say goodbye when you finally do part company. The duration of the show has something to do with it, of course, although the parting can be just as painful at the end of a short run as it is for a long run. The little farewell party we had for the *Flowers for Algernon* company in the Sea Horse pub in Soho was every bit as emotional and important a farewell as the gala that Cameron Mackintosh and the Really Useful Company and Andrew Lloyd Webber held for me at the posh Tavern on the Green in New York when I finished my Broadway run.

Something happens at those parties. A certain pang sets in as you suddenly realise that this is your last day in that theatre – you won't be coming in after the weekend to start up again, or put on sweats to work out and throw the banter about that stage, teasing and cajoling the other artists. All of us knew we'd probably run into each other again somewhere, sometime, but it would never again be quite the same. It's better just to hurry away.

I couldn't stay at home the next day because I knew I'd start clock-watching – *and that you mustn't do*. I had to get away and get something else going, another interest in my head, another distraction. So I jumped in the car and drove with Lucy and Sue Barbour across America, from coast to coast. It was a project designed with one thing in mind: to completely absorb my mind and concentration.

We drove at dawn almost from the first day, and each day afterwards. I used to wake Lucy and Sue up about five o'clock every morning, which did not endear me to them. Why all the rush? Where are we going that we have to leave at such an hour? 'We have to miss traffic,' was my lame excuse.

We arrived in Florida exactly one week later.

I looked at my watch – it was four-twenty on a Sunday afternoon – one-thirty pm on the West Coast. The company should just be arriving, putting their make-up on, warming up . . . I couldn't help myself. I had to make contact with my 'family' in Los Angeles again. I picked up the phone and called the backstage office at the Ahmanson Theater and spoke to the company manager.

'It's Michael,' I told him. 'I miss you all . . .'

'Michael?' he asked. 'Michael *who*?'

ACKNOWLEDGEMENTS

The author and publishers wish to offer thanks and acknowledgement to the following sources who have kindly provided pictures for this book. Our best efforts have been made to contact all copyright holders but should anyone be omitted or mis-credited we offer apologies and undertake to amend further editions. With thanks to the Children's Film & Television Foundation; BBC; 20th Century-Fox; Marie O'Connell; Michael White; Associated Newspapers; *Manchester Evening News*; Sue Knight; Michael Lamont; Richard Corkery; *People* magazine (US); Martine Peccoux/Gamma and Creston Funk. All other pictures are from the author's own collection.

We also wish to thank the following for allowing us to reproduce material in the book: BBC/Raymond Allen; BBC/Peter Lewis and Peter Dobereiner; and *Flowers for Algernon* by Daniel Keys with permission from Michael White Productions. For *The Phantom of the Opera*:

music – Andrew Lloyd Webber
lyrics – Charles Hart
additional lyrics – Richard Stilgoe
© copyright 1986 The Really Useful Group Ltd., London
All Rights Reserved. International Copyright Secured